CHILD SEXUAL ABUSE AND MENTAL HEALTH IN ADOLESCENTS AND ADULTS

Child Sexual Abuse and Mental Health in Adolescents and Adults

British and Canadian perspectives

CHRISTOPHER BAGLEY

Ashgate

Aldershot • Brookfield USA • Singapore • Sydney

Published by
Ashgate Publishing Company
Gower House
Croft Road
Aldershot, Hants
GU11 3HR
England

Ashgate Publishing Company
Old Post Road
Brookfield
Vermont 05036
USA

Ashgate website:http://www.ashgate.com

Reprinted 1999

British Library Cataloguing-in-Publication Data
Bagley, Christopher
    Child Sexual Abuse and Mental Health in
    Adolescents and Adults: British and Canadian
    Perspectives
    I. Title
    362.76

Library of Congress Catalog Card Number: 94-80260

ISBN 1-85628-943-5

Printed in Great Britain by Biddles Limited,
Guildford and King's Lynn

Contents

vi

Preface

This book is about victims and survivors — children and adolescents whose long term mental health has been undermined by sexual abuse and exploitation. I have lived and worked in several cultures — Britain, Canada, India, Hong Kong and The Philippines — and it is clear from various types of evidence that the sexual exploitation of children exists in all of these countries. Indeed, it is likely that children have been sexually exploited in various ways (including the violation of incest) since the dawn of humankind.

This book is a research monograph, reporting in detail on seven different research projects undertaken by colleagues and myself over a ten year period. Several of the chapters have been previously published in academic journals or in government reports. Often journal editors require substantial reductions in the length of papers to be published, even though reviewers have found the paper basically sound — most of the chapters present extended versions of the original journal articles, with additional tables and discussion. Chapter 3 is a much shortened version of a report commissioned by the Government of Canada.

Chapter 1 reviews and summarizes a number of published papers by colleagues and myself which are not included in this book. Several of the chapters are preceded with an abstract, and can be read and understood separately from other chapters. The final overview in Chapter 8 was specially written for this book.

This book has no overlap with previous texts on understanding and therapy of child sexual abuse victims (Bagley and King, 1990) and on the prevention of child sexual abuse (Bagley and Thomlison, 1991). Nevertheless, all of the chapters have implications for both prevention of child sexual abuse (particularly, Chapters 2, 3, 6 and 7) which are basically about the epidemiology, social context, and psychological sequels of abuse;

and the treatment of victims (particularly Chapters 4, 5 and 8 which are based on research in clinical and treatment settings).

My colleagues who have contributed to various chapters are:

Margaret MacDonald of University of the South Bank, London (Chapter 2);

Loretta Young of Alberta Children's Hospital (Chapters 2 and 4);

Olvina Naspini, Mehmoona Moosa-Mitha and Michael Wood of the University of Calgary (Chapters 7 and 8);

Gloria Rodberg and David Wellings of Alberta Family and Social Services (Chapter 8).

I gratefully acknowledge the permission of editors of the following journals to draw in whole or part on previously published articles:

Annals of Sex Research (Chapter 1);

Canadian Journal of Community Mental Health (Chapters 4 and 6);

Child Abuse and Neglect (Chapter 7);

Child Abuse Review (Chapter 8).

Just as Orlando was uplifted by the emotional and physical sustenance of his dear wife Grace, so am I continually uplifted by my dear wife Loretta. This book is dedicated to our kittens, and their safe and healthy development.

1 Measuring child sexual abuse and its long term psychological outcomes: A review of some British and Canadian studies of victims and their families

Introduction

What is extraordinary about child sexual abuse is not the extent of this aspect of the exploitation of children, but the fact that so many human cultures have tolerated (and may still tolerate) this practice. We owe our recent intellectual and moral insights into the history, nature, extent and effects of child sexual abuse to the historians of childhood, Lloyd de Mause (1974) and Florence Rush (1980) and to a number of feminist clinicians and writers, whose accounts Kathleen King and I have recently documented (Bagley and King, 1990).

The purpose of this book is not to offer any insights into the sociology of the knowledge which cultures and social systems have concerning child sexual abuse, or the dramatic changes in that understanding which have occurred in the past decade (on which see Bagley and Thurston, 1989; Bagley and King, 1990; Bagley and Thomlison, 1991), but to summarize a program of work begun in Britain in the 1960s, continued in Canada to the present time; and further extended into developing countries (Hong Kong and The Philippines) in the present decade.

Defining child sexual abuse

Arriving at a clear, precise definition of child sexual abuse for the purpose of clinical and sociological research has not been easy, and there has been disagreement between scholars on this issue (Finkelhor, 1984; Russell, 1986; Peters, Wyatt and Finkelhor, 1986). Indeed, part of our research has been to discover what kinds of sexual behaviour and contact in childhood have a statistically significant probability of being associated with

1

impairment of social and psychological functioning as an adult. We argue from our research that 'abuse' should be construed as an act which has a significant likelihood of resulting in harm, distortion or impairment of a young person's mental health development (Sorrenti-Little, Bagley and Robertson, 1984). Child sexual abuse, in this empirically derived model consists of at least physical contact with a child's unclothed genital area or breasts (including contact under clothing), contact which is unwanted by the child or young person. A 'child or young person' is further defined as someone who has not reached their 17th birthday (Bagley, 1989 and 1990a).

Child sexual abuse and incest

The work reported below arose directly from the teaching and influence of the anthropologist Robin Fox (Fox, 1980), who was my tutor in anthropology at Exeter University in the early 1960s. This work was begun in Britain in the late 1960s, and sought to understand why some individuals broke the traditional taboo on incest, and what implications this information had for understanding the taboo in general. Anthropological definitions (like legal definitions, which represent the formalization of explicit moral codes into enforceable rules) are quite different from the definitions of incest now proposed by some modern social researchers (e.g. Russell, 1986).

Traditional proscriptions of incest reflect the possibility that individuals closely related by blood (how close varies between cultures) might do two things: create biological offspring; and cohabit within a type of family, thus avoiding the need to seek new family members from other kinship groups. Both of these possibilities could be disastrous for the long term survival of human cultures. Legal definitions of incest usually follow the cultural proscriptions. In the British and Canadian legal codes for example, incest must involve completed intercourse between two people of opposite sex, closely related by blood (i.e. siblings, parent-child, grandparent-child, uncle or aunt with niece or nephew). Incest in this legal sense might occur between consenting adults, but it cannot occur between an adoptive father and daughter, between two males, or between a biological father or daughter where sexual assault did not amount to intercourse. Russell (1986) defines incest in much broader terms, to include sexual assault within family settings, whatever the biological relationship of the parties involved. While there is some logic in this, I prefer to follow legal definitions of incest, and use the broader generic term of 'child sexual abuse' to cover a variety of categories of sexual assault upon children.

In the British research (Bagley, 1969) I identified both published case histories of transgressions from the incest taboo as well as some 500 cases identified from social service records. It should be mentioned that although

2

Freud has been rightly criticized for his distorted interpretation of adult memories of child sexual abuse, his work on 'sexual perversion' does address the issue of the incest offender (Freud, 1977). Indeed, his chapter on 'Biologically immature persons as sexual objects' provides a prototype of the regressed offender identified by later researchers (e.g. Groth, 1979).

The typology of incest offenders identified (Bagley, 1969) identified five profiles, but this categorization is by no means exhaustive. The first type, functional incest has occurred in some well-described settings where out-marriage would involve breaking up viable family farms: the marriage of uncle and niece in such cases offends incest norms, but prevents the splitting of property. The second type, disorganized incest occurs in multi-problem families in isolated rural settings, or slum settings in decaying city areas. This can involve sexual assault on pre-pubertal females by older males, and is closer to a modern concept of child sexual abuse.

The third type, pathological incest occurs when one of the parties (usually an older male) has identifiable problems of mental illness or alcoholism and cannot function in normal roles, either outside or within the family. The fourth type, object fixation involves paedophile-like offenders who use their own children (as well as others) for sexual gratification, a need arising from their own arrested childhood development. The fifth type, psychopathic involves individuals who without any identifiable pathology in their backgrounds, callously use their own children for sexual purposes.

In later writing (Bagley and King, 1990), we propose a sixth group who may overlap with the psychopathic types of offender. This person we have termed a normative offender, someone who casually assaults a child in his family simply as an act of personal gratification or as an the expression of power. Given the high rates of child sexual abuse identified in the adult recall work (reviewed below), it is clear that the majority of those who offend against children cannot be classified into any but a residual, or normative category. However, regressed and fixated offenders remain important groups in terms of prevention, and clinical work (Bagley and Thurston, 1989).

The South London follow-up study

In the course of the research on violations of the incest taboo, we identified through social service sources 20 girls who had been removed from their family of origin after social workers had discovered that incest was being committed — all types of incest relationship defined by the criminal code were involved, but the majority were father-daughter cases. These adolescents were compared with 37 adolescent women removed from home because of physical abuse, neglect or family breakdown but for whom there

3

was no evidence of sexual abuse; and with 30 women of similar age and social background who had not been removed, but who grew up in seemingly normal families (Bagley and MacDonald, 1984). Most of these women came from similar areas of South London, in slum tenements of Southwark close to the River Thames. This area has since been demolished and redeveloped.

The 57 women (about 80 per cent of those originally identified) were followed up as young adults, and their mental health compared with those of the control respondents, in terms of various antecedent factors. Regression analyses indicated that the sexually abused women had very poor mental health outcomes, and were much more likely than others to lead disrupted lives (including prostitution, involvement in violent crime, and imprisonment). Physical abuse combined with sexual abuse in childhood had the worst outcomes; but physical abuse followed by removal from home without any sexual abuse apparent, had relatively good long term outcomes. We concluded that this study, the first follow-up from childhood of sexually-abused women, provided some persuasive evidence that the sexual abuse of children may well have a causal role in the development of adverse mental health and maladaption in adulthood (Bagley and McDonald, 1984).

Further follow-up work with 49 of the 57 women we in this follow-up study has been undertaken (Bagley, 1990a). The follow-up interviews were completed on average, 18 years after the original social service intervention to remove a child from home because of abuse of family breakdown. Nineteen of the 20 women known to have been sexually abuse were identified in this further follow-up, whose initial aim was to gather validity data on a new measure of child sexual abuse (Bagley, 1989a and b).

Fourteen of the 19 women for whom independent evidence indicated that serious, within family, sexual assault had occurred during childhood, did as adults recall events of such abuse, with details confirming data in social service files on who had abused them, how, and over what period. Two of the remaining women for whom independent evidence of abuse existed recalled that they had been subject to abuse of some kind, but could recall no details. However, three respondents for whom independent evidence of incestuous abuse existed did not report such abuse to the interviewer. Two of these women did say that there were long blank periods of childhood; these were in fact periods of their lives when we knew from independent evidence that combined and severe physical sexual assaults had taken place. The new and potentially more sensitive measure of child sexual abuse indicated that five of the 30 women whom we had previously considered (using social service records as a data source) not to have been sexually abused, had in fact been abused. Given that we had wrongly allocated some cases as 'not sexually abused' in previous work with this group (Bagley and MacDonald, 1984) we re-examined the data and found that in the earlier

4

research we had underestimated the long term, negative effects of child sexual abuse, since two of the most disturbed women amongst those whom we considered had not been sexually abused, had in fact been victims of long term, incestuous abuse. We further found that sexual abuse up to the age of 14 was the strongest predictor, all other factors controlled, of long term mental health problems in adulthood.

The Canadian studies 1: Child sexual abuse and student mental health

The first Canadian study to be reported was an attempt to replicate in a Canadian university (in Calgary), Finkelhor's (1979) work with students in Universities in the American North East, adding to Finkelhor's measure of sexual contacts in childhood a standardized measured of adult adjustment, the Tennessee Self-Concept Scale (TSSC). This work (Sorrenti-Little, Bagley and Robertson, 1984) has been used to define, in operational terms, whether any particular aspect of a child's sexual contact with another person (child or adult) could predict long term self-concept problems.

This method of adult recall deserves comment. Asking adults to review their childhood, and recall any particular events (including child sexual abuse) has a number of advantages over other methods such as the use of clinical referrals, or social service files. The bias of using prevalence estimates from clinic and agency populations is avoided, and one has the opportunity to access random sectors of the general population. But there are problems with such methods too. University students (even though they contain a much larger proportion of young adults in Canada than in Europe) are clearly not a random section of the population. Moreover, there is enough clinical evidence (reviewed by Bagley and Thurston, 1989; Bagley and King, 1990) to indicate that some of the victims of severe and prolonged child sexual abuse will drop out of school or at least will have poor motivation in learning programs, and will not enter university of college. Even random sampling of the general population (using voter lists, grid techniques, or telephone directories) will miss street and mental hospital populations, more than half of whom are likely to have histories of sexual abuse. Given these various problems, it is likely that the adult recall method will produce conservative estimates of the prevalence of child sexual abuse.

In the first study in Calgary we found, first of all (as did Finkelhor) that about two-thirds of children had some kind of sexual contact. But in the large majority of cases this was consensual contact with same-age peers, and usually did not proceed beyond mutual display and exploration. The issue of consent is a key one, and children are unlikely to be able to give consent

5

to a much older person, someone in a position of authority, or someone (of whatever age) who uses force or threat to achieve sexual contact.

Regression analyses with our university respondents (404 females and 164 males) indicated that a number of factors associated with sexual contact predicted a statistically significant diminishment of self-esteem. 'Abuse' in this operational definition involved someone at least three years older than the individual at the time of the sexual contact (which involved at least the handling of the child's genital area), or someone of any age using force, threat or structural authority (including family position) to achieve such contact.

We found that sexual abuse defined in this way was experienced by 19 per cent of females and nine per cent of males by the time they were 16; abused individuals of both sexes had significantly poorer self-concept than the non-abused — the strong correlations between impaired self-concept and earlier abuse (0.61 in females, and 0.46 in males) are in fact tautological, since the definition of sexual abuse was operationally derived from examination of individuals with poor self-concept levels (as measured by the total score on the Tennessee scale).

The Canadian studies 2: Follow-up of women in a community mental health survey in Calgary

This work arose from a study which randomly identified some 780 adults in the Canadian city of Calgary (population 700,000). This study was originally designed to investigate psychosocial correlates of suicidal ideas and behaviour (Ramsay and Bagley, 1985; Bagley and Ramsay,1985). These papers also describe the sampling procedures and the development and validity of the socio-demographic and mental health measures.

The opportunity arose to follow-up the women in this survey, and 377 of these women were located and interviewed about a year after the original survey. Questions about childhood events were asked right at the end of this second questionnaire, in order to avoid the possibility that asking adults to recall such events might colour there responses to the mental health measures (i.e. creating a negative response set). All of the women were seen in their homes, by skilled interviewers who offered initial counselling and referral where necessary.

The measure of sexual abuse was modified from that used by Finkelhor (1979), in the light of work with young adult students (Sorrenti-Little et al., 1984). At this stage, we did not ask subjects directly about 'unwanted' sexual contact in childhood, assuming that any contact that involved force or threat, someone three or more years older, or any authority figure, was abusive in nature.

6

In this community study, 22 per cent of the 377 women recalled some sexual abuse up to their 16th year (involving at least the unwanted touching of their unclothed genital area). Details were asked about first, second and third assaults by different perpetrators. We found, as had other investigators (e.g. Russell, 1986), that having been the victim of assault by one assailant put a victim at significant risk for further assaults by different individuals. Fifty-seven per cent of the abusive events were one time assaults however. Assaults by relatives or acquaintances accounted for nearly 80 per cent of the abusive events; the closer the relationship, the more likely it was that the assault would be serious, and would continue for a long time (Bagley and Ramsay, 1986).

Mental health outcomes for those recalling any kind of sexual assault in childhood were significantly poorer than in subjects who did not recall any abuse. It was found moreover, that respondents under 40 reported more abuse than older subjects (28 per cent versus 18 per cent), and that the negative effects of abuse were more marked in younger subjects. Analysis of the abuse victims found, as previous studies had predicted (e.g. Finkelhor, 1984) that seriousness of the assault, closeness of the relationship with the abuser, the degree of broken trust involved, and the length of the time over which the abuse occurred were associated with the worst mental health outcomes.

On a measure of depression (taken from the Middlesex Hospital Questionnaire — Bagley, 1980), 15 per cent of all the abuse victims reported serious depression in the previous year, compared with seven per cent of the non-abused. On the Centre for Epidemiological Studies for Depression scale (Radloff, 1977) administered in the follow-up study, an overlapping 15 per cent of the abuse victims were found to be seriously depressed at the time of interview, compared with five per cent of the non-abused.

In the previous 12 months, 11 per cent of abuse victims experienced serious suicidal feelings, compared with three per cent of the non-abused; five per cent of the abused and none of the non-abused had engaged in deliberate self-harm in the previous year. In responses to the Adult Coopersmith Self-Esteem Scale (Bagley, 1989a) 19 per cent of the abuse victims compared with five per cent of the non-abused had 'devastated' self-esteem. No less than 23 per cent of the former abuse victims had received medical treatment for a psychological condition (including serious depression or psychosis) in the past year, compared with three per cent of the non-abused.

The question remains as to whether the connection between sexual abuse in childhood and current psychological problems is a causal one. In order to explore this, we examined two other childhood factors known to be associated with adult mental health problems: permanent separation from a

7

parent (Akins, Akins and Mace, 1981); and lack of emotional support by parents combined with an excess of control or physical punishment by parents (Ross, Clayer and Campbell, 1983). Using Ross et al.'s (1983) measure of parental rearing style, and data supplied by informants on separation from a parent we undertook regression analyses to see if sexual abuse in childhood remained an independent predictor of adult psychological problems.

We found (in confirmation of ideas developed by Finkelhor, 1979) that girls who were subject to a cold, punitive and controlling regime during their childhood years were more at risk of sexual abuse, presumably because they had learned to obey adults without question, and because they lacked the confidence to approach an adult for help.

In addition, the role of separation from a parent, which has been shown by Russell (1986) to be a significant risk factor for child sexual abuse (especially if the separation from biological father is followed by the introduction of one or more unrelated adult males into the child's household) was also confirmed. Step-fathers, common-law husbands, and visiting boyfriends were particularly likely to sexually assault children who became available to them. Step-fathers and boyfriends of their mother accounted for 12 per cent of the assailants.

It is worth mentioning in this context that there does appear to be some natural protection for the child when the biological father remains present during her childhood years, especially if that father had a close, nurturing role and shared household and child care tasks with his wife (Parker and Parker, 1986). In our Calgary study (Bagley and Ramsay, 1986) we found that although sexual abuse by relatives was common, only a half of one per cent of sexual assault in childhood recalled by these subjects was by a biological father. While the fact that one out of every 200 children are likely to be sexually assaulted (or incestuously abused) by the biological father is a disturbing statistic, it is compatible with the idea that the incest taboo can inhibit sexual assaults imposed upon close relatives. Our subsequent community surveys in Calgary (see below) also support this view: biological closeness does appear to be a 'natural' inhibitor of sexual abuse and exploitation of children.

Trying to identify causal patterns through statistical analysis has both strengths and disadvantages. We found, following regression analysis that when the associations of poor mental health in adulthood with sexual abuse, emotional and physical abuse, and parental separation were controlled on one another, each remained an independent, statistically significant predictor of depression and suicidal ideas in adulthood. Combinations of sexual abuse, separation and emotional coldness did however predict poorer adjustment in some cases. We checked out possible causal sequences by re-interviewing 20 respondents for whom all three constraints existed. All had

8

mental health problems in adulthood. We asked these respondents to give elaborated or extended accounts of childhood events, and tried to date the onset of the apparently traumatic events. Analysis of this interview data indicated complex types of patterning in which the antecedent factors identified, all reinforced one another in contributing to the development of severely diminished self-esteem, learned helplessness, and depression in adulthood (Bagley and Young, 1990). While we do not have control data for this qualitative aspect of the study, we have little doubt that the adult problems of these individuals are fully explicable in terms of their childhood circumstances.

The Canadian studies 3: The family contexts of adolescent sexual abusers

We know from the Canadian surveys (see later chapters) that between six and eight per cent of boys will as adults recall unwanted sexual assaults before the age of 18. In addition, a study of university students has shown also that a history of unwanted sexual acts in childhood is associated with diminished self-esteem in young adulthood in both male and female victims (Sorrenti-Little et al., 1984). Research has suggested that males who are subjected to sexual assault in childhood (usually by a male assailant) are significantly at risk for becoming perpetrators of child sexual abuse (against both male and female victims) when they become adults (Bagley and Thurston, 1989).

We investigated these and associated problems in an study of a population of children and adolescents in residential treatment for serious behaviour problems, including extreme aggression against others and against themselves (Bagley and Dann, 1991). We reviewed the records of 620 individuals admitted to two residential centres in Alberta during the period 1978 to 1987 and among the males identified 65 individuals with a history of making a sexual assault, usually against children or adolescents. It is clear from the re-analysis of the national Canadian survey of unwanted sexual acts in childhood that between 18 per cent and 20 per cent of male perpetrators are themselves juveniles. It is clear too that a significant number of those who are later classified as 'dangerous sexual offenders' by the Criminal Code of Canada began their pattern of sexual offending while adolescents (Canada, 1984). Adolescence is a crucial time for intervention and therapy if the pattern of sexual assault is to be checked (Groth, 1979).

The 65 individuals with a history of sexual assault on our Alberta survey were compared with 220 control subjects of similar age and sex in the same residential centres, but who had no recorded history of sexual assault. Many significant differences were found. The sexually assaultive group

9

were more likely to have 'internalized' symptoms including depression, anxiety, and suicidal thoughts and behaviour. The comparison group by contrast, were much more likely to exhibit externalized aggression and delinquent behaviour. Sexual assault was isolated from other types of delinquency, and was also associated with much anxiety and self-doubt. The sexually assaultive youths were also much more likely to come from intact homes, whereas the remaining youths often came from broken or disorganized homes, often characterized by poverty. The sexually assaultive youth by contrast, usually came from intact blue-collar or lower middle-class homes in which the parents had stayed together.

We described these as hothouse families, because there were usually problems of alcoholism or mental illness in one or both parents in these intact homes. Children in these families were particularly likely to be victims of emotional, physical, or sexual abuse and over 50 per cent of these boys had experienced prolonged sexual abuse within their home or in the community, compared with less than 10 per cent of the comparison group. Another interesting finding was that 25 per cent of the assaultive youths, compared with less than 10 per cent of controls, had problems involving hyperactivity or a central nervous system problem requiring medication, and were much more likely to be grade retarded because of learning problems that had a physiological basis.

What was remarkable and disturbing in this study was the failure of treatment regimes to pay any significant attention to the sexual assault experienced by these children or to the sexually assaultive behaviour in which they were engaged. We had to read the files very carefully to find information about sexual assault and indeed, this information may not have been recorded in a number of cases. Therapists usually made comments which indicated that they thought that the sexual assaults were part of general development problems that did not merit particular attention; or, indeed, that the assaults were part of normal developmental behaviour in children from this type of family. Traumas resulting from sexual assault were rarely addressed in therapy. Therapists — social workers, psychologists, and psychiatrists — had neither the training nor the inclination to address problems of sexual assault.

Girls receiving treatment in these residential institutions, who had been sexually assaulted within their families, also tended to come from 'hothouse families' in which they were often assaulted in a variety of ways, and from which they often ran to escape abuse. Their acting out sexually, sometimes being recruited as juvenile prostitutes, seemed to be a reflection of these assaults. Indeed, those girls in many ways resembled the young adult women whom we had studied earlier who had drifted into prostitution (Bagley and Young, 1987, and the chapter below).

An international comparison: Psychosocial background of prostitution in Calgary and Manila

One of the questions which the Canadian research (reviewed above), raises is whether the dimensions, background and outcomes of child sexual abuse in Canada and Britain are specific to Western countries, or whether they can be generalized to other kinds of cultures. While our findings on teenage prostitution in Britain and Canada (Bagley, Burrows and Yaworski, 1990) are similar to American findings, the picture in a developing country in Asia may be quite different. Comparative research can be invaluable, for it can identify cultural and structural factors which can permit or inhibit child sexual abuse, and perhaps also the kinds of healing that can be practised (Bagley and Young, 1990).

The Philippines, like Thailand, is a country with a sexual subculture which seems to have arisen in response to the tourist industry from Japan, Australia, North America and Europe. Do the prostitutes who are recruited to serve these tourists resemble the adolescent prostitutes of North American cities?

Our initial answer to this question, after a period of research in Luzon, the northern-most island of The Philippines, is that they do not. Using a similar schedule to that used in the study of prostitutes in Canada, we found that 'only' 13.3 per cent of a sample of 45 adolescent prostitutes working in bar-brothels in Manila had experienced contact sexual abuse before being recruited into prostitution. Often these girls were sole supports of families living in desperate poverty in rural areas, and carried on prostitution with the troubled acquiescence of their families.

However, these girls were often cruelly exploited in the business of prostitution itself (and here they do resemble their North American counterparts). They were beaten, raped and abused, and sometimes robbed even of the small percentage of the customer's fee which they were allowed. If they became pregnant they were cast aside. And in a Roman Catholic society which has (unlike Thailand) disapproved of condom use, the risk of infection (including HIV positive status) appears to be high.

The generalization we make from this continuing fieldwork is that in cultures where women have very low status 'child sexual abuse' is a difficult concept to operationalize, particularly when female puberty is also the traditional age of marriage. In cultures where sexual exploitation of young adolescents is both cheap and socially acceptable, sexual abuse of children younger than adolescence may be relatively rare.

The Philippines does have a reputation as a source of young boys for adult paedophiles. Our information at the present time is that police have successfully intervened to stop the activities of some notorious paedophiles (particularly from Australia). Such paedophiles are also frequent targets for

exploitation, and blackmail. They will be shown a young boy and promised sexual contact if money is paid ahead of such contact. As soon as the man is alone in a hotel with the young boy police (acting in concert with the 'sting' operators) burst in, and the potential paedophile has to buy his way out of the situation. He will leave The Philippines penniless and humiliated.

Conclusions

The first conclusion is an ecological one: we have built up a systematic body of knowledge about the background of child sexual abuse in a large city in Western Canada in terms of prevalence, mental health outcomes, background factors, and ways in which child sexual abuse might be detected and prevented. Yet we know too that front line agencies for protecting children and helping families still see only a small proportion of those who have experienced serious abuse in childhood. In Calgary, service providers have just about kept pace with demand for services for children.

A further issue is whether the prevalence of child sexual abuse is in fact similar in different cultures (e.g. England and Canada) or whether England and other countries are facing rather different problems. The systematic methods of random surveying of adult recall which we have developed in Canada are useful in assessing whether there has been change in the overall prevalence of child sexual abuse — whether programs aimed at primary, secondary and tertiary prevention are actually working.

There is some evidence that European countries have regarded, and may still regard child sexual abuse differently (Chesnais, 1981; Cunningham, 1988). Chesnais (1981) argues that countries of Southern Europe (including Southern Germany and Southern France) have regarded the sexual use of children differently from their northern neighbours, and that it is only in the Protestant north (as in North America) that the sexual exploitation and use of children is regarded as a social problem.

It might be too that North America, with its numerous problems of violence and its many aspects of relatively unstable and still-evolving social structures, has overall a greater prevalence of child sexual abuse than the established and traditional societies of Europe.

A parallel to the adult recall survey of abusive events in childhood is the victim survey, which asks random samples of the population whether they have been subject to events (e.g. criminal acts) in a specified period. A recent comparative survey of 14 cultures (including Canada, England and Wales, Scotland, the United States, and several European countries) randomly sampled 2,000 adults in each country. It was found that the rate of sexual crimes (many of which were not reported to police) experienced by women was relatively low in England, Wales and Scotland, and was less

12

than one half the rate recalled by Canadian women (Mayhew, 1990). This would be compatible with the findings of Mrazek, Lynch and Bentovim (1983) who report a prevalence rate for child sexual abuse in the United Kingdom which is substantially lower than the figures obtained for Canada. However, different methods were used in the Canadian work, and a more exact methodology in cross-cultural surveys is required.

What is clear is that in all cultures a substantial minority (and perhaps a majority) of children who are subjected to serious, prolonged unwanted sexual assault will have long term impairment of mental health. While incest in traditional, legal terms appears to be relatively rare such sexual assaults are particularly likely to take a heavy psychological toll. But assaults involving a family member such as a step-father are just as likely to have negative outcomes for the victim. The mental health problems of victims have largely been unrecognized, and effective primary prevention would be a humanistic as well as a cost-effective approach (Bagley and Thomlison, 1991).

In order to increase both intellectual understanding of the phenomenon of childhood sexual exploitation, and to discover more effective ways of preventing and treating child sexual abuse we need much more comparative work, between a variety of types of culture. I pose some of the questions which such research might ask:

1   Are their links within particular cultures, between the non-recognition of sexual abuse as a problem, and the stigmatization of victims, as well as with the kinds of services provided? In other words, can the understanding of child sexual abuse, and the provision of non-stigmatizing services for victims be seen to emerge on a kind of evolutionary basis?

2   Do some cultures, in an ecological, political or structural sense, protect children of both sexes from sexual exploitation? Comparative work using the adult recall method could throw some light on this issue. We pose this question in terms of religion, culture and ethnicity since in our Canadian work on sexual abuse of male children, we have found that growing up in an Oriental, Indian or Islamic culture, in an orthodox, religious household (Christian or otherwise) is by no means an absolute guarantee that sexual abuse in childhood will not take place. But why is this so?

3   Comparative work on adolescent prostitution (which is in itself a form of child sexual abuse) and the backgrounds of the young men and women in this trade are needed. We still have relatively little

13

comparative knowledge on the nature of the institution of adolescent prostitution.

4   What is the role of cultural symbols (e.g. those depicting children and young people in sexual or pseudo-sexual roles) in providing normative support or direct triggers to childhood sexual exploitation? Now that virtually all world societies have made child pornography illegal, will the overall prevalence of child sexual exploitation decline?

5   Much more comparative research needs to be done on the nature and motivation of male sexual offenders against children. Are these offenders in most cultures, a pathological sub-group of the population, or are they supported explicitly or implicitly by mainstream values and cultural symbols?

6   How can we prevent male victims from repeating the cycle of their abuse, from going on to be themselves offenders?

7   Finally, the fascinating issue of dissociation and multiple personality needs to be addressed in a cross-cultural context. As Greaves (1980) put the matter: 'It is now considered that multiple personality is not a rare occurrence but a relatively common condition which is misdiagnosed with a high order for frequency. Recent research in ego psychology, particularly into the etiology of the borderline disorders, sheds considerable light on the origins of multiple personality . . . ' (Greaves, 1980, p. 577). This is a North American view. Is it also a culturally biased perspective, as psychiatrists in the Indian sub-continent (Adityanjee, Raju and Khandelwal, 1989) recently claimed?

In the writer's view, the evidence that the dissociative personality style (and its extreme manifestation, multiple personality disorder) is an important and likely trans-cultural outcome of severe abuse early in a child's life. In an important, metaphorical sense society in its collective consciousness split off from everyday understandings of ourselves and others the fact of sexual exploitation of children until the very recent past (Bagley and King, 1990). The individual victims of sexual abuse were ordered, encouraged or manipulated into doing the same.

Our task is to make the victims whole, ourselves whole, and our cultures into integrated, self-conscious, moral wholes in which we address the abuse and exploitation of children without silence, or hypocrisy.

14

2 Adult mental health sequels of child sexual abuse, physical abuse and neglect in maternally separated children

Abstract

A follow-up study is reported of the mental health and psychosexual adjustment in young adulthood of 57 girls who were removed from home in childhood by social service agencies because of abuse, neglect or family breakdown. Twenty of the girls had experienced sexual abuse within the family context before the age of 14. The 57 maternally separated girls were compared with 30 girls whose childhoods were not disrupted by known abuse, or by separation from a parent. Multiple regression analysis showed that early sexual abuse explained more of the variance in adult adjustment than either physical abuse and neglect, or maternal separation. It is concluded that subject to the limits of the sample, early sexual abuse within the family has severe long term implications for mental health in adulthood unless appropriate therapeutic intervention is offered. Combinations of sexual abuse with physical abuse or neglect commenced early in the child's life, have particularly adverse outcomes.

Introduction

A considerable amount of evidence has emerged from studies of clinical and deviant populations indicating that childhood sexual abuse within the family context has many adverse long term consequences which extend into adulthood (Bagley and King, 1990). The adult recall method (Chapter 1) also indicate that sexual abuse before age 17 is much more widespread than had previously been thought, and is a significant factor in adjustment in populations of young adults (Briere, 1989). However, since the early sequels of childhood sexual abuse are for some individuals quite

catastrophic, involving among other things, running away from home, self-mutilation, suicidal gestures and attempts, drug taking and juvenile prostitution (Silbert, 1982a and b), such individuals are unlikely to be included in surveys of college students such as those of Finkelhor (1979) and Bagley and Genuis (1991).

What is lacking in the literature are systematic follow-up studies of abused populations and controls. The lack of such longitudinal studies is not surprising however, given the difficulty of such studies, and the likely instability of some of the population which is to be studied.

The study described below had the original aim of exploring the idea outlined in Bagley (1969), that the psychological harm surrounding sexual abuse of children related as much to the action of authorities in removing a child from home as to the abuse itself. In forming these ideas we were influenced by the work of Bowlby (1951) which suggested that maternal separation is frequently harmful for long term psychological development. Although separation in infancy is thought to be most traumatic, separation at later stages of childhood can still have marked long term effects (Greer and Gunn, 1966), and can contribute to psychopathological outcomes in adulthood (Bagley and Greer, 1972). However, a reappraisal of the evidence (Rutter, 1979) suggests that maternal separation is by no means universally traumatic for children.

Methods

Subjects and procedures

A unique opportunity to undertake a long term study emerged in Britain in the late 1960s as a result of an extensive research project on aspects of incest behaviour (Bagley, 1969). The researchers had access to the case records of a social service department in a South London Borough, and were able to track a number of girls who had been sexually abused within the family context for a number of years. Policy in the 1960s on discovery of sexual abuse was usually not to prosecute offenders but to remove the child, usually permanently, from the home. Only in the grossest and most persistent cases, usually involving more than one child, were prosecutions instituted.

None of the cases of sexual abuse identified in the present study had involved prosecution. In over half of the cases the sexual abuse was discovered incidentally to other social service investigations. All of the girls came from economically poor families in slum areas (now demolished) close to London's dockland. The families in which physical or sexual abuse took place were in most cases considered by social workers to be generally

16

unstable and had been known to social services and other authorities for many years. Social workers in their case reports generally saw sexual abuse as a 'normal' hazard for children in such disorganized, multi-problem family circumstances.

In this study sexual abuse was defined as: manipulation or interference with the unclothed genitals of a female child aged 14 or less by a closely related male aged over 18 (father, uncle or brother) living in the same household as the victim; the assault taking place on more than three occasions, over more than a three-month period. The sexual abuse was verified at the time both by the child, and by the report of an adult familiar with the household. For purposes of the present study, only those cases were selected where the sexually abused child had been removed from home and separated from her natural mother for at least a year.

Three groups were studied in the present research: 32 sexually abused girls of whom 24 were traced and 20 interviewed; 59 separated girls who were not (to the knowledge of case workers) sexually abused, of whom 41 were traced and 37 were interviewed; and a 'normal' comparison group of 30 young women from the same geographical area, undertaking nurse training. The nurses were not part of a long term follow-up study, but all had grown up in the area from which the original sample was drawn. The mean age at maternal separation for the sexually abused group was 13.0 years, and for the separated group 11.9 years, a non-significant difference in the groups contacted at follow-up.

The two follow-up groups were aged between eight and 14 when the removal from home, for whatever reason, took place. The separations occurred between 1965 and 1970, and the follow-ups were completed at least eight years later in each case, when the young women were aged between 18 and 24.

Cases where there was not enough information to establish these various criteria were not included; nor were verified cases of sexual abuse in which the assailant, though living in the same household, was not biologically related to the victim. The study was originally designed as one investigating outcomes of incest, though we now accept the thrust of recent feminist arguments (Rush, 1981) that child sexual abuse is so widespread that it is unlikely that the incest taboo itself is being violated; rather, the taboo applies to sexual relations between closely related adults which are likely to result in pregnancy, and replace marital choice outside close kin.

The 32 sexually abused girls had suffered abuse ranging from manual interference and forced masturbation of the assailant through to completed intercourse. The known duration of the assault was greater than two years in six cases. In only six cases did social workers intervene to remove the child on the basis of known sexual assault alone. The most common reasons were obvious neglect of a child, or the child's acting out behaviour or

running away. The 32 girls were randomly selected from 140 sexual abuse cases known to social services in an urban area occupied by some 28,000 families in the five-year period during which records were monitored. Almost certainly the prevalence of family sexual abuse was much greater than this during the period in question, and the cases selected for study represent a special type: families in whom symptoms of disorganization led to both social service monitoring and the discovery of ill-concealed abuse. There exist other types of family sexual abuse, including a 'privatized' kind in which dominating fathers control families psychologically and are able to prevent the revelation of the abuse to others (Bagley, 1969).

The manifestly disturbed behaviour of some of the victims at the time of the sexual abuse probably contributed to the decision to remove the child from home in some cases, and indeed the stigmatization of the victim by placing her in the company of young delinquents may have been a factor contributing to poor prognosis. In order to explore aspects of this problem the maternally separated comparison group who were not sexually abused was selected on the basis of similarity of age, type of behaviour problem (if any) and type of placement at the time of being taken into care.

The maternally separated comparison group were drawn from a much larger pool of subjects taken 'into care' during the relevant period. All of the comparison group had been separated from both parents in childhood for six months or more, because of disorganization in the home, death or absence of the mother, or physical neglect or abuse. Many of the sexually abused girls had also suffered disorganized homes and physical neglect at the same time as being sexually abused. Three quarters of the separated group were separated from their mothers for more than two years.

The families of many of the girls had been rehoused in local authority 'council housing' which facilitated follow-up; and in many cases members of the extended family were still known to social services. In addition, girls who had spent extended periods in care were often traced through social service departments. Marriage records for the area were also checked, as well as prison, hospital and coroners' records.

In the original sexually abused group, one girl was known to have died (probably suicide), and one was serving a lengthy prison sentence for the manslaughter of a pimp. The majority of those traced in both groups agreed to be interviewed, and a completed interview rate of just over 60 per cent in both groups was obtained. This was judged adequate under the circumstances. Marriage and removal from the general area was the greatest cause of sample loss.

The survey was introduced as being about the experience of having been in local authority care as a child, and questions about sexual assault were introduced after rapport was established. Although the female interviewer knew from earlier access to case records which girls had been sexually

18

abused this information was not imparted to the respondent. Three of the 20 females with a previous history of sexual abuse failed to give any positive indication in response to the question, 'Were you sexually abused as a child?' However, we had prima facie evidence of prior abuse in these cases. Presumably the individual was repressing or at least denying this earlier event, and this mode of attaining an equilibrium of mental health should be borne in mind in retrospective studies. There are also ethical implications, since probing about traumatic early events may also have caused mental distress for an individual. All individuals in this study were in fact offered referral for specialized counselling with someone experienced in treating young women who had experienced earlier sexual abuse. A striking finding was that not one of the 20 females had been offered any help, therapy or counselling specifically related to the sexual abuse at the time it was reported (usually by a mother or sibling, rather than by the victim herself), nor indeed on any subsequent occasion, and the predominant mode of social workers and others was one of denial of the sexual abuse.

Contrary to expectation, none of the 37 maternally separated control group recalled childhood sexual abuse (thus supporting negative reports in the case records). Eighteen of these 37 had suffered significant physical neglect or abuse, as had six of the sexually abused girls.[1]

Instruments

The following instruments were completed by the subjects, including the nurse comparison group:

1   A shortened version of the Middlesex Hospital Questionnaire, which gives syndrome profiles as well as an overall measure of psychoneurosis of known validity and reliability (Bagley, 1980; Crisp, et al., 1979). This measure has been shown to be valid in discriminating populations with diagnoses of mental illness from non-psychiatric populations in Britain, the United States, the Caribbean and Israel (Crowne and Crisp, 1981). Work in Canada produced similar findings (Bagley, 1983b). This work showed, in a survey of 1,600 adults in an urban population that the measure of self-esteem used in the present study correlated strongly (0.55 to 0.68) with total score on the Middlesex Hospital Questionnaire, and the anxiety and depression subscales. It is probable that many scales in this area, including those of poor self-esteem, have strong intercorrelation and measure an underlying dimension of good mental health and positive self-evaluation versus negative self-evaluation, anxiety, and depression (Meites, et al., 1980).

19

2   A short version of the Coopersmith Self-Esteem Inventory (Bagley and Evan-Wong, 1975), since validated with a large population of young females in Canada (Bagley, 1983b).

3   A measure of psychosexual adjustment adapted from Hudson's (1974) 25-item instrument, but expanded to include questions on aversion to and avoidance of heterosexual relations as well as adjustment within sexual relations. This instrument did not explore adjustment in homosexual relationships.

These instruments were chosen because of their known validity and reliability, and our underlying assumption that mental health is a crucial dependent variable in examining long term effects of childhood disruption and trauma. Self-esteem was measured since it is taken to be a crucial, pivotal aspect of the adequacy of personal and social functioning (Bagley, et al., 1979). Problems in psychosexual functioning were assumed, by the time follow-up work was undertaken, to be a major possible outcome of early sexual abuse, a hypothesis based on retrospective studies in this area (Meiselman, 1978).

In the first analysis data from the three groups were combined, and a multiple regression analysis was used to test the hypothesis that when the influence of other factors (maternal separation; physical abuse; recent stress) was controlled, early sexual abuse would make a significant, independent contribution to variance in the adjustment variables (mental health, self-esteem, psychosexual adjustment). Stated in terms of the null hypothesis, long-lasting, negative effects of early sexual abuse are in fact confounded by accompanying or intervening variables.

Recent stress in this study was defined as an event of stress occurring apparently independently of the subject's action or volition in the previous two years, including serious illness or impairment of physical health; divorce or marital separation; enforced job loss; and death of a spouse, child, sibling or mother. Stress research is one fraught with difficulty, and has yielded elusive results so far as mental health is concerned (Billings, et al., 1983). Nevertheless, we felt it was sufficiently important to control for any effects of recent stress on mental health, and also to examine the interactions on childhood events (sexual and physical abuse, and maternal separation) with recent stress.

Results

It was found, contrary to expectation, that recent stress made no significant contribution to outcome measures, and did not interact with the measures of

earlier trauma (separation and abuse). Because of this, recent stress as a basis for categorization has not been utilized in Table 2.1.

Table 2.1 indicates that the most adverse outcome in terms of self-esteem, depression and psychoneurosis occurs in the six individuals who have suffered sexual abuse, physical abuse or neglect, and maternal separation for more than six months. On the measures of depression, self-esteem and sexual adjustment the sexually abused group as a whole have a poorer outcome than the other groups, and the 'normal childhood' control group of nurses has the best outcome on all measures.

It will be seen from Table 2.2 that all of the measures of adjustment intercorrelate at above 0.50. Being sexually abused has higher correlations with depression, sexual maladjustment and poor self-esteem than either physical abuse or neglect, or separation from mother.

Table 2.3 presents results of final stepwise multiple regression analyses, in which the correlation of the strongest predictor variable with each dependent variable is held constant while the correlations of the other predictor variables with the dependent variable are adjusted for their intercorrelations with one another.

Early separation is the strongest predictor of the combined symptom scale on the Middlesex Hospital Questionnaire (the measure of general psychoneurosis incorporating subscales of anxiety, phobia, depression and obsessionality) and after controlling, the correlations of the other predictors with psychoneurosis diminish to an insignificant degree. In the case of sexual maladjustment, poor self-esteem, and depression (a sub-scale of the MHQ) sexual abuse remains the sole significant predictor of the dependent variable.

These results show, in our opinion, that untreated child sexual abuse in the family context has in the population studied, serious long term consequences for mental health, particularly in terms of sexual adjustment, depression and self-esteem. Such consequences are more serious than those which follow physical abuse or neglect, and more serious than those stemming from separation from mother. Maternal separation is linked however to subsequent psychoneurosis, and to depression.

Our original presumption was that 'subcultural incest' (Bagley, 1969) which this imposition of sexuality on children involved would have relatively benign outcomes for a number of reasons. It was presumed that normative support or sanction for such sexuality in sub-cultural families would lessen the deviant, (and therefore the guilt-provoking) aspects of the behaviour for the child. It was presumed too that the many other stresses imposed upon the lives of these children would largely eclipse any ill-effects of sexual abuse. Our results seem to indicate that these presumptions were wrong. Guilt (represented by depression, low self-esteem, and disgust and aversion in sexual relationships) is a common feature of the lives of young women

who were sexually assaulted as children. Moreover, other stressful events of childhood have not eclipsed the effects of sexual abuse: rather sexual abuse has combined with these other factors to make outcome worse.

A problem in our design is that a non-separated control group of children from disorganized families was not obtained at the beginning of the study, so in essence an aspect of social class has not been properly controlled for: the nurse control group, although often of working class origin and from the same neighbourhood were unlikely to have come from disorganized, lower class families.

Table 2.4, predicting outcome in the maternally separated group shows that within this group early sexual abuse remains the significant predictor of three measures of adjustment after predictor variables have been controlled by multiple regressions.[2] Before controlling, physical abuse or neglect makes some contribution to variance in sexual maladjustment. After controlling, sexual abuse absorbs most of this variance: what this effectively means is that sexual abuse combined with physical abuse or neglect in childhood has a particularly deleterious effect on sexual adjustment in adulthood.

Surprisingly, such a combination does not emerge in the case of self-esteem or depression; however, early age at separation from mother (within the age range eight to 14) did predict poor self-esteem. This correlation 'merged' with the effects of sexual abuse after multiple regression. Since many of the children had behaviour problems (of various kinds, ranging from acute anxiety to extreme aggression and sexual acting out) this variable was included as a predictor (scored 0 for no disorder of any kind, 1 for some disorder, 2 for moderate disorder, and 3 for marked disorder — mean 1.1 for all 57 maternally separated subjects). These behaviour problems have moderate links to adult adjustment, and the correlations are absorbed within the effect of sexual abuse itself.

Further pieces of evidence, which have not been subjected to significance testing because of incomplete data, tend to confirm the extremely disadvantaged position of the sexually abused group. Five (25 per cent) of the 20 sexually abused females were known to have made a suicidal gesture or attempt compared with two (five per cent) of the 37 separated individuals who were not sexually abused. Two of the abused group had prolonged periods of depression or psychosis requiring hospitalization for more than three months compared with none in the other two groups. Five of the abused girls had worked for periods in prostitution, compared with none of the other subjects. Eleven of the abused girls (55 per cent) had experienced severe beating on more than one occasion at the hands of a husband, boyfriend or pimp, compared with three (eight per cent) of the early separated group.

The information in these areas emerged in personal histories given by the two abused groups. The personal interview data supplementing the formal measures suggests a pattern of drift into depressed helplessness on the part of the sexually abused group in which physical and sexual abuse in adulthood were heaped on one another.

Our small sample of sexually abused females, now adult, is unique in that it consists of the only follow-up study from childhood of which we are aware. The evidence we have suggests that (a) the adverse effects of untreated sexual abuse during childhood, within the family context are indeed frequent, gross and long-lasting; (b) those effects are intertwined with, but are distinguishable from the effects of other early trauma. Although the sexually abused individuals may to a greater degree be vulnerable and to experience particular kinds of stress in childhood, sexual abuse has a specific influence on later mental adjustment.

Physical abuse and neglect have long term adverse outcomes particularly in terms of psychoneurosis, while sexual abuse influences adverse outcomes in terms of poor sexual adjustment, depression and diminished self-esteem. In the face of such prolonged abuse, the majority of the sexually abused girls in our study seemed to retreat into hopelessness, depersonalization and psychological numbness, variously combined with guilt and chronic depression.

This hopeless and helpless attitude led many of these girls into abusing relationships as adults, and a number had experienced both physical and sexual abuse in relationships with males. The results of this study, while based on a small and selected sample, do interlock with a growing body of literature which demonstrates the long term harm which family sexual abuse can produce.

In interpreting these results, it should be borne in mind that the families from which the sample are drawn are quite similar to the subcultural, disorganized families in which child abuse of various kinds is frequent (Oliver and Cox, 1973). In his review of British and other materials Will (1983) identifies two types of incestuous families: the 'chaotic' family, and the 'endogamous' incestuous family. The girls we studied clearly came from 'chaotic' rather than 'endogamous' families. Whether long term psychological outcomes for victims of sexual abuse from these two types of sexually abusive families are different is a matter for further research.

Notes

1. Physical abuse was defined as a medically verified assault on the child, leaving bruises, cuts, burns, fractures or internal injuries detectable on examination at least one week after the event. Neglect was defined as under-nutrition and/or exposure to infection because of unsanitary conditions in the home for more than three

23

months, defined according to public health standards prevailing at the time. The nurse comparison group may also have experienced some earlier sexual assault, given the prevalence figure of at least 20 per cent of female populations having experienced some sexual assault or abuse before the age of 14 (Russell, 1983). This possibility was not investigated in the 'normal' comparison group, but should be born in mind in interpreting the results.

2. Results of multiple regression are heavily dependent on the variable which enters the regression procedure first. The strongest original predictor will, unless otherwise specified, always enter the regression equation first. Keeping sexual abuse out of the regression equation until the last step results in correlations with the three selected outcome measures which are reduced in magnitude, but remain significant.

    The regression program used here was Version 8 of the Statistical Package for the Social Sciences (Nie, et al., 1975).

Table 2.1
Mean values of indicators of maladjustment in combinations of sexual abuse, maternal separation and physical neglect or abuse in 87 females

Group	N	Variable	Mean	Standard deviation
Sexually Abused, Separated, and Physically Abused or Neglected	6	(1) Psychoneurosis	18.0	8.1
		(2) Psychosexual Adjustment	51.9	17.4
		(3) Self-Esteem	13.1	5.8
		(4) Depression	7.7	4.4
Sexually Abused and Separated	14	(1) Psychoneurosis	13.6	5.0
		(2) Psychosexual Adjustment	59.9	18.7
		(3) Self-Esteem	10.5	4.4
		(4) Depression	6.6	3.2
Separated and Physically Abused or Neglected	18	(1) Psychoneurosis	13.1	4.7
		(2) Psychosexual Adjustment	47.3	13.2
		(3) Self-Esteem	8.7	3.9
		(4) Depression	4.7	2.9
Separated only	19	(1) Psychoneurosis	13.25	4.3
		(2) Psychosexual Adjustment	44.3	12.7
		(3) Self-Esteem	8.9	3.7
		(4) Depression	5.2	3.4
Normal Childhood	30	(1) Psychoneurosis	11.1	3.7
		(2) Psychosexual Adjustment	36.8	9.2
		(3) Self-Esteem	7.5	2.2
		(4) Depression	3.5	1.8

Note: The higher the score, the poorer the adjustment.

Table 2.2
Correlation of variables in follow-up study of sexually abused, separated and normal childhood groups (N = 87)

		1.	2.	3.	4.	5.	6.	7.
1.	Sexually abused	-	-	-	-	-	-	-
2.	Separated from parent as a child	0.42	-	-	-	-	-	-
3.	Physically abused or neglected	0.04	0.47	-	-	-	-	-
4.	Recent Stress	0.02	0.09	0.18	-	-	-	-
5.	Psychoneurosis	0.28	0.31	0.24	0.01	-	-	-
6.	Sexual Maladjustment	0.54	0.32	-	0.09	0.52	-	-
7.	Self-esteem	0.36	0.35	0.21	-0.05	0.57	0.62	-
8.	Depression	0.60	0.55	0.19	-0.03	0.65	0.56	0.59

Note: Correlations of 0.24 to 0.27 significant at the 5% level.
Correlations of 0.28 to 0.35 significant at the 1% level.
Correlations of 0.36 and above significant at the 0.1% level and beyond.

Table 2.3
Multiple regression with adjustment as dependent variables, and earlier stress as predictor variables in 87 subjects

Predictor	Correlation before multiple regression (Simple Pearson's r)	Correlation after multiple regression	Beta
A. Dependent Variable: Psychoneurosis			
Early separation	0.31	0.31	0.22
Early sexual abuse	0.28	0.17	0.17
Early neglect or physical abuse	0.24	0.14	0.14
Recent stress	0.01	0.01	0.03
B. Dependent Variable: Sexual Maladjustment			
Early sexual abuse	0.54	0.54	0.46
Early separation	0.32	0.10	0.20
Recent stress	0.09	0.01	0.13
Early neglect or physical abuse	0.15	0.09	0.14
C. Dependent Variable: Poor Self-Esteem			
Early sexual abuse	0.36	0.36	0.27
Early separation	0.35	0.23	0.20
Early neglect or physical abuse	0.21	0.10	0.10
Recent stress	-0.05	-0.05	-0.05
D. Dependent Variable: Depression			
Early sexual abuse	0.60	0.60	0.44
Early separation	0.55	0.33	0.38
Recent stress	-0.03	-0.04	-0.06
Early neglect or physical abuse	0.19	0.00	-0.01

Note: Correlation of 0.24 and above after multiple recession are significant at the five per cent level or beyond. Beta is the standardized regression coefficient. Correlations after multiple regression are 'partial correlations' (Nie, et al., 1975, p. 332-334).

Table 2.4
Multiple regression with adjustment as dependent variables in 57 subjects from disorganized families

Predictor	Sexual maladjustment			Self esteem			Depression		
	Before m.r.	After m.r.	Beta	Before m.r.	After m.r.	Beta	Before m.r.	After m.r.	Beta
Sexual abuse	0.36	0.36	0.39	0.33	0.33	0.32	0.33	0.33	0.31
Physical abuse or neglect	0.25	0.20	0.20	0.15	0.10	0.11	0.10	0.11	0.10
Age Separated from mother	-0.11	-0.09	-0.09	-0.33	-0.10	-0.09	-0.15	-0.09	-0.19
Degree of behaviour problem before removal	0.25	0.05	0.04	0.25	0.17	0.16	0.26	0.07	0.06
Multiple correlation squared	-	0.15	-	-	0.14	-	-	0.15	-

Note: Correlations of 0.26 to 0.35 are significant at the five per cent level; correlations of 0.36 and above are significant at the one per cent level. Beta is the standardized regression coefficient, and correlations after regression are partial correlations (Nie, et al., 1975).

3 Child sexual abuse in Canada: Further analysis of the 1983 national survey

Abstract

A national survey of unwanted sexual acts experienced by a random sample of 2,135 Canadian adults aged 19 to 85 yielded data on 893 Canadian females, and 935 Canadian males. Defining sexual abuse as unwanted sexual touching, or attempted or achieved vaginal or anal intercourse indicated that 17.6 per cent of females, and 8.2 per cent of males experienced such abuse before their 17th birthday. For 10 per cent of female victims and 26 per cent of male victims these were assaults which continued over a long period of time. In the majority of cases (84 per cent for females and 72 per cent for males) the assailant was known to the victim. While father-daughter sexual abuse was relatively rare, abuse by other family members was not uncommon; but the most frequently mentioned group of abusers were acquaintances and family friends. Immediate emotional harm was experienced by nearly half of the female victims, and by 20 per cent of male victims. Similar proportions of male and female victims (some 80 per cent) failed to report the abuse to anyone. The most frequently cited reasons for not reporting were shame, fear of the abuser, and fear that the victim would not be believed. Almost all of those who abused a female victim were male, but 18 per cent of those with male victims were female. Thirty per cent of the assailants of both males and females were aged under 18. Juvenile assailants tended to use more force and threat, and more brutal methods of assault. Nevertheless, it was the more subtle assaults perpetrated by older males which caused the most emotional harm. Some demographic differences emerged in victimization experience. Male victims were somewhat more likely to come from urban, French-speaking backgrounds, while female victims were more likely to come from English-speaking, small town or rural backgrounds. However,

overall there was no socio-economic, ethnic, linguistic, religious or regional group which was not at risk for sexual abuse in childhood. Respondents born after 1950 were significantly more likely to have been victims of sexual abuse in childhood, and this may have been related to changes in family circumstances. In conclusion, these data carry some important implications for policy innovation and for further research, particularly that aimed to monitor changes in the prevalence of child sexual abuse and the effects of programs of prevention and integrated care.

Introduction: Adult recall studies of child sexual abuse

The Report of the Committee on Sexual Offences Against Children and Youth chaired by Dr. Robin Badgley, and published in 1984 under the auspices of the Minister of Justice and Attorney General of Canada and the Minister of National Health and Welfare, was a landmark document. The Report was based on a number of national surveys of the extent of and response to the problem and offered 52 well-reasoned recommendations, a number of which were accepted by the government of Canada, and were passed into law (Dawson, 1987; Wells, 1990). Among the surveys commissioned for the Badgley Committee was a survey of the extent of child sexual abuse recalled by a random sample of Canadian adults. This is the only national survey of the problem in North America, although a number of random surveys of child sexual abuse recalled by adults in local and special communities exist (Bagley and King, 1990).

The advantages of a study of sexual abuse recalled by an adult population is that one is able to obtain an estimate of the total prevalence of sexual abuse in childhood in a particular population or community. Adult surveys have both strengths and weaknesses however. Essentially, an adult survey provides historical information about the extent of child sexual abuse in the community in past years. The data provided can lead us however, to make informed guesses about the amount of current abuse by examining the amount of abuse recalled by younger respondents (say, those aged 18 through 25). Data in younger respondents can also give us some idea of change in the amount of abuse reported, provided that the samples of the different age groupings are large enough. These data on changes in prevalence are valuable in giving possible clues to sociological indicators which may underlie such changes.

The adult recall of events of childhood abuse is also a technique by which the success or otherwise of prevention programs, and programs encouraging the reporting of sexual abuse to protection authorities can be assessed.

Recall surveys with young adults as respondents also avoid the ethical and procedural problems involved in asking similar questions of children —

problems which involve gaining parental consent before asking such questions in a general, screening sense; and the need to involve child protection authorities when a child reveals abuse.

The methodology of adult recall studies has been extensively reported and explored by recent writers (Finkelhor and Hotaling, 1984; Finkelhor, 1984; Painter, 1986; Wyatt and Peters, 1986; Russell, 1986; Bagley and Ramsay, 1986). It is clear that estimates derived from child protection authorities and from police give a marked underestimate of the amount of child sexual abuse, and a biased picture of the nature of such abuse. Less than 20 per cent of victims (according to the adult recall surveys) report abuse to an adult, and only certain types of abuse (e.g. those defined by authorities as 'incest') may be referred to treatment agencies.

The methods of research used in adult recall surveys can influence the amount of abuse reported: surveys which involve a personal interview in which rapport is established with the respondent, and in which questions about abuse are asked in several different contexts, are likely to reveal the most abuse. The age range covered (e.g. abuse occurring before age 17 or 16) and the definitions of sexual abuse (e.g. including or excluding sexual threats or exposure without touching) and the exact wording of questions will also influence the amount of abuse which the study finally reports. Another factor which influences the final figure on 'abuse' which a study reports is the degree to which it is assumed that the young person exercised volition in a sexual relationship, and some complicated methods for assessing this have been devised (Finkelhor, 1979). The data from the national Canadian survey which we report below avoided this problem by asking respondents to report only unwanted sexual contact.

Bearing in mind these various methodological approaches and problems, we should note that the prevalence rates for abuse of females which have emerged in various studies range from six to 62 per cent in females, and from three to 21 per cent in males (Peters, Wyatt and Finkelhor, 1986). The median rate of abuse reported in 22 studies in North America is 22 per cent in females. The average rate of child sexual abuse in males, as reported in eleven North American studies, is eight per cent. The original estimates offered by Badgley (1984a) for serious sexual abuse were quite close to these averages, when only events of sexual touching and attempted or achieved penetration were considered. However, as will emerge from the reanalysis of the national Canadian survey presented below, for a number of reasons the initial estimates contained in the Badgley report have to be significantly revised.

In the initial publicity surrounding the issue of the Badgley Report in 1984, much was made in press handouts of the prevalence of sexual abuse which included exposure and threats as well as unwanted sexual contact, occurring at all ages and not just in childhood. The main report reinforced

31

the initial, sensationalistic, journalistic presentations which were followed by popular disbelief. The Report had suggested that when all types of abuse, at all ages were combined: 'About one in two females and one in three males had been the victims of sexual offences' (Badgley, 1984a, p. 193). While it was added that 'children and youths under 21 constitute a majority of the victims' (p. 193), the 'one in two' figure was at first greeted as an unqualified and spectacular estimate of the amount of child sexual abuse. In speaking to various community groups in Canada about the Report and the problem in general, I have come across many individuals who have been both astonished and sceptical about what they assume to be a 'one in two' figure of serious assaults against children.

The questionnaire and methodology of the national Canadian survey

The survey, undertaken by the Gallup Organization used the methods of stratified random sampling often associated with market survey work. The stratified random sample while not as statistically 'pure' as a straightforward random sample (in that sampling error is more difficult to estimate) has stood the test of time in terms of the validity of its results — for example, in the prediction of election outcomes. A stratified survey divides the area to be surveyed into districts according to known population parameters, and takes random samples within selected districts, stratified according to expected age and sex profiles (derived from census data) within these districts. Final choice of the sample, both of strata and of respondents within strata, is carried out by random methods of selection (Hoinville and Jowell, 1978).

The interviewers employed by the survey firm were appropriately experienced in market survey techniques, and specially briefed for this particular national survey. But they had no particular background in administering questionnaire on sensitive areas such as child abuse. In fact, the questionnaire was handed to the respondent with the assurance:

> Because of their personal nature, we ask you to answer the questions without the involvement of our interviewer, who has not seen the questionnaire, and will not be able to discuss them with you. . . . The information requested will be held in strictest confidence. There is no place on the questionnaire to identify yourself, and we ask that you do not do so . . . When you have completed the questions, there is an envelope inside for you to seal your answers. All questionnaires will be returned to the Canadian Gallup Poll, still sealed. (Badgley, 1984a, p. 177)

32

The survey was undertaken between the last week of January and the first week of February 1983. The Gallup Organization initially reported a return rate of 94.1 per cent (2,008 questionnaires returned of the 2,135 left with potential respondents). This, it should be said, is an exceptionally high return rate for this type of survey (Peters, Wyatt and Finkelhor, 1986). In fact, as we have discovered in a reanalysis of these data, only 1,833 questionnaires (85.8 per cent) provided usable or relatively complete information on the questions regarding sexual assault. Males were significantly more likely to complete the questionnaire, so although the sexes were equally balanced in the sampling procedure, 898 questionnaires from female respondents were finally analyzable, compared with 935 questionnaires from males.

The questionnaire was in four parts. The first section asked about knowledge of and attitudes to the availability and distribution of pornography. The second section asked about age at first sexual intercourse — it is not clear why this section was included, although a cross-classification with the sexual assault data indicates that about half the cases in which this experience occurred in someone under 17 involved an 'unwanted' sexual act. Virtually all of the cases of sexual intercourse in females under 13 were 'unwanted.' We could not detect any significant links between attitudes to pornography and sexual abuse experience, and data from that analysis are not reported here.

The third section of the questionnaire, and by far the longest, asked about 'unwanted sex acts.' The questionnaire is quite complex and detailed, and problems which might have been encountered by those who are functionally illiterate — some 15 per cent of the population according to one Canadian survey (Bagley, 1988d) — are not indicated by the Gallup Organization, nor by Badgley (1984a). Our own analysis does indicate a significant link between poorly completed questionnaires (with many gaps in the information provided) and completing fewer years of education. To the extent that people with less education have a greater risk of victimization as some research has suggested (Kelly and Scott, 1986), this survey will have underestimated the amount of child sexual abuse in Canada.

Other factors also mean that this survey will provide an underestimate of the true prevalence of the sexual exploitation of children. Some individuals, particularly older people, may be reluctant to talk about or reveal episodes of sexual abuse which took place in childhood. Older people may recall only the most serious and traumatizing events. It is known from clinical evidence that some individuals cope with the trauma of childhood sexual abuse by repression, the development of multiple personality, or borderline psychotic states of various kinds (Bagley, 1985a). Some individuals, therefore may simply not recall serious sexual abuse in childhood, even though that abuse has significantly impaired their adult adjustment. The

same may be said of abuse taking place before the child's fifth year, when memories are particularly likely to be confused (McFarlane, 1986).

Using customary techniques for sampling populations involves another problem. It is known that victims of severe and prolonged child sexual abuse are particularly likely to enter deviant populations (Bagley, 1985a; Bagley and Young, 1987, 1988). This means that they are found disproportionately amongst runaway youth, street kids, young prostitutes, and institutionalized populations of various kinds. However, normal sampling procedures will fail to identify these populations, so that a general population survey is likely to underestimate the amount of serious, long term abuse.

The fourth part of the questionnaire used in the national survey asked about the socio-demographic background of the respondent. The information gathered was fairly brief, with few questions about childhood family circumstances.

This national survey has both strengths and weaknesses. The questions about sexual abuse have the merit that they ask only about unwanted sex acts. Previous research (e.g. Finkelhor, 1979) had asked about all sexual acts in which under-age persons had participated. This yielded a great deal of data which was difficult to handle — since adolescents are often sexually active, for the most part voluntarily. Younger children too often engage in sexual play and exploration with peers, and these sexual acts are usually voluntary rather that abusive or unwanted. The researcher is left with the problem of deciding which of the events are actually abusive, and has to resort to complicated procedures such as establishing the age differences between the two parties (e.g. Finkelhor, 1979), or assessing psychological outcomes (e.g. Sorrenti-Little et al., 1984), or the amount of force, threat or abuse of authority involved. The Badgley definition asked only about unwanted sex acts, and so avoided many of the procedural problems which other researchers have had to face. The Badgley approach does however mean that some illegal sex acts — for example between an adult and a child, which the child decides, in retrospect were not 'unwanted' — will not be recorded by this method. In essence then this method is essentially conservative, and asks only about sexual incidents in childhood which have the possibility for causing some trauma or discomfort, both in the short and the long run.

We have recorded a maximum of one abusive event (the most serious) whenever a respondent reports more than one unwanted sexual approach on a different occasion. We have not considered exposure and threats separately, since we had no sure way of knowing whether or not these were aspects of more serious assaults, occurring at the same time, or earlier on. One problem with the national survey questionnaire is that respondents were asked to describe only the first unwanted sexual approach or act within any

category. Yet it is known from other studies that some children are victimized at separate times in their lives, by new assailants (Bagley and Ramsay, 1986). Once a child's victim status has been confirmed, these subsequent assaults are often more serious and more abusive. The national survey failed to ask specifically about subsequent sexual assaults by different assailants. This survey will, for that reason, be likely to have underestimated the seriousness of the sexual assaults experienced by victims in their childhood years.

In sum, the questionnaire and the survey method is likely to have both strengths and limitations. The completion of the questionnaire was not supervised or controlled, a factor which probably leads to under-reporting. There is no check on the validity of the information offered, but it is likely that respondents would be likely to under-report events of sexual assault, rather than to fabricate them. The design of the questionnaire is likely to underestimate the prevalence of serious sexual assaults. Only the most serious of the first-time assaults has been considered in the present reanalysis of the national survey data. Problems of sampling, including the failure to reach deviant or institutionalized adult populations mean that many events of the most serious abuse will have been missed in this national survey.

Methods of analysis

In the tables below we have condensed many pages of computer printout, and have not presented the degrees of statistical freedom (the compound of rows and columns in a cross-classification) for any table. Also, for reasons of space we have not given the exact value of Chi-Squared, which varies according to the degrees of freedom. The significance of Chi-Squared is presented in terms of the probability of a difference as large as the one presented in the table occurring by chance. Thus, the smaller the probability, the greater the significance. A probability level of 0.05 or a one in 20 chance possibility is assumed as the significance level in this study. The higher the level of Cramer's V, the greater the association between the two variables, with a theoretical range of zero (no association) to one (perfect association).

Analysis of the national survey data is exploratory rather than hypothesis testing, since the survey was not designed with any particular hypothesis in mind, being quasi-epidemiological in nature. We have, however compared variables related to assaults as well as some background variables, between age groups within the sexes, and between the sexes; and we have compared background variables between the abused and the non-abused. However, the

possible under-estimation of the amount of abuse is a factor working against statistical significance in comparisons.

The data have been set up for analysis by the Statistical Program for the Social Sciences, established within the Honeywell Multics System at The University of Calgary. The principal statistical test used was the well-known Chi-Squared test, which is a robust method of testing for non-random variations, and makes no assumptions about the linearity or 'normality' of any variable's distribution.

A measure of association derived from Chi-Squared is presented in most tables. This measure is Cramer's V, which is derived from Chi-Squared by a simple formula. In cross-tabulations with two cells and two columns, V is identical with the well-known statistics Phi, Rho and Pearson's r. The multiple regression analyses presented do make linear assumptions for data, and for this reasons a restricted range of variables has been considered, with a reordering of categories for some variables into a smaller number so that an approximation to a normal distribution can be obtained. These various statistical methods and tests are well described in Nie et al. (1975).

Results: Female victims

The prevalence and types of child sexual abuse in females in the national Canadian survey

We have defined sexual abuse in childhood in this national Canadian sample as unwanted touching or interference with the child's genital area, buttocks or breasts which occurred prior to the child's 17th birthday. According to this definition, 158 of the 898 females in the national survey for whom reasonably complete information was available, reported abuse of this type, or 17.6 per cent. For the various reasons indicated above, this must be regarded as a conservative estimate of the prevalence of child sexual abuse.

Table 3.1 indicates the types of assaults experienced by the female respondents, compared between respondents aged less than 13, and aged 13 to 16. In general, the types of assault experienced by the two age groups were rather similar, although younger respondents reported more touching of the crotch or vagina, while older respondents reported somewhat more attempted vaginal insertion by the assailant, although younger respondents actually reported more achieved vaginal insertion. This could reflect the lack of ability in younger respondents to resist or limit the assault. This is probably reflected too in the fact that somewhat more of those who were younger when the assaults began endured the assaults for a longer frequency. More older respondents reported touching of breasts; this presumably reflects developmental factors, although it should be noted that

36

as many of the younger victims reported oral-breast contact as did those who were older when the assault began.

Finally, it should be noted that the rate of assault is higher in those who were aged between 13 and 16 at first assault: there were 93 assaults in total, or an average inception of 23 cases per year at risk in the victims aged 13 to 16, compared with an average inception rate of nine cases per year for the younger victim group, making the conservative assumption that assaults which did not continue past the child's fifth year could not be recalled. It is possible too that some respondents whose assault began when they were less than 13 were subject to fresh assaults (by a new assailant) in their teenage years — but this will not usually be recorded in the present survey. It is known from clinical studies (e.g. Russell, 1986) however, that this is a distinct possibility.

Trauma which resulted from the assault on female respondents

Table 3.2 presents the comparisons of psychological and physical outcomes for the younger and older female victims. Nearly two-thirds of those aged less than 13 reported immediate emotional trauma as a result of the abuse, compared with 31 per cent of the older victims. However, significant physical harm was much more likely to result from the assaults on the older respondents. Some 10 per cent of the older victims became pregnant as a result of the assaults; not all of these pregnancies were carried to term.

The factors which are associated with a report of significant emotional harm at the time of the assault are reported in Table 3.3. In this multiple regression analysis (which calculates the correlation of each of the variables considered after its correlation with all the other predictor variables is controlled for) being younger at the time of the assault, the seriousness of the assault, and betrayal of trust in a relationship all combined to predict the individual's report of emotional harm. The physical harm which resulted was relevant only for older victims however. These variables compound one another, and a combination of these factors is much more likely to result in emotional harm.

Characteristics of the assailants of female victims

The data (Table 3.3) show that those who carried out the abuse of these female victims were overwhelmingly male. What is surprising however is that some 13 per cent of assailants acted together with other males. There are no significant differences in this respect between younger and older victims. We do know, however, that these 'gang' situation usually involved groups of older adolescent males, or older boys. Although many victims were unable to recall or report the age of the aggressor, it is clear that a

significant minority (some 30 per cent) of those reporting the age of assailant reported that the assailant was younger than 18. It could be that age is more likely to be recalled, or recalled accurately when the assailant is a known peer. Nevertheless, these findings are of particular interest and have emerged clearly in some previous adult recall surveys (Bagley and Thurston, 1988).

There is a statistically significant association between the age of victim and the age(s) of the assailant(s) — younger victims were assaulted by somewhat younger assailants.

The interpersonal circumstances of the assault did not differ significantly between the two age groupings of victims. For both, physical threat, direct force, and/or verbal threat emerged as the most prevalent factors associated with the assault. The simple use of authority by an older person was not mentioned, since it was not presented to respondents as an option in the questionnaire.

Table 3.5 indicates a significant difference in the relationship of victim to the abuser between the two age groups of victims: the younger age group were much more likely to be victimized by a family member or a relative, while the largest category for the older victims was an acquaintance of some kind. The largest difference between the two age groups with respect to family relationship was that more of the younger victims had been assaulted by a father, grandfather or uncle. When these categories of relationship are combined, there is a highly significant difference between the two age groups with respect to biological relationship with the assailant. Overall, 14 cases of sexual assault on a female child by her biological father were identified in this national survey, or 1.6 per cent of all of those surveyed. Non-victims were not asked to report their family circumstances in detail so it is not known precisely how many of the non-victims were reared away from their biological father, or with a stepfather. We cannot therefore estimate the risk factors for sexual assault by a biological father, as opposed to the risk of abuse by a step-father. The unadjusted estimate of 1.6 per cent for father-daughter 'incest' in the Canadian population does suggest however that the problem is less prevalent than some clinical workers have asserted; this estimate does however accord with that offered in another random sample of Canadian adults (Bagley and Ramsay, 1986).

It should be noted that abuse by a total stranger occurred in only some 13 per cent of cases of sexual assault. Children and young persons are most likely to be assaulted by someone they know, and in the case of girls under 13, someone they trust as well.

Actions taken by the female victims following the assault

The most striking finding with respect to action taken (Table 3.6) is that the majority of victims took no action — 77 per cent of younger victims and 86 per cent of older victims did not tell anyone about the assault. However, younger victims (15.4 per cent) were more likely to tell someone immediately afterwards. The main reason given by the younger victims for not telling anyone was being afraid of the person who carried out the abuse. Stranger abuse was most likely to be reported to someone; abuse by a close family member was least likely to be reported. Being ashamed, and assuming that others would not believe them were also given as reasons for not reporting by the younger victims. The most prevalent reasons given by older victims were being too ashamed, and the matter being too personal to tell anyone.

Those victims who did inform an adult were unlikely to be helped. The numbers are too small to be put in tabular form: only five assailants (to the victim's knowledge) were interviewed by police, but only two were charged, one offender being finally jailed. Three of the female victims who reported continued to be sexually assaulted, even after they had told an adult about the sexual abuse. Failure to report abuse to anyone occurred at fairly even rates in victims of all ages. There is no evidence from this survey that there was a greater tendency to report abuse by victims who mere assaulted after 1970 when, in theory at least, recognition and understanding of the problem of child sexual abuse had increased.

Demographic profiles of female victims

It is important to establish whether victims are in general similar in demographic terms in those in the general population who were not assaulted. It is often claimed in the literature that child sexual abuse has no barriers in terms of region, social class or ethnicity. While the Canadian data show that this generalization is true, there are also some groups who appear to be somewhat more at risk than others.

In terms of region, there are some significant differences, with a trend for there to be somewhat less sexual abuse of females in the Atlantic and Quebec regions, and slightly more in the other regions of Canada. Large cities are somewhat under-represented in terms of adult females recalling events of sexual abuse in their childhood; but residents of smaller towns are somewhat more likely to recall such abuse. There is no over-representation of those living in highly rural and farm areas, however.

Those women who grew up speaking French or another language than English were somewhat less likely to recall sexual abuse before their 17th

39

year. Protestants are over-represented amongst those who recall such abuse, and Catholics are under-represented.

Age is a significant variable associated with a recollection of sexual abuse in childhood. Women who are younger at the time they were interviewed were more likely to report sexual abuse in childhood. Thirty-one per cent of women aged 43 or less when interviewed reported sexual abuse occurring before their 17th birthday, compared with 15.4 per cent of women aged 44 and over. This trend is consistent with some previous reports (e.g. Russell, 1986), but is difficult to interpret. It could mean that younger women are more ready or more able to report events of sexual abuse in childhood (in which case this survey will have significantly underestimated the overall amount of sexual abuse in the childhood of the older population); or it could mean that the prevalence of child sexual abuse is actually increasing.

Three key variables distinguishing victims from non-victims — age, community and linguistic background — have been combined in a multiple regression analysis predicting a history of childhood sexual abuse (Table 3.15). These variables contribute significantly to an additive model in predicting the prevalence of abuse. Women born in larger urban communities before 1950, and whose home language was French had a rate of abuse of 12.4 per cent; but those born in smaller, English-speaking communities after 1950 had an average abuse rate of 35.6 per cent. This finding is a most interesting one in historical terms, and we cannot advance any particular explanation for the somewhat higher rate of abuse in smaller, English-speaking communities. However, changes in family structure since 1950 could well explain the higher rate of abuse in the younger respondents.

Results: Male victims

The prevalence and types of child sexual abuse reported by males in the national canadian survey

Table 3.8 indicates that 8.2 per cent of the 935 males for whom reasonably complete data exist in this national Canadian survey reported sexual abuse before their 17th birthday, which involved at least the touching of their genital area or buttocks. The commonest type of assault for both age groups (assault occurring before age 13 or between ages 13 and 16) was a manual and/or an oral assault on the victim's penis. Younger victims were somewhat more likely to be subject to such an assault, while older victims were more likely to experience attempted or achieved insertion by a finger, object or penis into their anus. Younger victims experienced a greater frequency of abuse overall, although there was sub-group of older victims who were subjected to very regular assaults.

40

Nearly twice as many cases of first time assault were reported to have occurred during the teenage years, compared with assaults occurring before age 13. As with females then, adolescence is a particular time of risk for unwanted sexual acts for males.

Trauma which resulted from the assault on male respondents

Nineteen per cent of male victims experienced significant emotional hurt following the unwanted sexual act; this is a lower proportion than in females. Unlike females, a higher proportion of emotional hurt was experienced in males by the age group 13 to 16 years. Only assault involving the child's anus resulted in significant physical harm.

Characteristics of the assailants of male victims

The data (Table 3.10) indicate the surprising finding that 18 per cent of the assailants on these under-age males were females. In every case where age of assailant is reported, the female was older than the victim. These female assailants included both teenagers and adults. In a number of cases (eight per cent) the assailants were males acting in a group. Thirty per cent of assailants were under the age of 18, although this figure must be read in the light of the fact that in a significant number of cases the age of the assailant was not recorded. As with females, assault by peers and acquaintances may have involved a more accurate recall of age. A special analysis of characteristics of assault by individuals aged less than 18 is presented later on in this chapter.

For males aged 12 or less at the time of the first assault, the most frequent reasons given for participation in the assault was the encouragement of someone other than the assailant. For older victims, the drinking behaviour of the assailant was most frequently cited as a factor (in 16 per cent of cases). Physical force or threat was cited rather infrequently in both victim age groups.

Assault by a stranger occurred somewhat more frequently in younger victims than in older male victims (31 versus 26 per cent of cases). For both groups assault by a stranger had greater frequency than for females. Assault by a close relative was relatively rare, and the most frequently cited groups were acquaintances, family friends, neighbours and peers. There was a significant difference in this respect between the victim age groups: those over 12 were more likely to cite a peer or peers as the assailant(s), and less likely to cite a neighbour. No biological fathers were cited as assailants; the only categories of relatives identified were uncles and step-fathers.

Actions taken by the male victims following the assault

Male victims infrequently told anyone about the assault: 73 per cent of the younger victims and 80 per cent of the older victims told no one (Table 3.12). Those who said they did inform someone were generally, unforthcoming in the questionnaire about the details; however, no victim reported telling the police or anyone in authority about the assault, and none of the assailants was reportedly charged.

Among the reasons given for not reporting, fear of or threats by the assailants were an infrequently given reason. However, younger victims cited the fact that the assault 'didn't bother me' as the most frequent reason, while older victims cited the fact that they were 'too ashamed' most frequently. Reports of emotional harm were strongly correlated with these feelings of shame, which were reported by four per cent of younger victims, and by 20 per cent of older victims.

Demographic profiles of male victims

There are a number of significant socio-demographic differences between victims and non-victims in this national Canadian sample of males. However, the victim population is too small to make comparison between older and younger victims meaningful, in comparison with the remaining population (Table 3.13).

Some slight but statistically significant regional differences occur: the prevalence of assault reported by males is somewhat higher in Quebec, somewhat lower in British Columbia, and about at par in Ontario, the Prairies and the Atlantic region when proportions in the sample across the regions are compared. Prevalence rates were significantly lower in rural and small communities, and higher in communities of more than 100,000 residents. Male respondents growing up in a French-speaking and/or a Catholic environment reported significantly more abuse in childhood.

Age of respondent at interview is also a statistically significant predictor of assault experience in males. Respondents born after 1960 (aged between 18 and 23 at the time of interview) reported a higher prevalence of abuse: 25.3 per cent of these younger respondents reported serious sexual abuse occurring before their 17th birthday. In contrast, 7.6 per cent of male respondents aged 44 and over, reported serious sexual abuse in childhood or adolescence. It could be (as with females) that older respondents are more reluctant than younger respondents to talk about or reveal abuse; or the higher prevalence in younger respondents could be a reflection of statistical factors (an unknown sampling error); or the difference could be a real one, and reflects sociological factors not yet identified.

Further statistical analysis (not shown in tables) indicates that the other significant difference between the two groups (abused and non-abused) are a reflection of age differences. The younger respondents (amongst whom abuse victims are over-represented) are more likely to have white collar jobs, have more years of education, somewhat higher incomes, and larger household sizes.

In Table 3.16 we have undertaken a multiple regression of three variables which predict the prevalence of assault experience in males. These variables both interact with and add to one another in a predictive equation: the overall correlation between these three variables and the experience of abuse 0.27. The highest risk factors were for a man now aged 18 to 23 living in a large city in Quebec, and speaking French: the assault rate recalled by such individuals in this survey was 32.1 per cent.

Comparison of differences between male and female victim groups in the national Canadian survey

In Table 3.14 we present a statistical comparison between male and female victim groups on a number of variables, selected because of their salience or presumed importance. When males are assaulted, they are more likely to be victims of an assault continuing over a longer time. However, stranger assault is more common in males, and these tend to one time assaults. Relatives or close family members are much more likely to be the assailants in the case of females. Males are most at risk from acquaintances and peers, and it is these relationships which tend to be associated with continued, unwanted sexual acts. Significant emotional and/or physical hurt immediately following the abuse was significantly more likely to be reported by female rather than male victims.

No significant differences were found when reported age of assailants was compared: for both males and females, about 30 per cent of assailants were aged less than 18. Similar proportions of victims in the male and female groups were aged less than 13 when the first assault occurred. Similar, high proportions in both groups failed to report the assault to anyone. Overall, reasons given for not reporting were generally similar.

A comparison of demographic factors between the male and female victims revealed both similarities and differences. Age profiles were generally similar, with victimization rates being highest in those born after 1959. Regional profiles showed no statistical differences, although proportionately more male than female victims came from Quebec. Significantly more male victims than female victims came from a French-speaking background; and proportionately more female victims came from English-speaking backgrounds. Community of residence also indicated

significant male-female differences: victimization of females was more prevalent in smaller communities; while victimization of males was more prevalent in larger communities, with more than 100,000 inhabitants.

In terms of language and community then, male and female victims show some opposite characteristics. Female victims are more likely to come from English-speaking, smaller communities while male victims are more likely to come from larger, French-speaking communities. It should be stressed that overall, these differences although statistically significant, are relatively small. Sexual abuse of children has occurred, according to this survey to a substantial degree in all communities however large or small, and in all linguistic and religious groups. While the differences observed are of sociological interest, they do not carry any immediate policy implications.

Sexual assaults committed by minors

The fact that about 30 per cent of assailants (where age was identified by the victim) were aged less than 18 is a matter of both sociological and substantive interest (Table 3.17). Prevention strategies may have to address this population differently if it can be shown that the characteristics of this population are different from older offenders. Indeed, it has been argued that adolescence is a crucial time for intervention, at a time before their behaviour becomes confirmed or fixated, and difficult or impossible to treat (Stenson and Anderson, 1987).

Table 3.18 shows the kinds of assaults which perpetrators of various ages inflicted on female victims. Although younger assailants were more likely to indulge in manual assaults on the victim's genitalia, and were slightly less likely to engage in attempted or achieved intercourse or insertion, nevertheless their assaults were as gross or as threatening as those of older assailants. The pattern is somewhat different with regard to assaults on males (Table 3.19): juvenile assailants were more likely to attempt or achieve anal insertion, and were less likely to indulge in manual or oral sex involving the victims penis. We can speculate, without direct evidence, that the juvenile assailants were often using their victims as a proxy for unavailable female partners, while the adult assailants had a more direct sexual interest in their victims and used methods of assault more traditionally associated with adult paedophilia.

Table 3.20 summarizes the statistically significant associations of assault by a juvenile (aged less than 18) on a female victim aged less than 17. First of all, there is some consonance between age of victim and age of assailant: young assailants are more likely to choose as victims girls younger than themselves, so the victims aged less than 13 were more likely to be assaulted by a juvenile (who was usually a teenager).

The assaults by juveniles on females were more likely to be one-time or infrequent assaults, and were more likely to result in threats of violence to prevent the victim reporting the event. Victims were in fact, somewhat more likely to report an assault by an adult. Some interesting demographic associations of being the victim of a juvenile occurred in female respondents. Victims of a younger assailant were more likely (by the time they were adults) to have completed fewer years of education, and to have a currently lower occupational status, and to be currently living in a small town (less than 10,000) or in a rural area. There may be some significant ecological factors in the type of peer group culture in which the victims of juvenile assailants grew up. Finally, it should be noted that juvenile assailants were more likely to act in groups, in a 'gang rape' type of situation.

The situation with regard to male victims (Table 3.21) shows both similarities and differences when comparisons are made with female victims (Table 3.20). Male victims of assault by juveniles also by adulthood had completed fewer years of education, and at the time of interview had lower occupational status, and lower income. Adult assailants with male victims were more likely to use persuasion or gifts to achieve their assault, while juveniles were more likely to use force. Despite this, assault by an adult was more likely to result in emotional harm to the male victim. This seems to reflect relationship to the abuser: assault by an adult involving 'gentle' persuasion, bribery and emotional manipulation was more likely to continue for some time, and more likely to result in emotional hurt. Juvenile assailants used more threats and brutality, and more often attempted or achieved anal insertion. But it was the more subtle, rather more gentle assault by an adult relative or family friend which resulted in the most emotional harm to male victims.

Conclusions, and implications for policy and further research

The Canadian national survey of adult experiences of sexual abuse occurring in childhood has provided a valuable picture of the nature and extent of the problem; and although the survey is retrospective in nature, it does have some implications for current social policy.

The survey is essentially historical in that it asks about events of abuse which happened in the past, sometimes long ago. The earliest event of abuse in this survey was reported by a woman in her seventies, and took place in 1908, while the latest event of abuse occurred in 1981. The majority of abusive events occurred after 1950, and respondents aged 18 through 20 actually reported the highest number of abusive events. This means that although child sexual abuse is certainly not a new problem in

45

society, it may be occurring with greater frequency today (although older individuals might be more unwilling to recall abuse).

We have some detailed profiles of abuse from this survey occurring as recently as the mid and late 1970s and the early 1980s, and this information certainly has implications for current social policy. The proportion of sexual abuse by stepfathers and other close family members (but not by biological fathers) seems to have increased during the century. Overall, the amount of abuse by strangers seems to have remained fairly constant during the present century, judging by the events of sexual abuse in childhood recalled by the respondents.

For a variety of reasons (both those inherent in adult recall surveys and those specific to the Canadian survey) the figures provided are almost certainly an underestimate of the amount of child sexual abuse. A particular problem with the Canadian survey is that since it asked only about the first event of sexual abuse in childhood involving contact, rather than any subsequent and potentially more serious incident, it tended to underestimate the amount of serious abuse in the population. In addition, the method of administering the questionnaires and the failure to control for any reading or comprehension difficulties experienced by respondents may have contributed to under-reporting of abuse, or non-completion of the questionnaire, factors which may be associated with a further underestimate of the amount of child sexual abuse of children recalled by Canadian adults.

Despite these problems of estimating the true rate of past abuse, the Canadian national survey does indicate a significant amount of sexual abuse occurring in the childhood of both males and females: 8.2 per cent of males, and 17.6 per cent of females reported abuse (involving at least unwanted sexual touching) occurring before their 17th year. These estimates are compatible with those obtained in number of community surveys carried out in Canada, Europe, New Zealand, Central America and the United States in recent years (Finkelhor, 1984).

One striking feature of the Canadian survey (a finding reflected in several community studies in Calgary, reported in other chapters) is that regardless of current aged, sex of social status, reporting of the abuse to an adult at the time it occurred was a relatively rare occurrence. When reporting did occur, it was in turn unusual for any effective action to be taken against the abuser in terms of therapy or action by the criminal justice system.

Victims whose abuse occurred in the 1970s and early 1980s were no more likely to report abuse to an adult than were individuals whose victimization occurred in earlier decades. Whatever recognition of the problem has been achieved in recent years, any change in thinking and attitudes by professionals had not affected the victims to a noticeable degree.

Two findings from the national survey deserve comment and interpretation, since they have some implications for current policy

46

formation. These findings relate to teenagers as victims, and as assailants. According to the national survey, the majority of under-age victims (both male and female) were aged between 13 and 16 when the abuse first occurred. This finding has a number of implications for prevention strategies, including educational programs addressed to both potential victims and potential abusers. The survey data also show that some 30 per cent of the assailants of both sexes are aged under 18. Sometimes too, teenagers act with others in groups in the assault of younger boys and girls. It is possible that some of the lone, teenage assailants (including the female teenagers who assault younger males) were themselves former victims. Recent clinical and community studies have suggested this possibility (see later chapters).

There are implications from such findings for intervention and education programs aimed at adolescents, including education which might enhance non-sexual and non-sexist behaviour and attitudes, which could inhibit or control the more brutal expressions of male aggression and sexuality. It is implied too that schools are useful arenas for the early detection and appropriate referral of victims of sexual abuse, and that special training for teachers, and resources in terms of counsellors (and child care workers in elementary schools) would be valuable.

The increasing prevalence of child sexual abuse by step-fathers which the results of this survey imply has a number of implications for family policy, including education and support programs which can advise and support women and men entering second marriages and relationships, as well as a strengthening of existing family counselling services.

While some statistically significant trends have emerged in the survey data with respect to the demographic backgrounds of abuse victims, these differences are too small and too difficult to interpret to have any clear policy significance, although they are intriguing enough to invite further research. What can be said is that the problem of child sexual abuse in Canada, from the evidence of this national survey is a widespread problem, and invites a major commitment by health and welfare programs and services. It is a problem which seriously affects all regions, and potentially threatens all types of individuals from whatever social class, ethnic, linguistic or religious background. Given the comparability of rates of child sexual abuse across many different cultures (Finkelhor, 1994) it is probable too that the nature and impact of such abuse may be broadly similar. This could lead to culturally adapted programs of prevention and treatment which have as the common premise: sexual exploitation of children and adolescents is morally and psychologically wrong, and may have very harmful long term consequences for the victims.[1]

Notes

1. In recent work in Hong Kong we have adapted a Canadian approach for school counselling of distressed teenagers — in both cultures sexual abuse is a major source of stress and suicidal ideation, but requires culturally different counselling approaches — see Bagley (1992) and Tse, Bagley and Mak (1994).

Table 3.1
Nature of assaults in 158 female victims of Unwanted Sexual Acts prior to age 17 (in 898 female respondents in a national Canadian survey)

Type of assault	In 65 respondents aged under 13	In 93 respondents aged 13-16	Cramer's V	Signi-ficance
Breasts touched	61.5%	80.6%	0.36	0.000
Crotch/vagina touched	56.9%	34.4%	0.27	0.000
Buttocks touched	38.5%	43.0%	0.20	0.036
Anus touched	10.8%	1.1%	0.23	0.012
Vagina kissed/licked	7.7%	4.3%	0.10	0.421
Breasts kissed/licked	6.2%	6.5%	0.02	0.832
Anus kissed/licked	1.5%	0%	0.06	0.637
Attempted insertion of finger, object or penis into vagina	30.8%	37.6%	0.17	0.050
Attempted insertion of finger, object or penis into anus	4.6%	3.2%	0.05	0.733
Achieved insertion of finger, object or penis into vagina	18.5%	15.4%	0.12	0.406
Achieved insertion of fingers, object object or penis into anus	7.6%	2.1%	0.20	0.058

Frequency

Once	33.8%	49.5%		
Twice	18.5%	19.3%	0.19	0.055
3 - 5 times	18.5%	18.2%	(combined categories)	
6 - 9 times	15.4%	6.5%		
10+ times	13.8%	6.5%		

Note: Cramer's V is a measure of association derived from Chi-squared. Calculations by SPSS (Nie et al., 1975).

Table 3.2

Immediate trauma following sexual assault in childhood in 172 females in a national random sample of 898 Canadian females

Variable	In 65 respondents aged under 13	In 93 respondents aged 13-16	Cramer's V	Significance
Significant emotional hurt	64.6%	30.9%	0.38	0.000
Significant physical harm	10.8%	35.5%	0.24	0.005
Bruises and scratches	6.1%	11.8%	0.11	0.172
Cuts and bites	0%	2.1%	0.05	0.219
Irritation or redness of anus or vagina	0%	9.7%	0.20	0.044
Bruised and torn vagina or anus	3.1%	2.1%	0.04	0.318
Infections of vagina or anus	0%	2.1%	0.05	0.478
Discharge and bleeding from vagina	4.6%	3.2%	0.03	0.496
Became pregnant	2.1%	9.7%	0.16	0.049

Note: Cramer's V is a measure of association derived from Chi-squared. Calculations by SPSS (Nie et al., 1975).

Table 3.3
Multiple regression analysis of factors predicting immediate emotional hurt resulting from sexual assault in childhood in 867 Canadian females

Variable	Simple r	Partial r	Combined r
Age at which assault first occurred	0.38	0.38	0.38
Seriousness of assault(s) (touching/ attempted insertion/ achieved insertion)	0.35	0.17	0.42
Physical harm or pregnancy resulted from assault(s)	0.32	-0.14	0.44
Relationship (stranger/ acquaintance/ relative/close relative)	0.13	0.12	0.47

Note: A number of cases had to be excluded, since they contained missing data. Correlations of 0.1 and above are significant at the one per cent level or beyond. Regression analysis carried out by SPSS, Version 8.0a (Nie et al., 1975). No particular order of entry of variables into the regression equation was specified.

Table 3.4
Assailants and circumstances of sexual assault in childhood in 158 females in a national random sample of 898 Canadian females

Variable	In 65 respondents aged under 13	In 93 respondents aged 13-16	Cramer's V	Significance
Assailant was male	78.5%	84.9%	0.13	0.567
Assailant was female	0%	2.1%	(combined	
Assailants more than			categories)	
one male	18.5%	9.7%		
Assailants male and				
female	0%	1.1%		
Did not state	3%	2.2%		

Estimated Age of Assailants

14 or less	12.3%	4.3%	0.30	0.002
15 to 17	12.3%	30.1%	(combined	
18 to 24	6.1%	24.7%	categories)	
25+	7.6%	16.1%		
Did not state	61.7%	24.8%		

Estimated Age of Second Assailant

14 or less	3.1%	0%	0.11	0.213
15 to 17	4.6%	2.1%	(combined	
18 to 24	1.5%	6.4%	categories)	
25+	10.8%	4.3%		
Not stated/not relevant	80%	87.2%		

Interpersonal Circumstances

Encouraged by the person	6.2%	5.4%	0.13	0.221
Encouraged by someone else	0%	7.7%	(combined	
Promised a gift or favour	10.8%	5.4%	categories)	
Threatened verbally	15.4%	9.7%		
Threatened with a weapon	1.5%	1.1%		
Physically forced to do it	15.4%	11.8%		
Assailant had been drinking alcohol	4.6%	12.9%		
Any physical threat or force	15.4%	12.9%	0.14	0.175

Table 3.5
Relationship to assailant, in 158 child victims of sexual assault in a national random sample of 898 Canadian females

Variable	In 65 respondents aged under 13	In 93 respondents aged 13-16	Cramer's V	Signi- ficance
<u>Assailant Was:</u>				
A stranger	12.3%	16.4%	0.48	0.001
An employer	0%	4.3%	(combined	
A co-worker	0%	0%	categories)	
An acquaintance	0%	25.8%		
A neighbour	15.4%	4.3%		
A family friend	4.6%	7.5%		
A boyfriend/girlfriend	1.5%	12.9%		
A relative	32.4%	8.4%		
A close family member	33.8%	20.4%		
<u>If A Close Family Member Or Relative:</u>				
Natural father	18.5%	2.1%	0.07	0.181
Stepfather	9.2%	4.3%	(combined	
Natural brother	7.7%	1.1%	categories)	
Step-brother	0%	0%		
Foster brother	3.2%	0%		
Grandfather	4.6%	1.1%		
Uncle	23.2%	17.0%		
Cousin	3.2%	1.1%		
Other relative	4.6%	2.1%		

Table 3.6
Actions taken in relation to sexual assault in childhood in 158 females in a national random sample of 898 Canadian females

Variable	In 65 respondents aged under 13	In 93 respondents aged 13-16	Cramer's V	Significance
Did not report/tell about assault to anyone	76.9%	86.0%		
Told someone immediately afterwards	15.4%	5.4%		
Told someone within 1 day	0%	2.1%		
Told someone within 3 days	0%	2.1%	0.29	0.001
Told someone within one week	0%	0%		(combined categories)
Told someone after more than one week	3.1%	2.1%		
Told a family member	18.5%	9.6%	0.17	0.052
Told a friend	1.5%	4.6%	0.07	0.650
Told police	2.1%	1.1%	0.08	0.551
Told clinic/hospital	0%	0%		
Told family doctor	1.5%	3.2%	0.09	0.419
Told teacher/counsellor	0%	0%		
Told social worker	3.1%	0%	0.12	0.194
Told distress centre/rape centre/help line	0%	0%		
Told other person (priest, lawyer, nurse, other)	0%	0%		

(Note: More than one person sometimes told)

Reasons for not reporting

Too personal a matter to tell anyone	9.2%	20.4%		
Afraid I wouldn't be believed	13.8%	9.6%		
Too ashamed	18.5%	21.5%		

Table 3.6 (Continued)

Variable	In 65 respondents aged under 13	In 93 respondents aged 13-16	Cramer's V	Signi- ficance
Too young to know it was wrong	15.4%	2.1%	0.25	0.004
Felt partly responsible	7.7%	11.8%	(combined categories)	
Wasn't important enough to do anything	10.8%	3.2%		
Didn't bother me that much	3.1%	2.1%		
Didn't want to hurt family members	6.1%	10.7%		
Didn't want to hurt person who did it	4.6%	10.7%		
Afraid of person who did it	23.1%	10.7%		
Threatened not to tell by the person who did it	6.1%	6.4%		
Too angry to do anything	1.5%	4.3%		

(Note: More than one reason for not reporting often given)

Table 3.7

Demographic associations of unwanted sexual acts in childhood, in a national sample of 898 Canadian women

Variable	In 65 respondents aged less than 13 when assault occurred	In 93 respondents aged 13-16 when assault occurred	In all remaining 740 respondents	Cramer's V P
Region				
Atlantic	6.2%	9.7%	10.8%	0.09 0.013
Quebec	21.5%	24.7%	27.8%	(combined
Ontario	41.5%	35.5%	35.5%	categories)
Prairies	15.4%	19.3%	16.2%	
British Columbia	15.4%	10.8%	9.7%	
Urban-Rural Community				
500,000+	32.3%	34.4%	37.8%	0.16 0.008
100,000 - 500,000	18.5%	15.0%	14.0%	(combined
10,000 - 100,000	10.8%	12.9%	14.9%	categories)
1,000 - 10,000	13.8%	15.0%	10.1%	
Under 1,000 and farm	24.6%	22.7%	23.2%	
Language of Childhood				
English	73.8%	79.6%	64.8%	0.19 .000
French	20%	17.2%	26.8%	(combined
Other	6.2%	3.2%	8.4%	categories)
Marital Status				
Single	23.1%	19.3%	16.7%	0.17 0.000
Married	56.9%	61.3%	69.6%	(combined
Co-habiting	3.1%	7.6%	3.5%	categories)
Widowed	0%	2.1%	4.8%	
Separated/ Divorced	16.9%	9.7%	3.6%	

Table 3.7 (Continued)

Variable	In 65 respondents aged less than 13 when assault occurred	In 93 respondents aged 13-16 when assault occurred	In all remaining 740 respondents	Cramer's V P
Religious Preference				
Protestant	55.4%	46.3%	43.2%	0.16 0.005
Jewish	0%	0%	0.9%	(combined
Roman Catholic	32.3%	40.9%	47.5%	categories)
Other	0%	5.4%	1.3%	
None	10.8%	7.5%	7.1%	
Respondent's Current Occupation				
Prof/Executive	9.2%	7.5%	11.8%	0.11 0.369
Sales/Clerical	32.3%	31%	26.2%	(combined
Manual Work/ Other	9.2%	18.3%	17.9%	categories)
Not currently employed/ unknown	49.3%	43.2%	44.1%	
Education				
Grades 0-8	13.3%	8.7%	12.6%	0.10 0.051
Grades 9-13 completed	60%	54.3%	54.4%	(combined) categories)
Post-secondary but, not completed university	10%	26.1%	12.8%	
Completed university	16.7%	10.9%	8.1%	
Household Size (including respondent)				
1	4.7%	4.3%	7.9%	0.11 0.055
2	12.3%	25.8%	22.1%	(combined
3	24.6%	12.9%	21.7%	categories)
4	33.8%	45.2%	26.9%	
5+	24.8%	11.8%	21.4%	

Table 3.7 (Continued)

Variable	In 65 respondents aged less than 13 when assault occurred	In 93 respondents aged 13-16 when assault occurred	In all remaining 740 respondents	Cramer's V P
Children Under 7				
0	40.0%	49.2%	64.7%	0.20 0.009
1	30.8%	25.8%	21.2%	(combined
2	12.3%	17.2%	12.3%	categories)
3+	16.9%	7.8%	1.7%	
Year of Birth				
Prior to 1939	20.0%	19.4%	31.9%	0.22 0.001
1940 to 1949	33.8%	24.7%	25.6%	(combined
1950 to 1959	27.7%	33.3%	14.3%	categories)
1960 to 1965	18.5%	22.6%	14.7%	
Household Income				
Less than $10,000	21.5%	17.2%	13.5%	0.12 0.011
$10,000 - $14,999	6.1%	11.8%	13.5%	(combined
$15,000 - $19,999	12.3%	17.2%	15.5%	categories)
$20,000 - $29,999	24.6%	26.9%	24.2%	
$30,000 - $39,999	7.9%	12.9%	16.1%	
$40,000+	27.6%	14.0%	17.3%	

Table 3.8
Nature of assaults in 77 male victims of unwanted sexual acts prior to age 17 (in 935 male respondents in a national Canadian survey)

Type of assault	In 26 respondents aged under 13	In 51 respondents aged 13-16	Cramer's V	Significance
Penis touched	80.8%	64.7%	0.30	0.017
Buttocks touched	26.9%	25.5%	0.04	0.272
Anus touched	15.4%	5.9%	0.12	´0.178
Kissed/licked penis	30.8%	27.4%	0.04	0.192
Kissed/licked anus	3.8%	5.9%	0.09	0.389
Attempted insertion of finger, object or penis into anus	26.3%	29.4%	0.03	0.200
Achieved insertion of finger, object or penis into anus	11.5%	13.7%	0.02	0.190
Frequency				
Once	38.5%	19.4%		
Twice	11.5%	13.7%		
3 - 5 times	15.3%	21.6%	0.30	0.009
6 - 9 times	19.2%	3.9%		(combined
10+ times	15.5%	31.4%		categories)

Note: Cramer's V is a measure of association derived from Chi-squared. Calculations by SPSS (Nie et al., 1975).

Table 3.9
Immediate trauma following sexual assault in childhood in 77 male victims prior to age 17 (in 935 male respondents in a national Canadian study)

Variable	In 26 respondents aged under 13	In 51 respondents aged 13-16	Cramer's V	Significance
Significant emotional hurt	15.4%	21.6%	0.15	0.225
Significant physical harm	7.7%	11.8%	0.06	0.484
Bruises, scratches, cuts or bites	0%	0%	-	-
Irritation, bruising or redness of anus	7.7%	9.7%	0.04	0.521
Infection	0%	2.0%	0.05	0.579

Note: Cramer's V is a measure of association derived from Chi-squared. Calculations by SPSS (Nie et al., 1975).

Table 3.10
Assailants and circumstances of sexual assault in childhood in 77 male victims in a national random sample of 935 Canadian males

Variable	In 26 respondents aged under 13	In 51 respondents aged 13-16	Cramer's V	Significance of Chi-Squared
Assailant was male	61.5%	60.8%		
Assailant was female	15.4%	19.6%		
Assailant more than one male	11.5%	5.9%	0.18	0.417
Assailant more than one female	0%	3.9%	(combined categories)	
Did not state	11.5%	9.8%		
Estimated Age of Assailant				
14 or less	11.5%	2.0%		
15 - 17	30.8%	21.6%		
18 - 24	26.9%	29.4%	0.26	0.213
25+	11.5%	9.8%	(combined categories)	
Did not state	19.3%	37.2%		
Estimated Age of Second Assailant				
14 or less	0%	0%		
15 - 17	0%	2.0%		
18 - 24	0%	0%	0.12	0.420
25+	11.5%	3.9%	(combined categories)	
Did not state/not relevant	88.5%	94.1%		
Interpersonal Circumstances				
Persuaded by the person	7.7%	13.7%		
Encouraged by someone else	15.4%	9.8%		
Promised gift or favour	3.8%	7.8%		
Threatened verbally	2.8%	2.0%	0.16	0.111
Threatened with a weapon	0%	2.0%	(combined categories)	
Physically forced	7.7%	2.0%		
Assailant had been drinking	0%	15.7%		
Any physical force or threat	10.5%	6.0%		

Table 3.11
Relationship to assailant, in 77 male victims of sexual assault in a national random sample of 935 Canadian males

Variable	In 26 respondents aged under 13	In 51 respondents aged 13-16	Cramer's V	Significance
Assailant Was:				
A stranger	30.7%	25.5%		
An employer	0%	2.0%	0.24	0.042
A co-worker	0%	2.0%	(combined categories)	
An acquaintance	30.9%	23.5%		
A neighbour	19.2%	0%		
A family friend	3.8%	17.6%		
A boyfriend/girlfriend	0%	17.6%		
A relative	7.7%	1.8%		
A close family member	7.7%	0%		
If a Close Family Member or Relative				
Stepfather	7.7%	0%		
Uncle	7.7%	9.8%	0.15	0.165
Cousin	0%	2.0%		

Table 3.12
Actions taken in relation to sexual assault in childhood in 77 male victims in a national random sample of 935 Canadian males

Variable	In 26 respondents aged under 13	In 51 respondents aged 13-16	Cramer's V	Signi- ficance
Did not report/tell about assault to anyone	73.1%	80.4%		
Told someone immediately after	7.7%	0%		
Told someone within one day	0%	0%	0.18	0.221
Told someone within three days	0%	3.9%	(combined categories)	
Told someone within one week	7.7%	3.9%		
Told someone after more than one week	7.7%	3.9%		
Did not state	3.8%	7.9%		
Person Told:				
Family member	0%	2.0%		
Told a friend	0%	0%		
Told police	0%	0%		
Told clinic/hospital	0%	0%		
Told family doctor	0%	0%		
Told teacher/counsellor	0%	0%		

Table 3.12 (Continued)

Variable	In 26 respondents aged under 13	In 51 respondents aged 13-16	Cramer's V	Signi- ficance
Told social worker	0%	0%		
Did not state	26.9%	17.6%		
Too personal a matter to tell anyone	7.7%	17.6%		
Afraid I wouldn't be believed	7.7%	5.9%		
Too ashamed	3.9%	19.6%	0.20	0.056
Too young to know it was wrong	7.7%	0%	(combined categories)	
Didn't bother me that much/wasn't important	23.1%	11.8%		
Didn't want to hurt family members	3.8%	3.9%		
Didn't want to hurt person who did it	15.4%	3.9%		
Afraid of person who did it	7.7%	0%		
Threatened not to tell by the person who did it	0%	0%		
Too angry to do anything	0%	3.9%		

(Note: More than one reason for not reporting often given.)

Table 3.13
Demographic associations of unwanted sexual acts in childhood in a national sample of 935 Canadian males

Variable	In 77 respondents aged less than 17 when assault occurred	In all remaining 858 respondents	Cramer's V P
Region			
Atlantic	9.1%	10.5%	
Quebec	29.9%	26.2%	
Ontario	33.8%	34.6%	0.09 0.041
Prairies	18.2%	16.5%	(combined categories)
British Columbia	9.1%	12.1%	
Urban-Rural			
Community 500,000+	42.9%	37.6%	0.10 0.027
100,000 - 500,000	19.5%	12.8%	
10,000 - 100,000	20.4%	14.7%	(combined categories)
1,000 - 10,000	6.5%	9.7%	
Under 1,000 and farm	20.8%	25.2%	
Language of Childhood			
English	63.6%	65.0%	
French	29.9%	24.9%	0.11 0.008
Other	6.5%	10.1%	(combined categories)
Marital Status			
Single	39.0%	26.1%	
Married	50.6%	64.2%	
Co-habiting	5.2%	4.7%	0.18 0.000
Widowed	0%	1.9%	(combined categories)
Separated/divorced	5.2%	3.1%	
Religious Preference			
Protestant	32.5%	40.8%	
Jewish	1.3%	0.6%	0.09 0.051
Roman Catholic	48.0%	42.1%	(combined categories)
Other	3.9%	1.8%	
None	14.3%	14.7%	

65

Table 3.13 (Continued)

Variable	In 77 respondents aged less than 17 when assault occurred	In all remaining 858 respondents	Cramer's V P
Respondent's Occupation			
Prof/Executive	37.7%	35.5%	
Sales/Clerical	18.9%	8.5%	0.14 0.000
Manual work/Other	35.1%	38.7%	(combined
Not currently employed/unknown	10.3%	17.3%	categories)
Education			
Grades 0-8	3.9%	11.0%	
Grades 9-13 completed	40.3%	40.6%	0.11 0.002
Post-secondary, but not completed university	27.2%	25.3%	(combined categories)
Completed university	28.6%	23.1%	
Household Size (including Respondent)			
1	7.8%	7.3%	
2	22.1%	22.6%	
3	14.3%	22.0%	0.14 0.000
4	23.4%	25.0%	(combined
5+	32.4%	23.0%	categories)
Children Under 7			
0	68.8%	68.6%	
1	25.0%	17.5%	0.08 0.097
3+	5.2%	11.4%	(combined categories)
Year of Birth			
Prior to 1939	24.7%	29.2%	
1940 - 1949	19.5%	23.1%	0.14 0.019
1950 - 1959	29.9%	30.3%	(combined
1960 - 1965	25.9%	9.2%	categories)
Household Income			
Less than $10,000	11.7%	11.2%	
$10,000 - $14,999	10.4%	10.2%	
$15,000 - $19,999	13.0%	13.7%	0.05 0.361
$20,000 - $29,999	20.8%	26.2%	(combined
$30,000 - $39,999	19.5%	18.2%	categories)
$40,000+	24.6%	20.5%	

Table 3.14
Selected differences between males and females reporting sexual abuse in childhood in a national Canadian sample

Variable	In 158 females	In 77 males	Cramer's V	Signi-ficance
Frequency of Assault:				
Once	43.0%	32.5%		
twice	19.0%	13.0%	0.27	0.009
3 - 5 times	18.3%	19.5%	(combined categories)	
6 - 9 times	10.1%	9.1%		
10+ times	9.6%	25.9%		
Assailant Was:				
A stranger	14.6%	27.3%		
A known person, not a relative	42.4%	59.7%	0.33	0.002
A relative	18.3%	10.4%	(combined categories)	
A close family member	24.7%	2.6%		
Assault Resulted In:				
Significant emotional hurt	44.9%	19.5%	0.40	0.001
Significant physical harm	19.0%	10.4%	0.23	0.023
Estimated Age of Assailant				
13 or less	7.6%	5.2%		
14 - 17	23.4%	24.7%	0.20	0.219
18+	29.7%	38.5%	(combined categories)	
Did not state	39.3%	31.6%		
Respondent's Age at First Assault				
12 or less	41.1%	33.8%	0.08	0.351
13 to 16	58.9%	66.2%	(combined categories)	
Reporting of Assault				
Did not tell anyone	82.3%	77.9%	0.05	0.751
Afraid I wouldn't be believed	11.4%	6.5%	0.07	0.439
Too ashamed to tell anyone	20.2%	14.3%	(combined categories)	

Table 3.14 (Continued)

Variable	In 158 females	In 77 males	Cramer's V	Signi- ficance
Region				
Atlantic	8.2%	9.1%		
Quebec	23.4%	29.9%	0.08	0.277
Ontario	38.0%	33.8%	(combined categories)	
Prairies	17.7%	18.2%		
British Columbia	12.7%	9.1%		
Urban-Rural				
Community 500,000+	33.5%	42.9%		
100,000 - 500,000	16.5%	19.5%	0.12	0.049
10,000 - 100,000	12.0%	10.4%	(combined categories)	
1,000 - 10,000	14.6%	6.5%		
Under 1,000 and farm	23.4%	20.8%		
Language in Childhood				
English	77.2%	63.6%		
French	18.3%	29.9%	0.15	0.037
Other	4.4%	6.5%	(combined categories)	
Religious Preference				
Protestant	50.0%	32.5%		
Jewish	0%	1.3%	0.17	0.022
Roman Catholic	37.3%	48.0%	(combined categories)	
Other	3.2%	3.9%		
None	8.9%	14.3%		
Year of Birth				
Prior to 1939	24.7%	20.2%		
1940 - 1949	19.5%	28.5%	0.09	0.137
1950 - 1959	29.9%	31.0%	(combined categories)	
1960 - 1965	25.9%	20.3%		

Table 3.15
Multiple regression analysis of demographic predictors of sexual assault in childhood in 847 women in a national Canadian survey

Variable	Simple r	Partial r	Combined r
Year of Birth: born before 1940 versus born 1940 or later	0.26	0.26	0.26
Community: 10,000 plus versus smaller than 10,000	0.14	0.11	0.27
Language: French versus English or other	0.13	0.10	0.31

Note: Regression carried out by SPSS version 8.0 (Nie et al., 1975). Correlations of 0.1 and above are significant at the one per cent level or beyond. Some cases with missing data were excluded.

Table 3.16
Multiple regression analysis of demographic predictors of sexual assault in childhood in 895 men in a national Canadian survey

Variable	Simple r	Partial r	Combined r
Year of Birth: born before 1940 versus born 1940 or later	0.23	0.23	0.23
Community: 10,000 plus versus smaller than 10,000	–0.12	–0.10	0.18
Language: French versus English or other	–0.11	–0.08	0.27

Note: Regression carried out by SPSS version 8.0 (Nie et al., 1975). Correlations of 0.1 and above are significant at the one per cent level or beyond. Some cases with missing data were excluded.

4 Juvenile prostitution and child sexual abuse: A controlled study

Abstract

This study presents a Canadian replication of the work of Silbert and Pines (1982a) on entry to prostitution. Our results, like those of the American workers, point to a picture of multiple abuse and degradation of the 45 former prostitutes interviewed, both before and after entry to prostitution. The Canadian work of Badgley (1984b), apparently showing juvenile prostitutes are no more likely to experience child sexual abuse than members of the general population, has been criticized on methodological grounds. The present study indicates 73 per cent of prostitutes were sexually abused in childhood, compared to 29 per cent of a control group obtained in a random population survey. Comparison with control respondents indicated severity of sexual abuse in childhood was a significant contributor to the currently poor mental health and diminished self-esteem of the former prostitutes.

Introduction

This research was originally conceived to explore the idea that prostitution, in particular that practised by adult women, was both the enterprise of normal, decent individuals and was also capable, through legal reform, of becoming a normative institution. This presumption was based on an historical perspective (Otis, 1985) and on cross-cultural experiences and understanding: in non-Moslem parts of West Africa the prostitute is an esteemed member of the community, free and independent; and in India the subcaste of the <u>devadesis</u>, prostitutes whose calling is ordained by God and sustained by religious ritual, still survives (Bagley, 1979). In some

70

European countries too, certain types of social structure foster the independent and non-stigmatized practice of prostitution: for example, in fieldwork on the adaptation of ethnic minorities in The Netherlands, we encountered prostitutes in Amsterdam who were free and independent entrepreneurs, tolerated within a complex plural society in which conservative and extremely liberal values co-exist (Bagley, 1973, 1983c). Research by Kiedrowski and Van Dijk (1984) provides some supportive evidence suggesting officially liberal attitudes to prostitution in The Netherlands result in a profession which is to some extent self-governing and self-regulating, excluding both the entry of juveniles and the practice of pimps.

This rather optimistic perspective has been tempered by a growing number of research reports which suggest that prostitution is not, by and large, a voluntary activity but usually involves a juvenile (someone under 18) who has fled from an abusive or rejecting home, reluctantly turning to prostitution as a means of economic survival; has become a prostitute through the coercions of a boyfriend or pimp; or has entered as a secondary activity to support drug addiction (James and Meyerding, 1978; Silbert and Pines, 1981, 1982b; Badgley, 1984b; Fraser, 1985).

Our concern in this respect has been paralleled by disillusionment with an associated hypothesis. We had argued (Bagley, 1969) that the observed harmful effects of sexual relationships between adults and juveniles might, in many cases, be a reflection of the intervention of external authorities rather than due to the relationship itself. The study we designed to test this hypothesis completely disconfirmed this idea. We found, contrary to expectation, that sexual abuse of children by adults had independent, long term harmful effects to a greater or lesser degree, for all of the children involved (Bagley and MacDonald, 1984). Data from a community mental health survey which enquired about abusive events in childhood confirmed that sexual abuse in childhood has significant links to poor mental health as an adult (Bagley and Ramsay, 1986). In addition, evidence from clinical studies has produced clear evidence of the harmful sequels, for the children involved, of coerced sexual relationships with adults (Bagley, 1985a).

Recent North American research on juvenile prostitutions

Uncharacteristically, there has been more research on juvenile prostitution emerging from Canada than from the United States in recent years (Bagley, 1985a). While the growing American literature on outcomes of child sexual abuse (Able-Peterson, 1981; Geisser, 1979; Herman, 1981; Linedecker, 1981) has frequently mentioned cases of sexually abused children entering prostitution, these have been largely based on clinical studies of a few cases.

71

An alternative method, used by James and Meyerding (1978), Silbert and Pines (1981), and Badgley (1984b), has been to interview a group of individuals known to have practised prostitution, asking questions not only about current lifestyle, but also about factors antecedent to prostitution. This approach has both strengths and weaknesses. While such studies can yield valuable psychological and social data, it is clear that defining the population to be accessed presents major difficulties. In North America, prostitution is a deviant and often clandestine activity, and groups large enough for study purposes are often difficult to obtain. Trying to gain the time and confidence of women working on the street may put them in physical danger from pimps. Male researchers will be initially mistaken for clients, police, or potential pimps, and treated with great cynicism. Female researchers may be regarded as social workers or other prostitutes, and may well be in physical danger from pimps.

Current ethical procedures for most scholars usually require that the researcher seek parental permission before interviewing someone under 18: this makes research with juvenile prostitutes extremely difficult! In addition, child welfare laws in many provinces and states require professionals who learn of the sexual abuse of a juvenile to report this knowledge to an appropriate authority. Again, abiding by the letter of this regulation will make research with prostitutes extremely difficult, since it is clear from a variety of studies that the majority of practising prostitutes are aged under 18 (Fraser, 1985).

In our review of the literature (Bagley, 1985a), one piece of research stood out from all others, in terms of the quality of research methods, and the depth of material elicited. This is the work by Mimi Silbert and her colleagues at the Delancey Street Foundation in San Francisco (Silbert, 1982b; Silbert and Pines, 1982a, 1982b, 1983).

Silbert's (1982b) respondents were women approached by 'a self-help residential facility nationally known for its successful treatment of prostitutes, criminals and drug addicts' (p. 6). All of the 200 women in this study (ranging in age from 10 to 46) had practised prostitution before seeking or being-offered the refuge of the Delancey Street Foundation. An important aspect of this research was the use of a standardized questionnaire which included checks (asking the same questions, worded in slightly different ways, at different points in the three-hour interview) which indicated the general reliability of the information given.

Silbert's survey found 60 per cent of the 200 female prostitutes were victims of juvenile sexual exploitation: most respondents started prostitution after running away from home because of sexual, physical, or emotional abuse. Once in the streets, they were victimized by pimps; they were beaten, raped, robbed, and abused. In addition to victimization in prostitution, they were victimized in situations that had nothing to do with

their street work. Three-quarters of the respondents were raped, in most cases by total strangers, in rapes often involving brutal force. Despite the fact that virtually all the victims described physical injuries and extremely negative emotional impact, very few reported their victimization to authorities or sought help (Silbert, 1982b). Seventy-eight per cent of the women became prostitutes while they were still juveniles. Two-thirds of those who were sexually abused were abused by father figures. Seventy per cent of the women who were sexually abused as children said this assault had a definite influence on their entry to prostitution.

In Canada, a federal committee on Sexual Offenses Against Children and Youth (Badgley, 1984b) carried out a number of surveys, including a prevalence study of the amount of child sexual abuse (through a survey of a nationally representative sample of adults who recalled events of sexual abuse in their childhood); and a survey of 229 male and female juvenile prostitutes in Canada's major cities. The Badgley Report concluded, *inter alia,* that:

> Young prostitutes . . . were at no more risk when they were growing up than other Canadian children and youths of having been victims of sexual offenses . . . it cannot be concluded that having been sexually abused as a child was, by itself, a significant factor that accounted for their subsequent entry into juvenile prostitution. (p. 978)

The basis for this conclusion is the apparent finding that the juvenile prostitutes reported no more sexual abuse in childhood than did the adults in the national prevalence survey. We have criticized Badgley's conclusions in this respect (Bagley, 1986) on the following grounds:

1   The two samples were not comparable — one was a national random sample of adults; the other was a 'snowball' sample of prostitutes aged 20 or less. The interviewers for the prostitute sample were a variety of temporary workers, including students and at least one ex-police officer! The interviewers for the national sample were adults regularly used by a national poll organization. We are not told what questions were asked in the survey of prostitutes, nor in what setting; nor are we told the response rate. The wording and presentation may have been different from that in the national sample.

2   The two groups were not comparable in age — the average age of the prostitutes was 17.8 years when interviewed. Respondents in the national sample were on average in their late thirties when interviewed. Groups with different ages and contrasted sexual histories might well describe childhood events differently.

73

3   A crucially important error in Badgley's comparison appears to be the differential period at risk for sexual abuse within the family. Once they had entered prostitution, within-family abuse would be extremely unlikely, since the young prostitutes were (as Badgley shows) unlikely to be living at home. The average age at entry to prostitution was 16 for both boys and girls in Badgley's survey; 48 per cent had engaged in prostitution for the first time when they were 15 or younger; 14 per cent of males and 19 per cent of females began prostituting at age 13 or younger. Furthermore, many of these young people were recruited into prostitution only after they had run from home, often more than once. By the age of 14, 76 per cent had run from home at least once; 52 per cent had run away 'several times' or 'continually.' Children who are not in the home cannot, of course, be sexually assaulted within the home, and are also likely to be removed from the adult relatives and acquaintances who, from other evidence in the Badgley Report often impose themselves on children.

Putting these various pieces of evidence together, it appears that at least two-thirds of children who became prostitutes were hardly present at all in their homes after the age of 12. If they experienced the same amount of sexual abuse as children in the general population, as the Badgley Committee asserts, then this sexual abuse seems likely to have taken place before their twelfth year. In contrast, the majority of children in the general population experience assault after their twelfth year. Other evidence in the report indicates the assaults experienced by the general population group were — both before and after age 12 — of a less serious nature.

It is paradoxical that the Badgley Committee argues young prostitutes have experienced no more sexual abuse than the general population sample, and then argues that being a prostitute at age 12 through 16 constitutes 'the most severe forms of the abuse of children' (p. 1061). Looked at in this way, the severest forms of sexual abuse of young prostitutes take place after they enter prostitution. The case study evidence suggests entry to prostitution is not, by and large, a voluntary decision but reflects a pattern of pre-teen and young teenage children trying to escape emotionally, physically, or sexually abusive homes by running to the streets where they are sucked into lifestyles involving drugs and disorganized sexuality, and enter prostitution due to the coercion of poverty, homelessness, and social relationships with street figures, including pimps. On the street and at the margins of prostitution it is likely that virtually all young people who finally enter prostitution, suffer serious sexual abuse.

Our reading of the evidence presented in the Report on Sexual Offenses Against Children is that the overall prevalence of 'ordinary' sexual abuse of young people prior to their entry to the street life is probably at least twice

that in the general population, because of their much shorter period of risk. Street life involves exposure to special kinds of sexual abuse, and prostitution itself is sexually abusing for the young teenager.

In some ways then, the findings of the Badgley Report (1984b) parallel those of Silbert's (1982b) study: the young prostitutes in both studies experienced considerable abuse, both before and after entering prostitution. But in Badgley's study that abuse was emotional and physical, with sexual abuse-being no more prevalent (at about 15 per cent) than that reported in the general population. Clearly, further research is needed to throw more light on discrepant findings on prior sexual abuse in the lives of young prostitutes, in the contrasted studies of Badgley and Silbert. We had hoped that the special studies commissioned for the Fraser Committee on Pornography and Prostitution in Canada could throw some useful light on this discrepancy in findings. Unfortunately, these studies, on Ontario (Fleischman, 1984), Atlantic Canada (Crook, 1984), Quebec (Gemme, Murphy, Bourque, Nemeh and Payment, 1984), the Prairies (Lautt, 1984), and Vancouver (Lowman, 1984) did not use a uniform methodology or set of questions. Gemme et al. (1984) report that of the 82 Quebec prostitutes they studied, 'most' came from unhappy family backgrounds and poor environments. No estimate was made of the amount of child sexual abuse experienced by the prostitutes. Crook (1984) studied a sample of 47 prostitutes in the Maritimes, reporting that only 13 had experienced prior sexual abuse. The differential prevalence by sex in this mixed male and female sample was not given, nor were the research methods or questions asked clearly specified. Lautt (1984) studied 36 female prostitutes in Prairie cities, but made no estimate of prior sexual abuse. Lowman (1984) reported that of 48 prostitutes interviewed, one half confirmed sexual abuse had occurred in their childhood prior to entry to prostitution. Of the 23 respondents confirming prior child sexual abuse, 13 thought the abuse had 'a significant impact on their subsequent involvement in prostitution,' while a further 10 of these 23 abused women could give no direct opinion on this topic. It is, of course, often difficult for even the most sophisticated respondents to recall with analytic accuracy what factors influenced even relatively simple decisions which took place some years before. Reviewing the Fraser Committee studies in light of Silbert's (1982b) methodologically sophisticated work, the best we can conclude is that entry to prostitution is influenced by isolation from customary peers and normative networks, and an isolation fostered by abusive events in the home, including sexual abuse. Silbert and Pines (1982a) indicate:

> . . . the street prostitute is a victim of an abusive home who starts prostituting because of survival needs, rather than as a willing participant. (p. 488)

The picture which Silbert and her colleagues paint is one of a despairing, isolated drift into prostitution. In many ways Badgley's (1984b) research confirms such a picture, except he appears to underestimate the amount of prior sexual abuse in the matrix of family abuse which undermines the self-confidence and adequate functioning of young women who enter prostitution.

Young women especially seem to enter prostitution because their survival options become extremely constrained. This may be so to a lesser degree for young men who enter prostitution (Benjamin, 1985), but it seems safe to conclude from recent American and European studies (Sereny, 1985; Weisberg, 1985) that the majority of teenage prostitutes can hardly be said to exercise free choice in choosing this particular 'profession.'

The present study

Methods of research

As Silbert (1982b) has observed, a truly representative sample of prostitutes is impossible to obtain. All studies will be biased to a certain degree, and the 'high class' prostitutes, the elite of the profession (Gemme et al., 1984) are rarely described. It is likely that studies of prostitutes are biased toward the most easily available groups, particularly street prostitutes. But these women may also be the most psychologically and socially marginal groups among the profession.

The present study differs from previous research in the population accessed. Although we used the same questionnaire as Silbert (1982b) with similar methods of administration and coding, our respondents were somewhat older than Silbert's (Table 4.1). We studied 45 women aged 18 or more, all of whom had previously been prostitutes but who were no longer practising prostitution. All of the women were interviewed by women associated with various helping agencies in Calgary and Edmonton with whom the former prostitutes were in contact. We contacted the complete 'universe' of respondents available in the cooperating agencies. Fifty-two respondents were available: 4 had left town or could not be traced; 3 declined to be interviewed; and 45 cooperated fully in the interview procedure.

All of the respondents had given up prostitution at least three months earlier — the average time since leaving prostitution was 9.5 months (range: three to 27 months). All respondents were interviewed by social work or counselling professionals with whom they had previous contact. All interviews were conducted in a relaxed, private setting. We are reasonably

confident that respondents gave as accurate a review of their lives as they were able.

A unique feature of this research has been the availability of comparison respondents who had never engaged in prostitution. These control or comparison respondents were drawn from a community mental health study of 679 individuals randomly selected from the adult population of Calgary (Ramsay and Bagley, 1985). These individuals completed a number of standardized measures of mental health and psychological adjustment, and answered questions about childhood and current circumstances antecedent to particular types of psychological adjustment (Bagley and Ramsay, 1985). These mental health measures were added to the Silbert Questionnaire and provide a useful check on the validity of the self-concept measure used in Silbert's study. In addition, female respondents were interviewed and completed the mental health measures a second time a year later. At that time, they also completed a previously developed questionnaire about sexual abuse in childhood (Sorrenti-Little, Bagley, and Robertson, 1984). The controls were randomly selected on the basis of age alone, to produce two groups whose mean ages were not significantly different.

A second set of control or comparison respondents was drawn, for 33 of the 45 former prostitutes who reported sexual abuse in childhood. The comparison group consisted of all the women aged under 40 in the community mental health survey who reported sexual abuse in childhood. These 36 women were significantly older than the ex-prostitute group (27.4 years versus 22.4 years), but did provide a valuable comparison group with regard to the nature of child sexual abuse and its possible influence on entry to prostitution.

Results

The ex-prostitute group (referred to hereafter as EX) were somewhat but not significantly younger than the community comparison or control group (hereafter referred to as CON). The EX group contained somewhat more women from minority ethnic backgrounds (Table 4.2). This is characteristic of street prostitutes in Prairie cities (Lautt, 1984). The EX group had completed significantly fewer school grades, and had frequently been in trouble in school. Although rates of pregnancy were the same, the EX group were much more likely to have had a termination of pregnancy and to have become pregnant before age 17. The EX group were much more likely to have grown up in inner-city areas; on average they came from larger families, and were much less likely to have grown up in a conventional, two-parent household. Drinking problems among family members, physical abuse and neglect, emotional abuse, and sexual abuse were significantly more frequent in the EX group than in the community

77

controls. Nearly three-quarters of the EX group had been sexually abused, compared with 28 per cent of the CON group. All of the EX group had experienced either sexual or physical abuse, or both, compared with 35 per cent of the CON group.

Three-quarters of the EX group left homes riven by strife, drunkenness, and abuse by the time they were 16: none of the controls left home at this age. Sexual abuse was the most frequent reason given by the EX group for leaving home. A third of the EX group had been sexually abused by two or more individuals in childhood, compared with seven per cent of controls.

The mental health of the EX group was dramatically poorer than that of the controls. They were three times as likely to have made a suicide attempt, and more than four times as likely to have poor mental health (on the Middlesex Hospital Questionnaire — Bagley, 1980), and devastated self-esteem (as measured by Coopersmith, 1981). The Coopersmith Scale and the Middlesex Questionnaire sub-scales correlate with the semantic differential measure used by Silbert (1982b) on average 0.56, lending some validity to Silbert's work on the importance of restoration of self-esteem in the psychological rehabilitation of former prostitutes.

Table 4.3 compares the abuse experienced by the 33 ex-prostitutes reporting sexual abuse in childhood (up to age 16), with that of the 36 women aged less than 39 in the community sample who also reported sexual abuse in childhood. It is immediately obvious that the EX group were much more likely than the controls to have experienced sexual abuse by more than one abuser. The EX group was abused by the same range of individuals (although more frequently by a biological father). The EX group experienced abuse which began at a significantly earlier age, was more frequent, and lasted for longer periods.

The differences in types of assault are dramatic. The EX group were subjected to a greater range of assaults, and to more serious assaults. Three-quarters of the EX group who were victims of child sexual abuse had to submit to completed intercourse, compared with 11 per cent of controls. Fifteen per cent of the sexually assaulted EX group had been required to be involved in sado-masochistic practices (including practices involving beating, mutilation, or burning of the individual), and an overlapping 15 per cent had been required to pose for pornographic materials. None of the sexually-abused controls had been treated in this manner.

The sexually abused group of ex-prostitutes reported a much more negative reaction to the abuse than did the controls. Cross-classifications indicate depressed self-image was strongly related to a combined index of the severity of the abuse; the nature, frequency, and duration of the abuse; and the number of separate abusers.

Some of the factors which may influence entry to prostitution emerge in the profiles of the group of ex-prostitutes (Table 4.4). For more than half,

child sexual abuse resulted in negative feelings about sex: yet despite or because of this, for more than half, the experience of sexual abuse was judged to be a significant factor in becoming a prostitute. The sexually abused children became sexually active at an early age, and more than half had intercourse with four or more males before entering prostitution in their teen years. No less than 29 per cent had intercourse with 20 or more boys or men before entering prostitution, and many of these girls earned the reputation of being 'easy' or 'sluts' while at school. Many of these girls were also raped as teenagers (before becoming prostitutes). Ninety per cent of the ex-prostitutes had been sexually abused and/or raped before entering prostitution. The majority of respondents began prostitution before their sixteenth birthday, and the ages at which these girls began prostitution were similar to those which emerged in other studies (Benjamin, 1985).

The main reasons given for entering prostitution was the need for money — to survive, or for drugs. Relatively few of the women were persuaded to enter prostitution by boyfriends or pimps. Eighty per cent of the women felt they did not have any alternative to entering prostitution given the weight of multiple problems they faced. For almost all, the entry to prostitution was a hateful experience, leaving them scared, inadequate, worthless, and confused. All left prostitution as soon as they could, either of their own volition or with the aid of another person. None had gained any economic advantage from being prostitutes; but many had experienced emotional and physical trauma, and had been beaten and raped.

The picture which emerges from this gloomy survey is similar to that which emerged in Silbert's (1982b) study — a picture of abuse, exploitation, and learned helplessness. In many ways our results are similar to those of Silbert (Table 4.1). The differences which do emerge (including a greater prevalence of physical and sexual abuse in the Alberta study) might be attributed to the fact that our respondents left home later than the San Francisco respondents, and were thus at greater risk of abuse in the home.

In looking for a model to explain entry to prostitution, we combined the data from the 45 ex-prostitutes and the 45 community controls (Table 4.5). The multiple regression technique used selects the variable which explains the maximum amount of the variance of the other predictor variables with the dependent variable (in this case, entry to prostitution). No particular order of entry was specified, except the amount of variance explained by each independent variable. The variable selected by the statistical analysis was separation from a biological parent before age 12, a factor which acts as an indicator of many other problems in childhood, including physical and sexual abuse, and physical neglect. Sexual and physical abuse remain significant predictors of entry to prostitution, even when the effects of parental separation are controlled for. It should be noted that abuse experiences were coded according to their severity, not simply as present or

absent. Thus, sexual abuse was coded by assigning a zero if no abuse of any kind was experienced, a weight of one if abuse of any kind was experienced, and an additional weight of one for each of the following events: assault amounting to intercourse or other kinds of bodily penetration, assault involving sado-masochist activity, assault by more than one assailant on separate occasions, assault on more than 20 different occasions, assault(s) continued for more than six months at the hands of any assailant. For the controls, the mean sexual abuse score was 0.40; for the ex-prostitutes it was 2.31. Physical abuse and neglect, and emotional abuse were measured by the EMBU, a 'memories of childhood' measure known to be valid and reliable (Perris, Jacobson, Linstrom, Van Knorring and Perris, 1980) and shown to be predictive of adult adjustment in a parallel study in Calgary (Bagley and Ramsay, 1986).

Another issue to be addressed in this chapter is whether the experience of prostitution per se contributes to the markedly poorer mental health observed in the ex-prostitutes in comparison to the community controls (Table 4.2). We carried out a further multiple regression analysis to address this problem (Table 4.6), with total score on the Middlesex Hospital Questionnaire (MHQ) as the dependent variable (Bagley, 1980). The MHQ is a well-validated measure used in community mental health studies, and discriminates between various DSMIII categories.

The regression analysis (Table 4.6) shows severity of sexual abuse is the strongest predictor of poor mental health. While being a prostitute takes its toll on mental health independent of other factors, there were some ex-prostitutes in our sample with relatively good mental health. Without exception, these women had suffered neither physical nor sexual abuse, but in the majority of cases ran from home to avoid emotional conflict and the alcoholism of a parent.

The regression analysis with poor mental health as the dependent variable was repeated for the 45 ex-prostitutes (Table 4.7). Again, the severity of sexual abuse in childhood explains the greatest amount of the variance in the measure of poor mental health. When the correlation of other potential predictors with child sexual abuse are controlled for, two variables remain significant predictors of poor mental health: time spent in prostitution, and separation from a parent for five or more years before age 12.

Discussion

The results of this study indicate a high proportion of prostitutes experienced sexual abuse in childhood. In this respect our results resemble those of Silbert (1982b) (whose questionnaire we used), rather than those of Badgley (1984b). These results also tend to support our methodological critique of

Badgley, although the problems of obtaining comparable samples of prostitutes should be borne in mind.

Our own sample was drawn from various helping agencies, and it might be that those ex-prostitutes who cooperate with agencies are those with the most traumatic histories. This is but speculation, and it must be said that our original expectation was that those women able to leave prostitution after a relatively short time on the streets would be the least traumatized. Contrary to this expectation, the interviews revealed an astonishing picture of family disorganization, multiple abuse, and running from home. Once on the streets these young women were abused again, and the experience of prostitution contributed yet further to the psychological bondage of these women.

Comparison with the community control group indicated that the mental health of these former prostitutes was dramatically poorer. In a parallel study of links between childhood circumstances and current adjustment in a large community sample (Bagley and Ramsay, 1986), we found three factors were significantly intercorrelated: sexual abuse, physical abuse, and permanent separation from a parent. Children in disrupted homes were at significantly greater risk of physical neglect and emotional, physical, and sexual abuse. But when the intercorrelations of these factors were controlled for in multiple regression analysis, three factors — sexual abuse, physical abuse, and separation from a parent — each had some independent and statistically significant power in predicting current mental health. The present study (Tables 4.6 and 4.7) has produced similar results.

An English study (Bagley and MacDonald, 1984) of children removed from their homes and raised permanently in care because of physical abuse, sexual abuse, or family breakdown, found each of these background factors (sexual abuse, physical abuse, parental separation) predicted adjustment in adulthood. The general conclusion from these various studies, including the present one, is that psychological adjustment in women is influenced by the interaction of a number of factors reflecting family disruption. In prostitutes, the traumatic effects of child sexual abuse often seem to transcend and independently influence adult mental health, in comparison with the influence of the degradation and trauma of prostitution itself. It should be emphasized, however, that we are not certain about cause in this respect, which has not been established beyond doubt in this or indeed in any other study.

Silbert (1984) showed ex-prostitutes improved in self-esteem and self-confidence following counselling. Our own study (Table 4.7) shows a positive but non-significant correlation between time that has elapsed since leaving prostitution and improvement in mental health. This could be, as in Silbert's work, a reflection of counselling or it could simply reflect the amount of time lived in a more stable situation.

81

Does the experience of child sexual abuse influence entry to prostitution? This is a difficult question to answer, notwithstanding the fact that over 70 per cent of the ex-prostitutes in this study had been seriously sexually abused as children. Only 40 per cent of the women felt child sexual abuse was 'definitely' a factor in their entry to prostitution. Yet it appears sexual abuse may have caused social and psychological isolation and/or maladaptive sexual behaviour in at least two-thirds of those interviewed. Stigmatized, running from home, isolated, drawn into drug subcultures, these teenagers drifted into prostitution. None really chose to be prostitutes. All hated doing it, and left as soon as they could. The present sample, biased as it may be, completely disconfirms our earlier notion that there is such a thing as 'normal' prostitution, or rational social and economic choice about entry.

The model of entry to prostitution which has emerged from this study is something as Figure 4.1. Family disruption and family violence undermine children's capacity to avoid prevalent sexual and physical assaults. Sexually abused children act out in various ways; physically abused children react by running. Children who have been both physically and sexually abused are doubly at risk. On the streets these traumatized children have little psychological strength to resist the predators who lead them into drug and prostitution subcultures. The girl who finally tries prostitution is one who is already degraded and demoralized, in a state of psychological bondage, with grossly diminished self-confidence. The experience of prostitution further degrades her.

Table 4.1
Comparison of aspects of Silbert's San Francisco sample (N=200) with the Alberta sample (N = 45)

Variable	San Francisco	Alberta	Significance of difference
Under 21 at time of interview	70%	44%	$p < .01$
Father or mother absent for 5+ years by 12th birthday	40%	42%	N.S.
Grew up in urban area	77%	73%	N.S.
Grew up in inner city	54%	44%	N.S.
White	69%	82%	$p < .05$
Black	18%	4%	$p < .05$
Native Indian	1%	13%	$p < .05$
Drinking problems in father and/or mother	58%	53%	N.S.
Regular violence between adults in the home	40%	38%	N.S.
Child physically abused	45%	62%	$p < .05$
Child sexually abused	61%	73%	$p < .05$
Average age of leaving home permanently	14.0 years	15.4 years	$p < .01$
Started prostitution while aged less than 16	62%	51%	N.S.
Negative feelings about self starting prostitution	94%	95%	N.S.
Raped (other than by a client) while a prostitute	70%	62%	N.S.

Table 4.2
Comparison of 45 ex-prostitutes and 45 community controls

Variable		Former prostitutes	Control respondents	Statistical significance of difference
Age:	18-21	44.4%	40.0%	Not
	22-25	28.8%	22.2%	significant
	26-29	20.0%	22.2%	
	30-36	6.7%	15.5%	
Ethnicity:	White	82.2%	95.5%	Not
	Indian or Metis	13.3%	2.2%	significant
	Black	4.4%	2.2%	
Highest School Grade:	6-7	11.1%	0%	
	8-9	28.9%	15.5%	$p < .01$
	10-11	42.2%	17.8%	
	12-13	17.8%	66.7%	
Expelled or Suspended From School More Than Once		55%	Not asked	-
Ever Pregnant		55%	48.9%	N.S.
Termination of Pregnancy		53%	13.3%	$p < .01$
Pregnant Prior to Age 17		31%	2.2%	$p < .01$
Grew up in:	Inner city	44.4%	22.2%	
	Suburb of city	28.9%	37.8%	$p < .05$
	Small town	8.9%	28.9%	
	Rural area or reserve	17.8%	11.1%	
Siblings:	0	11.1%	8.9%	
	1-2	40.0%	68.9%	$p < .05$
	3-4	35.5%	20.0%	
	5 +	13.3%	2.2%	
Raised by (majority of childhood, up to age 12):				
	Mother and father	42.4%	80.1%	
	Mother alone	31.1%	17.7%	$p < .01$
	Sibling	4.4%	0%	
	Other relative	6.7%	2.2%	
	Foster home	15.5%	0%	
Drinking Problem in an Adult in Household when Child:				
	Father/stepfather	48.8%	11.1%	
	Mother	13.3%	0%	$p < .01$
	Other relative	17.7%	0%	

Table 4.2 (continued)

Variable	Former prostitutes	Control respondents	Statistical significance of difference
Physical Abuse (excessive beating at least once a month)	62.2%	6.7%	$p < .01$
Physical Neglect (often hungry or left unattended for 8 hours or more)	22.2%	0%	$p < .01$
Emotional Abuse (excessive criticism and or failure to meet emotional needs)	66.7%	8.9%	$p < .01$
Sexual Abuse by an Adult (18+) up to 16th Year	73.3%	28.9%	$p < .01$
Two or More Types of Abuse (emotional, physical or sexual)	100%	35.5%	$p < .01$
Fights Between Adults (including drunken brawls) at Least Weekly Before 16th Year	66.7%	4.4%	$p < .01$
Age Left Home Permanently:			
13-14	13.3%	0%	
15-16	66.6%	2.2%	$p < .01$
17-18	15.5%	11.1%	
19+	4.4%	86.7%	
Main Reason Left Home:			
Conflict between adults	15.5%	2.2%	
Sexual abuse	48.9%	0%	
Physical abuse	17.8%	0%	$p < .01$
Emotional abuse	13.4%	2.2%	
To attend college	0%	11.1%	
To marry	0%	40.1%	
To work elsewhere	4.4%	44.4%	
Sexual Abuse in Childhood:			
None	26.7%	71.1%	
One assailant	40%	22.2%	
Two assailants (on different occasions)	22.2%	6.7%	$p < .01$
Three assailants	6.7%	0%	
Four assailants	2.2%	0%	
Five assailants	2.2%	0%	

Table 4.2 (continued)

Variable	Former prostitutes	Control respondents	Statistical significance of difference
Suicide Attempt or Act of Deliberate Self-Harm by Age 21	26.7%	8.9%	$p < .05$
Self-Esteem (Coopersmith Adult Scale)			
Devastated or very low self-esteem (clinical criteria-score of 30 or more)	71.1%	6.7%	$p < .01$
Semantic Differential Self-Concept Measure			
Very low self-esteem (below two standard deviations from mean for community sample)	51.1%	6.7%	$p < .01$
Middlesex Hospital Questionnaire			
Psychoneurosis (total scale) - Score in range of clinical group	80%	17.8%	$p < .01$
Depression Sub-Scale	80%	15.5%	$p < .01$
Somatic Anxiety Sub-Scale	71.1%	20%	$p < .01$
Phobic Anxiety Sub-Scale	62.2%	17.8%	$p < .01$

Table 4.3
Comparison of former prostitutes (N = 33) and community controls
(N = 36) sexually abused up to age 16

Variable	Former prostitutes N=33	Control respondents N=36	Statistical significance of difference
Number of Abusers:			
One only	54.5%	77.8%	
Two (on different occasions)	30.3%	19.4%	
Three abusers	9.1%	2.8%	$p < .01$
Four abusers	3.0%	0%	
Five abusers	3.0%	0%	
Assailant in Sexual Abuse in Childhood:			
Biological father	21.4%	4.4%	
Stepfather, cohabiter, or mother's boyfriend	26.8%	31.1%	
Brother, uncle, or other relative	25%	31.1%	$p < .01$
Acquaintance or family friend	10.7%	22.3%	
Foster parent or teacher	7.2%	0%	
Stranger	8.9%	11.1%	
Number of assailants, on which percentages based	56	45	
Age at Commencement of First Abuse:			
less than 6	18.2%	6.7%	
6-7	18.2%	11.1%	
8-9	36.4%	28.9%	$p < .05$
10-11	15.1%	35.5%	
12-13	9.1%	13.3%	
14-16	3%	4.4%	

Table 4.3 (continued)

Variable	Former prostitutes N=33	Control respondents N=36	Statistical significance of difference
Frequency of Sexual Abuse in Childhood (in longest lasting abuse):			
once only	9.1%	33.3%	
2-4 times	15.1%	38.9%	
5-9 times	15.1%	13.9%	$p < .01$
10-19 times	18.2%	8.3%	
20 + times	42.5%	5.5%	
Longest Duration of Sexual Abuse by One Abuser:			
Single abuse on one day	9.1%	33.3%	
Over one month	21.2%	30.5%	
Over six months	18.2%	16.7%	$p < .01$
Over one year	6.1%	16.7%	
One to four years	15.1%	0%	
Five or more years	30.3%	2.80%	
Nature of Child Sexual Abuse:			
Fellated assailant	66.7%	25%	
Cunnilungus on victim	87.9%	25%	
Penetration of vagina by penis	75.7%	11.1%	$p < .01$
Penetration of anus by penis	30.3%	5.5%	
Penetration of vagina or anus by object	24.2%	8.3%	
Masturbated assailant	100%	55.5%	
Masturbated by assailant	100%	58.3%	
Kissing/fondling of unclothed breasts	60.6%	41.7%	
Involvement in fetishism or sado-masochism	15.1%	0%	
Posing for pornographic pictures or movies	15.1%	0%	

Table **4.3** (continued)

Variable	Former prostitutes N=33	Control respondents N=36	Statistical significance of difference
Subjective Reaction: Effect on Self-image of Sexual Abuse in Childhood:			
Very negative feelings about self	84.8%	55.5%	
Somewhat negative	6.1%	27.8%	p < .01
Numb; no reaction	6.1%	13.9%	
Felt positive	3.0%	2.8%	
What Did You Do, if Anything, to Stop the Sexual Abuse?			
Nothing/didn't know what to do	57.5%	52.8%	
Ran from home	21.2%	0%	
Revealed to family member, friend, or relative	36.4%	50%	p < .05
Revealed to police or professional	3.0%	5.5%	
Tried to commit suicide	9.1%	0%	

Table 4.4

Questions relevant to prostitution, asked only of 45 former prostitutes

Variable	Number	Percent
Effect on Feelings About Sex, Following		
Experience of Child Sexual Abuse:		
No abuse-not relevant	12/45	26.7%
Very negative	10/45	22.2%
Somewhat negative	16/45	35.5%
No reaction	7/45	15.5%
Positive reaction	0/45	0%
Felt that Sexual Abuse as a Child was a		
Significant Factor in Becoming a Prostitute:		
No abuse-not relevant	12/45	26.7%
Definitely not	5/45	11.1%
Perhaps/not sure	7/45	15.5%
Probably, yes	3/45	6.7%
Definitely, yes	18/45	40%
Age at First Sexual Intercourse (other than		
in child sexual abuse, or in prostitution):		
10-11	4/45	8.9%
12-13	16/45	35.5%
14-15	21/45	46.7%
16-17	4/45	8.9%
Number of Boyfriends with whom Respondent		
had Voluntary Sexual Intercourse Prior		
to Prostitution:		
0 - 1	5/45	11.1%
2 - 3	10/45	22.2%
4 - 5	6/45	13.3%
6 - 9	4/45	8.9%
10 - 14	4/45	8.9%
15 - 19	3/45	6.7%
20 +	13/45	28.9%
Considered "Easy" or "Promiscuous"		
When at School	9/45	20%
Raped (in addition to any event of		
child sexual abuse):		
Before entering prostitution	14/45	31.1%
After entering prostitution	28/45	62.2%
Reported rape to police	6/40	15%
Raped more than once and/or		
experienced sexual abuse before		
entering prostitution	40/45	88.9%

Table **4.4** (continued)

Variable	Number	Percent
Type of Prostitution Ever Practised:		
Street only	30/45	66.7%
Street and bar	8/45	17.8%
Street and bar and massage parlour	5/45	11.1%
Escort agency and other	2/45	4.4%
Call girl	0/45	0%
Age Started Prostitution:		
12-13	6/45	13.3%
14-15	23/45	51.1%
16-17	16/45	35.5%
18 +	0/45	0%
Age First Regularly Working as a Prostitute:		
12-13	4/45	8.9%
14-15	22/45	48.9%
16-17	12/45	26.7%
18 +	7/45	15.5%
Main Reason for Starting Prostitution:		
Needed money to survive	15/45	33.3%
Needed money for drug habit	18/45	40%
Coerced or persuaded by pimp or boyfriend	6/45	13.3%
Drifted into prostitution because of example/influence of friends	6/45	13.3%
Did You Consider You Had any Alternative to Entering Prostitution?		
Yes	6/45	13.3%
No (forced, or did it to survive)	36/45	80%
Unsure	3/45	6.7%
Feelings Following First Prostitution Experience:		
Depressed	32/45	71.1%
Inadequate/worthless	34/45	75.5%
Confused	25/45	55.5%
Scared	25/45	55.5%
(more than one type of feeling usually reported)		
Number of Problems Faced Prior to Entry to Prostitution:		
None	1/45	2.2%

Table 4.4 (continued)

Variable	Number	Percent
1	3/45	6.7%
2-3	17/45	37.8%
4-5	12/45	26.7%
6 +	12/45	26.7%
('Problems' included drug habit; money and shelter needs; psychological confusion and dependency on a dominant person; runaway situation following emotional, physical, or sexual abuse at home)		
Severely Beaten (causing scarring, confusions, fracture, and/or considerable blood loss) at Least Once by Trick, Own Pimp, Other Pimp, Police, or Other Person:		
No	3/45	6.7%
Yes	42/45	93.3%
Time Spent in Prostitution		
Less than a year	4/45	8.9%
12-23 months	6/45	13.3%
24-35 months	16/45	35.5%
36-59 months	12/45	26.7%
Five years or more	7/45	15.5%
Reason for Leaving Prostitution:		
To escape physical beatings, own volition	5/45	11.1%
Had enough, wanted out, left of own volition	28/45	62.2%
Became 'born again' Christian through street evangelist	1/45	2.2%
Helped to leave by women's group or sexual assault centre	5/45	11.1%
Boyfriend helped to leave	3/45	6.7%
Social services, probation, or other agency helped	3/45	6.7%
Financial Status Now:		
Poor, struggling, on social assistance or student loan, or in minimum wage job	28/45	62.2%
Working, reasonably well off	13/45	28.9%
Married, living at home in reasonable comfort	4/45	8.9%
Independently wealthy	0/45	0%

Table 4.5
Multiple regression analysis of factors predicting entry to prostitution in 90 respondents

Variable	Original correlation with entry to prostitution	Partial correlation	Multiple correlation	Proportion of variance
Separation from a biological parent for 5 + years before age 12	0.54	0.54	0.54	29%
Severity of sexual abuse before age 16	0.50	0.37	0.65	42%
Severity of physical abuse before age 16	0.42	0.36	0.74	55%
Ran from home before age 16	0.40	0.25	0.80	64%
Severity of physical neglect before age 16	0.36	0.15	-	-
Severity of emotional abuse before age 16	0.30	0.07	-	-
Age of respondent	-0.30	-0.15	-	-

Note: All correlations were significant before multiple regression. After multiple regression, the first four variables with correlation greater than 0.20 remained significant predictors of entry to prostitution. Multiple regression was carried out using SPSS version 8.0 (Nie, Hull, Jenkins, Steinbrenner and Bent, 1975). The last three variables, being non-significant predictors, were not included in the regression equation.

Table 4.6
Multiple regression analysis of factors predicting poor mental health in 90 respondents

Variable	Original correlation with poor mental health	Partial correlation	Multiple correlation	Proportion of variance explained
Severity of sexual abuse before age 16	0.61	0.61	0.61	37%
Practised prostitution	0.54	0.35	0.71	50%
Separated from a biological parent for 5+ years before age 12	0.49	0.22	0.75	56%
Severity of physical abuse before age 16	0.40	0.25	0.76	58%
Severity of emotional abuse before age 16	0.28	0.09	-	-
Age of respondent	-0.25	0.10	-	-

Note: All correlations were significant before multiple regression. After multiple regression, the first four variables with correlations greater than 0.20 remained significant predictors of poor mental health.

Table 4.7
**Multiple regression analysis of factors predicting poor mental health
in 45 ex-prostitutes**

Variable	Original correlation with poor mental health	Partial correlation	Multiple correlation	Proportion of variance explained
Severity of sexual abuse before age 16	0.40	0.40	0.40	16%
Months in prostitution	0.33	0.30	0.44	19%
Separated from a parent for 5 + years before age 12	0.30	0.28	0.50	25%
Age at entry into prostitution	0.35	0.19	-	-
Severity of physical abuse before age 16	0.29	0.11	-	-
Severity of physical neglect before age 16	0.20	0.04	-	-
Severity of emotional abuse before age 16	0.15	0.01	-	-
Time since leaving prostitution	-0.14	-0.14	-	-
Age	0.08	0.06	-	-

Note: Correlations of 0.27 were significant before multiple regression. After multiple regression the first three variables above remained statistically significant, and were included in the regression equation, which explained 25 per cent of the variance in the index of poor mental health.

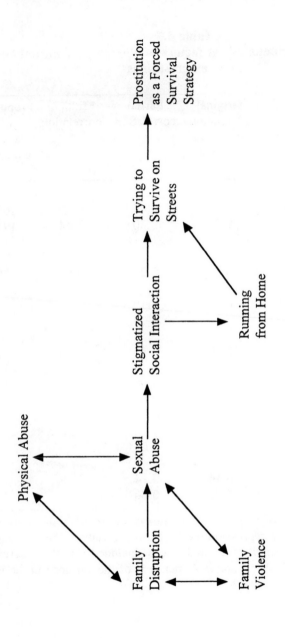

Figure 4.1   A model of entry to prostitution

5 When incest is revealed: A mental health crisis for mothers

Abstract

It is argued, from a representative sample of 20 mothers in families where incestuous abuse of a child has taken place, that there is no evidence of connivance or collusion in the sexual abuse by these mothers. Comparison with control respondents indicated that these mothers had significantly poorer mental health following the revelation of abuse, and came from backgrounds where abuse and early marriage were more common. Once in therapy these mothers made excellent progress, and began to self-actualize. The mother's recovery of mental health is an essential component in therapy for her daughter.

Introduction

Feminist critiques of conventional clinical and social work approaches to families in which a child has been sexually abused have led us to reappraise traditional descriptions of the role of the mother in such families (McIntyre, 1981; Wattenberg, 1985; Gavey, Florence, Pezaro and Tan, 1990). There should, hopefully, be a movement away from practice which reflects textbook statements such as that of Glick and Kessler (1980):

> In many cases of frank incest, the study of the family interactions involved a covert acceptance by the uninvolved spouse of the sexual relationship between parent and child. The mechanisms involved often are relatively complex, but they seem to permit the uninvolved spouse to avoid sexual relations. . . . (p. 207)

Emerging empirical evidence on mothers of incest victims indicates that the majority immediately support their daughters; the dilemma for a minority of women is not that of having sanctioned the incest, but of believing the victim and the role dilemma of choosing between daughter and father in an acute dilemma of loyalty (De Jong, 1988a and b; DeYoung, 1994a and b; Everson, Hunter, Runyon, Edelsohn and Coulter, 1989; Johnston, 1992; Sirles and Franke, 1989).

There is also some evidence that mothers of incest victims are more likely than other women to have themselves been victims of incest (Goodwin, McCarthy and DiVasto, 1981; Cooper and Cormier, 1982; Sheldon, 1988). While writers in the Freudian tradition have interpreted such prior abuse as a motivation in unconscious collusion with abuse of their own daughters (Pincus and Dare, 1980) we can find no good empirical evidence that this has led to women to collude (consciously or unconsciously) with their husbands in the sexual abuse of their daughter. An alternative explanation from the few empirical studies available is that vulnerable women (perhaps entering a cycle of learned helplessness — see Muram, Rosenthal and Beck, 1994) were easy to coerce and easy to deceive by the men who already had an interest in the exercise and abuse of gross power in their relationships with women (Bagley and King, 1990).

What is clear is that the role of the mother is crucial in supporting her daughter through the difficult stages of disclosure, court hearings and therapy. There is also some evidence that for some mothers the revelation can precipitate a mental health crisis. For these reasons, it is important to give psychological support to mothers of victims so that they can in turn support the healing process for their daughters (Bagley and King, 1990).

A study of 20 mothers of victims and 41 controls

This study examines various aspects of the crisis which revelation of sexual abuse in a daughter presents for a mother. The 20 women studied were referred by child protection workers in Calgary to an agency specializing in a modified humanistic model for treating families in which child sexual abuse had occurred. This model is described by Anderson and Mayes (1983). A parallel study of 122 cases of child sexual abuse in the same city in 1987 shows that this particular agency received referrals which were similar to all other child sexual abuse cases seen by child protection services in terms of the nature of the abuser, family structure, the type and seriousness of the abuse, and other victim characteristics (Bagley, Rodberg, Wellings, Moosa-Mitha and Young, 1994).

The personal accounts (based on extended interviews, often lasting for several hours) of the consecutive series of 20 mothers whose daughters had

been referred to the family treatment agency give a consistent picture: the revelation of the child's sexual abuse causes a crisis for the mother — a crisis involving personal relationships, values and personal mental health. But after a period of counselling, most mothers seemed to have recovered their self-esteem, and many seemed more self-assured and in control of their lives than they had ever been before (Naspini, 1988).

Present study: Methods

In the present chapter we explore in a quantitative design the hypothesis that on initial referral to the counselling agency, mothers of victims will have significantly poorer mental health than age-matched controls. The comparison group of women were obtained from a community mental health study which randomly sampled 680 adults (420 of them female) in Calgary (Ramsay and Bagley, 1985). The survey asked a wide range of questions, including those pertaining to recent mental health, past suicidal feelings and behaviour, and current levels of self-esteem. In a follow-up of the women in this study, questions were asked about long term mental health problems in relation to a variety of factors, including separations from a parent during childhood, and events of child sexual abuse. Data were obtained on 380 women in this second stage of the survey (Bagley and Ramsay, 1986).

We obtained control respondents for the 20 mothers who are the primary focus of this study from this second stage sample. Age, by year of birth, was exactly matched between the mothers and all available control respondents. One control respondent was available for each of four of the mothers; two controls were available for each of nine mothers; three controls for each of six mothers; and four controls for one mother, giving 44 control respondents in all. Since comparisons were made on a group rather than an individual basis, the fact that some mothers were compared with more than one control was unlikely to result in any distortion, especially as the mean age levels of the two groups were identical.

The measures used by Ramsay and Bagley (1985) which were utilized in the study of mothers included the Middlesex Hospital Questionnaire, a well-validated instrument which has been used in a number of community mental health studies (Bagley, 1980), and which has been used to predict or detect psychiatric morbidity in general populations (Crowne and Crisp, 1981).

A further measure utilized was the Coopersmith Self-Esteem Inventory for use with adults. This is a scale of known reliability and validity, and correlates with many aspects of social functioning (Bagley, 1989a). In addition, a measure of suicidal ideas and behaviour was used which was developed by Ramsay and Bagley (1985) from earlier measures.

99

The Middlesex Hospital Questionnaire asks questions designed to give profiles which will enable general practitioners to establish which of their patients need further investigation for particular types of psychiatric condition. The questionnaire contains a number of scales, but only two of them have been utilized in this study — the scale total score, giving an overall profile of psychoneurosis (including depression, somatic and free-floating anxiety, phobia and obsessionality), and the depression sub-scale. The MHQ asks 'about your feelings in general . . . during the past year.' Questions relating to depression for example, ask 'Did you ever find yourself needing to cry . . . often,' and 'Did you experience long periods of sadness . . . often.'

The questions about suicidal ideas and behaviour asked about the whole of an individual's lifetime, with such questions as 'Have you ever made an intentional attempt to take your life?' The self-esteem measure, asking respondents to comment on such statements as 'I have a low opinion of myself,' did not specify a particular time frame, but was clearly asking the respondent about contemporary self-evaluation, since all questions were posed in the present tense.

Results: Comparison between mothers and controls

A comparison of the significance of difference between the two groups, using the t-test, is presented in Table 5.1. First of all, it is clear that mothers of victims have much higher scores on all of the measures indicating much poorer mental health and adjustment than controls (in previous months). Mothers also have significantly higher scores on the measures of suicidal ideas and behaviour over a lifetime. Nine mothers (45 per cent) had made either an act of deliberate self-harm or a suicide attempt, or both, compared with four (nine per cent) of controls during the period of their lifetime. Just over 30 per cent of controls had experienced some suicidal ideas or thoughts in their lifetime, compared with 19 of the 20 mothers (95 per cent).

When we compare self-esteem scores however, we see that mothers and controls have identical levels of self-esteem (see Table 5.1). The most likely reason for this is that the time spent in therapy has enabled the mothers to develop normal levels of self-esteem, even though in the recent past they experienced crises which were associated with devastated mental health, depression, suicidal feelings and, in some cases, actual suicidal behaviour.

A number of other interesting differences emerge from the comparisons — women in the 'mothers of victims' group married at a significantly earlier age than the controls (2 were married at 14, 1 at 16, 3 at 17, while only 5

were married past the age of 19). The average age of marriage of the mothers was 18.1 years, compared with 21.4 in the controls.

Sixty-five per cent of the mothers had experienced sexual abuse in their own childhood, compared with 36 per cent of controls, using similar definitions. In addition, a somewhat greater number of mothers had been abused within their immediate or extended family. Slightly more mothers than controls had experienced separation from a parent before their 17th year, for at least three months. Previous research (Bagley and McDonald, 1984; Bagley and Ramsay, 1986) has shown that both sexual abuse in childhood, and separation from a parent are independent though often overlapping contributors to poorer mental health in adulthood.

Table 5.2 presents the correlations of the Psychoneurosis Score for three groups (mothers, controls, and both groups combined). It is clear that the total score on the MHQ (measuring global aspects of psychoneurosis) has strong and significant links to other aspects of mental health in both groups. This result was to be expected in the light of the results obtained by Ramsay and Bagley (1985) from a larger sample. It will be noted that age at marriage, early separation, and sexual abuse in an individual's childhood are related to some extent to poor mental health outcomes in both mothers and controls. In particular, mothers who married in their early or mid-teen years were particularly likely to have poorer mental health, and were also more likely to have experienced both prior separations and sexual abuse.

Table 5.3 indicates that time that elapsed since the revelation of sexual abuse (27 months, on average) was, as expected, negatively correlated with the self-esteem measure in the mothers. Since a high score on this scale indicated poorer self-esteem, this means that there is a significant tendency for the longer the time that has elapsed since the revelation, the better the mother's self-esteem level is likely to be.

Multiple regression analysis (table not shown) has been carried out for the mothers and controls combined (N = 64). This analysis, which partials out or controls for the intercorrelation of variables predicting an outcome (in this case, psychoneurosis) shows that when the effect of the revelation of the sexual abuse of the daughter is taken into account, the significant correlation of both separation and sexual abuse in one's own childhood are considerably diminished. This analysis does tell us, however, that mothers who were themselves sexually abused carry an additional mental health burden.

Discussion and conclusion

These statistical analyses have been useful in reinforcing the descriptive accounts obtained from the mothers (Naspini, 1988). The analysis does show that at the time of interview the self-esteem levels of the mothers were

at a normal level, presumably having been at an abnormal level in previous months and years.

When this study commenced, we had no expectation that the mothers would as a group, have married so young. Nor did we expect such high rates of sexual abuse in the mothers' own childhood. The implications of these factors in understanding the mother's reaction to her daughter's sexual abuse were not, in consequence, explored fully in the extended interviews. We have a clear impression from the interviews, however, that some mothers married very young in order to escape abusing and neglectful family situations. Mothers who had themselves been sexually-abused often saw their own marriages in unrealistic terms, as ideal relationships which contrasted with their unhappy childhoods. Some women, too, were probably trapped in the cycle of 'learned helplessness.' They rarely knew about the sexual assault of their own daughter, but often it was not difficult for their husbands to browbeat and deceive them.

It is possible, too, that some of the husbands who married very young wives had some paedophile impulse, which they transferred to their daughter as their wives grew older. It is worth noting that the husbands of the mothers group were on average 4.5 years older than their wives, significantly higher than the age difference of 3.1 years in the controls.

These findings carry implications for further research, and for therapeutic intervention on behalf of mothers as key caregivers in therapeutic intervention for sexually-abused children. Whether or not fathers (after experiencing judicial consequences, and after admitting and making amends for the abuse) should be readmitted to the family, the bond between mothers and daughters should be an enduring one, of women healed in their respective roles, and self-actualizing their own lives. Treating mothers of victims is as important as treating victims themselves, yet this model is only atypically addressed in the social work and the clinical literature (Bagley and King, 1990). Indeed, there is evidence that some social workers can still engage in 'mother blaming' when child sexual abuse is disclosed (Ringwalt and Earp, 1988).

Interventions with victims must also prevent women entering into the passive cycle of 'learned helplessness' in which they are so easily deceived and brow-beaten by the men who select them as partners, or as victims (Bagley and Thomlison, 1991). The sample used in this study is small, and further work needs to the undertaken with larger samples of mothers of victims to explore more fully how they can be healed, and how mothers in general can, through an expanded, feminist consciousness, protect their child from exploitation with the family.

There is clearly a need for more studies such as our own, using an empirical methodology with larger populations. Generalizations based on prejudice rather than on fact continue to prevail. Thus, in 1987, a leading

public health journal in Canada could publish an article on incest containing the following gross and unsubstantiated allegations:

> The mother is . . . both a victim and a party to the incestuous drama . . . such a mother rejects her role and does not attempt to protect her child. Had she been made aware of the situation by her daughter, she would have scolded her and refused to believe her. . . . In some cases, she will ask her daughter to play the parts she gave up, in the home and with her younger children. (Rodrigue, 1987, p.4)

Table 5.1
Comparison of means and proportions for mothers and control respondents

Variable	Mean value in 20 mothers (standard deviation in brackets)	Mean value in 41 controls	Significance of difference between means
Total Psychoneurosis score on Middlesex Hospital Questionnaire	71.7 (17.4)	52.7 (14.2)	0.000
Score on Middlesex Hospital Questionnaire depression	12.8 (4.2)	9.2 (2.5)	0.002
Score on Suicidal Ideas Questionnaire (range 0 to 6)	4.15 (1.7)	0.8 (0.6)	0.006
Number of suicide attempts in lifetime (range 0 to 2)	0.7 (0.5)	0.1 (0.1)	0.004
Coopersmith Self-esteem Score	39.0 (9.8)	38.5 (10.2)	N.S.
Age at research interview	35.7 (3.4)	35.9 (3.6)	N.S.
Age at marriage	18.2 (2.3)	21.4 (2.2)	0.000
Number of separations from a parent up to age 16	1.0 (0.5)	0.3 (0.4)	0.050
Victim of sexual abuse up to age 16	65%	38%	0.036

Table 5.2
Correlations of psychoneurosis score (scale total) of the Middlesex Hospital Questionnaire

Variable	Mothers (N=20)	Controls (N=44)	Both Groups (N=64)
Mothers (scored 1) versus controls (scored 0)	-	-	0.41
Depression score in MHQ	0.71	0.59	0.63
Suicidal ideas score	0.44	0.48	0.47
Suicidal attempts in lifetime	0.30	0.19	0.25
Coopersmith Self-esteem Score	0.61	0.66	0.63
Age when interviewed	-0.20	0.01	-0.05
Age when married	-0.44	-0.13	-0.21
Ever separated from a parent before age 17	0.30	0.19	0.25
Sexual abuse in own childhood	0.28	0.30	0.30
Time since revelation of child's abuse	-0.20	-	-

Significance:
- For mothers (N=20), correlations of 0.45 and above are significant at the five per cent level or beyond.
- For controls (N=44), correlations of 0.29 and above are significant at the five per cent level or beyond.
- For mothers plus controls (N=64), correlations of 0.24 and above are significant at the five per cent level or beyond.

Table 5.3

Correlations of selected variables in mothers (N=20) and controls (N=44)

Variable	Time since revelation	Sexual abuse		Separations		Age at marriage	
	Mothers	Mothers	Control	Mothers	Control	Mothers	Controls
Psychoneurosis total score in MHQ	-0.20	0.28	(0.43)	0.35	(0.23)	-0.44	(-0.13)
Depression score in MHQ	-0.19	0.10	(0.39)	0.16	(0.14)	-0.15	(-0.10)
Suicidal ideas	-0.17	0.23	(0.34)	0.39	(0.19)	-0.22	(-0.10)
Suicidal attempts in lifetime	-0.05	0.25	(0.34)	0.25	(0.03)	-0.47	(-0.19)
Coopersmith Self-esteem Score	-0.37	-0.06	(0.06)	0.24	(0.10)	-0.26	(-0.11)
Age when interviewed	0.23	0.17	(0.07)	-0.26	(0.30)	0.33	(0.30)
Age at marriage	-0.26	-0.43	(-0.43)	-0.45	(0.43)	-	-
Separated from a parent in own childhood	-0.08	0.20	(0.49)	-	-	0.45	(-0.43)
Sexual abuse in own childhood	0.25	-	-	0.25	(0.49)	-0.43	(-0.43)

Note:
- Higher scores on mental health and self-esteem scales indicate poorer mental health.
- Correlations in brackets are those for control respondents.
- For mothers, correlations of 0.45 and above are significant at the five per cent level or beyond.
- For controls, correlations of 0.29 and above are significant at the five per cent for level or beyond.

106

6 The prevalence and mental health sequels of child sexual abuse in a community sample of women aged 18 to 27

Abstract

A community mental health survey of 750 women aged 18 to 27 in a large urban centre established mental health profiles, using a variety of measures, as well as investigating any history of child abuse (including sexual abuse, defined as the unwanted fondling of the child's genital area, or attempted or achieved penetration of the child's body before the person was 17). Overall, 32.0 per cent of respondents recalled abuse of this type. Of the 750 women, 6.8 per cent had experienced sexual abuse which went on for more than one week. This long term category included virtually all of those who experienced abuse by a trusted, authority figure. The Trauma Symptom Checklist (TSC) was found to be the most useful instrument amongst the several used in identifying sexual abuse histories. Scores of 30 or more on the TSC identified 72 per cent of victims of long term abuse, while 23 per cent of those with scores of 30+ had experienced short term sexual abuse. Seven per cent of individuals with 30+ scores had never experienced (or did not recall) sexual abuse. No particular sub-scale of the TSC had better utility in identifying former victims than did the scale total.

Introduction

It is now clear from a number of research studies that sexual abuse in childhood may have serious consequences in adulthood, in terms of a variety of mental health and adjustment indicators (Bagley and King, 1990). As Finkelhor, Hotaling and Yllo (1988) have argued, what are now needed are studies which can identify linkages between different aspects of the sexual abuse experience, and the nature and degree of mental health problems in

adulthood. Another research task is that of developing instruments which can screen for the long term sequels of sexual abuse in childhood, since it is clear that a failure to address the traumatic memories of the abuse may well undermine the efforts of conventional psychiatric intervention (Gold, 1986).

There is a growing research literature in this area which has been reviewed extensively elsewhere (Bagley and Thurston, 1989; Bagley and Thomlison, 1991). Many clinical problems in this field remain unsolved however (Bagley and King, 1990), and we are particularly impressed with Briere's (1989b) approach to 'therapy for adults molested as children.' Our own approach in this area is based on a combination of the humanistic approach to therapy, and a research method based in a humanistic social psychology (Bagley and King, 1990).

Research plan and methods

The present study does not formulate direct hypotheses; rather, it aims to explore, by means of the analysis of data from a relatively large sample of young women in the general population, whether there has been any increase or decrease in the experience of sexual abuse in childhood, in terms of prevalence and type of abuse (Bagley, 1990a, b and c); whether risk factors for sexual abuse in childhood can be identified or verified; whether measures of adjustment in adulthood can identify or reflect a history of child sexual abuse; and whether there are specific types of psychological problem which can be linked to sexual assault in childhood.

The present study is based on research methods and instrument validation developed in a number of previous studies based in Calgary and in other urban and rural areas, on aspects of community mental health; and on the extent, nature and long term sequels of child sexual abuse (Sorrenti-Little, Bagley and Robertson, 1984; Bagley and MacDonald, 1984; Ramsay and Bagley, 1985; Bagley and Ramsay, 1985 and 1986; Bagley and Young, 1987 and 1990; Bagley, 1989a and b).

The mental health instruments validated in these previous studies, and in the present work include a measure of suicidal ideation (Ramsay and Bagley, 1985); the Middlesex Hospital Questionnaire (MHQ) which measures psychoneurosis in general terms, with specific sub-scales for the measurement of anxiety, depression and neurosis (Bagley, 1980); the Centre for Epidemiological Studies in Depression scale, for the measurement of depression (CESD-scale) developed by Radloff (1977); the childhood memories scale (EMBU) developed by Arrindell, Emmelkamp, Monsma and Brilman (1983) in Europe, and validated cross-culturally (Arrindell, Perris, Hjordis, Eisemann, Van der Ende and Von Knorring, 1986) for the retrieval

of memories of emotional neglect and excessive punishment by a parent; and the Coopersmith adult self-esteem scale (Bagley, 1989b).

The choice of these instruments reflects their known reliability and validity, and their importance as screening instruments in epidemiological and community mental health surveys.

The method of assessing whether those interviewed had experienced sexual abuse in childhood was derived from that used in a national Canadian survey (Bagley, 1989a). After various socio-demographic and mental health measures have been completed, the respondent is asked: 'When you were growing up — that is before your 17th birthday — did anyone even touch or interfere with sex parts of your body in a way you didn't want?' ('Sex parts' are defined for respondents in a standardized way, in answer to any query). The detailed questionnaire is found in Bagley (1988).

Asking only about unwanted sex acts in childhood and adolescence could in theory lead to a conservative estimate of the amount of 'abuse' when this method is compared with the method pioneered by Finkelhor (1979), which asks respondents about any sexual events in childhood. Sexual abuse is defined in Finkelhor's method by age differences, and by force in the relationship. We found, however, in a Canadian replication (Sorrenti-Little, Bagley and Robertson, 1984) that the mass of data generated by Finkelhor's method is difficult to code, and operationalize in terms of a single measure of child sexual abuse that would be useful for epidemiological purposes.

In addition to the previously used and validated instruments, a new measure was used, Briere's Trauma Symptom Checklist (TSC). This instrument was devised as a result of the clinical work of Briere and his colleagues (Briere, 1989b; Briere and Runtz, 1987 and 1988a, b and c) comparing clinical populations with and without a history of child sexual abuse. These comparisons allowed Briere and his colleagues to identify symptom clusters which occurred with particular frequency in sexual abuse survivors, and which usually distinguished victims from non-victims in clinical situations at a statistically significant level.

As a result of these comparisons, five sub-scales (measuring Dissociation, Anxiety, Depression, Post-traumatic Stress, and Sleep Disturbance) were incorporated into a 33-item scale. Briere and Runtz (1987) report satisfactory internal reliabilities for the measures, as well as construct validity (significant correlations with duration of abuse, number of perpetrators, and presence of intercourse).

Further data on the TSC-33 are presented in Briere (1989b), but it is clear that further work needs to be done on this potentially important instrument, which is however quick to complete, non-intrusive, and identifies a wide range of current distress which can be addressed in counselling. We should emphasize, however that at this stage we regard the TSC-33 as a useful

instrument for screening purposes in large scale surveys, rather than as an instrument for use once therapy was commenced.

The women in the present study were identified by a stratified, random sampling procedure. Neighbourhoods in the city of Calgary known to contain a high proportion of young women were identified. Five such communities were randomly selected, being stratified by the average income levels in the area, so that each of the five communities represented a different SES level. The areas ranged from one including many owner-occupied homes and high quality rental apartments, with a high income per capita, to an area with much subsidized housing, a high proportion on welfare, and low average per capita income. The reverse telephone directory listings (containing 97.3 per cent households) were used as the sampling frame within each community. Random sampling of numbers was continued until each community yields one-fifth of the total number (750) of interviews planned for in the study design.

Each telephone call established whether or not there was a woman aged 18 to 27 living in the household. Of the 750 women identified in the first phase of this research, 66 per cent of those contacted agreed to participate in a study asking about 'current adjustment in relation to childhood circumstances.' The major reason (in two-thirds of rejections) given for not participating was lack of available time to meet the interviewer. The other main reason for declining was a simple lack of interest in such a study. Lack of available time was a reason given much more frequently in potential respondents in low SES areas; the highest rate of initial co-operation occurred in the highest SES area, with 80 per cent of women contacted agreeing to an interview. This meant that women in the lower SES areas have had to be oversampled. After the first 120 interviews had been completed, we were able to access a funding source which enabled us to offer each respondent $10 (whether or not the interview was completed). This offer of payment for an hour's interview nearly doubled the acceptance rate to our telephone inquiries in the two lowest SES areas.

All respondents were interviewed in their own homes by specially trained workers (all female), who were human science or nursing graduates. Interviewers also offered initial counselling and referral for any individuals who appeared to have very poor mental health, or who wished to talk to a therapist about any issues, including child abuse. Anonymity was assured, and the interview was introduced with the statement: 'We are interviewing a sample of young adults about events which occurred before age 17, which might be considered abusive or unpleasant in some way.' The issue of sexual abuse was not raised however, until the very end of the interview. The rationale here was that talking about sexual abuse earlier in the interview might have elicited a negative affect which could have influenced the completion of the mental health measures.

Data have been analyzed by SPSS (Nie, Hull, Jenkins, Steinbrenner and Bent, 1975). The measure of association reported, Pearson's r assumes relative normality of distribution in the two measures co-varied. All measurements have been checked by rank order correlations, and by Cramer's V (derived from chi-squared, making no assumptions about normal distribution). In the tables below Pearson's r has been compared with these two measures, and gives very similar results.

The obvious limitations of this method of estimating the prevalence and correlates of child sexual abuse must be stressed. This kind of study gathers information on assaults which took place up to 20 years earlier, and the relevance of such information for current social policy may be in question. Because formalized and coherent memories do not usually emerge until about the age of four or five, abuse occurring before this date may not be recalled (Benedek and Schetky, 1987). Clinical studies indicate that some kinds of seriously traumatic sexual abuse are repressed, and lost to conscious recall (Bagley and King, 1990). Some individuals are so damaged by abuse that the life style they lead means that their usual residence (streets, half-way houses, prisons, hospitals, institutions) will not be reached by normal sampling techniques (Bagley and Young, 1987). In addition, very mobile individuals and those without a current telephone number may not be reached by normal sampling techniques — but such populations may contain a higher proportion of victims of childhood trauma (Bagley and King, 1990).

It is possible too that those individuals who agree to take part in surveys of this kind are those who are troubled by childhood events, and seek the interview as a means to therapeutic resolution or referral. On balance however, we would judge that community surveys of this type will underestimate the actual amount of child sexual abuse.

Results and discussion

Of the 750 women, 240 (32.0 per cent) reported some kind of unwanted sexual contact before their 17th birthday. While this figure is higher than that reported in the national Canadian study (Chapter 3), it is consistent with the data in that survey which indicated that women under 40 recalled a much higher prevalence of sexual abuse than did older women. Another Calgary study (Bagley and Ramsay, 1986) also found this, as did Russell (1984) in a study in California. The reasons for this higher prevalence in younger women are not clear, but could reflect a change in risk situations (more families disrupted by divorce and the introduction of non-related males into the household; changes in sexual norms, involving a loosening of controls on sexuality involving children; reluctance of older women to reveal sexual

111

assaults; greater recall of recent assaults in younger respondents; and changing definition in younger people concerning what is 'unwanted' in terms of adult or peer activity.

These prevalence figures, high as they seem, are compatible with those obtained in other adult recall studies of younger women (Bagley and King, 1990), and must be considered as underestimates. Most previous studies (reviewed by Finkelhor and Associates, 1986) defined sexual abuse inter alia, by age differences or abuse of authority. But in the present study we asked only about unwanted sexual contacts, with someone of any age.

Cross-classifying various aspects of abuse (type, duration, who abused, amount of threat or persuasion, amount of force, age abuse started, number of separate abusers, whether victim was able to tell anyone) we found that duration of abuse had the greatest communality or predictive power amongst these measures. In other words, duration of abuse had the highest average correlation of any indicator with other aspects of abuse.

A threefold classification yielded the most utility in terms of co-variance with other measures (see Table 6.1). This classification includes: no abuse recalled (68.0 per cent of respondents); abuse commenced and completed in less than a week — usually a single assault, on one day (25.2 per cent); and abuse continued for more than a week — the range was from one week to seven years (6.8 per cent). It was this 6.8 per cent which contained virtually all of the cases in which a relative or authority figure had used subtle threats, rewards or persuasions to impose and continue the assault. The longer the assault went on, the more likely it was to proceed from fondling to intercourse, although not all of the victims of long term abuse had experienced bodily penetration.

The majority of the unwanted sexual acts were single acts of fondling or attempted penetration by a close-in-age peer, a relative, baby-sitter or a stranger. Sexual assault in adolescence by other adolescents was relatively common (c.f. Ageton, 1983). These assaults often resulted in penetration, but did not usually carry long term consequences in terms of later adjustment, provided the victim was able to tell someone who could offer helpful support. Usually the person told was a supportive peer or peers, and it is was relatively rare for authorities to be involved in any of these assaults. Fifty-five per cent of these one time assaults were reported to someone, compared with less than a fifth of the assaults occurring over a longer period. Police or social workers were involved in only 8.3 per cent of any of the cases of unwanted sexual contact.

Table 6.1 shows the product moment correlations between the Trauma Symptom Checklist (TSC) and its sub-scales, with child abuse variables and with the other mental health indicators used in this study. TSC total score has a correlation of 0.40 with the duration of sexual abuse; this is higher than any other correlation of the TSC with other aspects of sexual abuse,

112

and higher than any correlation of the TSC sub-scales with aspects of child sexual abuse. We conclude that the TSC total scale is better at identifying former victims of child sexual abuse in community surveys such as this, than any of the other measures, including the TSC sub-scales. It should be noted too that a TSC score derived only from extreme responses ('very often') correlates 0.43 with duration of abuse.

None of the other mental health measures employed (correlations not shown) has a correlation with any aspect of sexual abuse which is higher than 0.34. Hypothetically the utility of the TSC lies in the fact that it measures both general psychoneurosis (in particular, symptoms of depression and anxiety) and symptoms (e.g. flashbacks, spacing out, nightmares) which are more specifically associated with some types of prior sexual abuse. The TSC is not however the best predictor of the EMBU, a measure of physical and emotional abuse in childhood — although the TSC correlation of 0.25 with the EMBU is highly significant, the Middlesex Hospital Questionnaire (MHQ) total score correlates at a somewhat higher level (0.27) with the EMBU.

The face validity of the TSC total scale (TSC-33) is indicated by its correlations with other mental health measures: the highest correlations are 0.59, with the MHQ psychoneurosis scale; and 0.55 with the CESD depression scale. It should be mentioned that the CESD measures the occurrence of symptoms in the past week, while the MHQ reviews the experience of the past six months, and the TSC the past two months. The Suicidal Ideation Scale measures suicidal ideas, plans and behaviour in the previous six months.

Concurrent or face validity of the Anxiety and Depression sub-scales of the TSC is also indicated by reasonably high correlations with Anxiety and Depression sub-scales of the MHQ. Principal components analysis (not shown) of mental health variables and the childhood variables (excluding the auto-correlated sub-scales) indicates a strong, general factor on which all of the clinical variables, and the childhood abuse and stress variables load at greater than 0.35.

In Table 6.2, we explore the degree to which various measures, and various cut-off points identify sexual abuse history. For this purpose sexual abuse has been divided into two types: 'short term' (defined by any unwanted sexual contact which was not repeated beyond a six-day period); and 'long term' (any unwanted sexual contact continuing for more than a week). This 'long term' category includes 95 per cent of cases of abuse by a close, adult relative (grandfather, father, step-father). This is the type of abuse which is most frequently described in the clinical literature as impacting negatively on mental health (Bagley and King, 1990).

The 'short term' category is heterogeneous in nature and includes many single incidents in which a relative, neighbour or other authority figure

fondled the child's genitalia, as well as incidents of one time sexual assault by an adolescent peer which often resulted in penetration. All stranger abuse categories are included in the 'short term' abuse category. It should be stressed that inclusion in the short term abuse category is no means a guarantee of lack of long term impairment of mental health; however, in statistical terms longer term assaults were much more likely to be associated with negative sequelae in young adulthood.

The TSC is the most useful measure in terms of minimizing 'false negatives' (missing serious abuse when it did actually occur). In this population the Trauma Symptom Checklist full scale (TSC-33) measure has a range of 0 to 57, with a mean for all respondents of 18.57 (SD 6.7, N=750). The size of the standard deviation gives an indication of some abnormality of distribution — there was a cluster of individuals with very low scores, and a cluster with very high scores. The median for all respondents was 15.10, and the failure of median and mean to converge confirms a somewhat uneven distribution of scores.

The TSC-33 mean for the women in the short term abuse category was 18.58, and for the long term abuse group, 33.49, a difference significant at less than the 0.000 level (Table 6.4). Nearly 35 per cent of all respondents had TSC-33 scores of 20 or above; 14.8 per cent had scores of 30 or more; and 7.7 per cent had scores of 40 or more. Using a score of 30+ on the TSC-33 identified 72.5 per cent of the serious, long term abuse group; 23.8 per cent of the short term abuse group; and 8.2 per cent of the group who recalled no abuse in their childhood. The cut-off point of 20+ is relatively more efficient in identifying true positives (particularly in the short term abuse group), but identifies 28 per cent false positive (individuals with scores of 20 or more who recalled no sexual abuse in childhood). The mental health questionnaire (MHQ) total score is particularly prone to identify false positives.

Two case histories support the possible usefulness of the TSC-33 as a screening instrument for workers who have a particular interest in identifying and treating the long term mental health sequelae of child sexual abuse:

> Case 1: A 23-year-old women had a score of 53 on the TSC-33, and high scores on all of the other mental health indicators. She had engaged in an act of deliberate self-harm (overdose of about a dozen aspirin) in the previous six months, but had not sought help from a psychiatrist or counsellor. She recalled no sexual abuse in childhood, but did remember a childhood in which parents were cold and excessively punitive. We obtained a rapid referral to a psychiatrist associated with this research. Six months after commencing treatment, she contacted the original interviewer and told her that she had been

systematically and cruelly sexually abused by a close relative over a long period. This memory had been lost to conscious recall, but was recovered during therapy.

Case 2: This 19-year-old woman had a TSC-33 score of 35, poor self-esteem, and some indicators of depression and anxiety in the MHQ. She told the interviewer that she had never been sexually abused. Her symptoms were not considered to be serious enough to justify psychiatric referral. Two months after interview, she called requesting a further interview. With some agitation and guilt she told her interviewer that she had indeed been sexually abused (by a brother over a period of months when she was 12) but felt too ashamed to talk about it. She also felt very guilty because she had concealed the fact of this abuse from the interviewer. We referred her to a women's therapy group.

Both of these cases had been included in the statistical analysis above in the 'no abuse' category, and underline the conservative bias against obtaining significance in the statistical analyses. Both cases also illustrate the difficulty of getting accurate prevalence rates of earlier sexual abuse from recall data — a factor which implies a conservative bias, acting against significance in estimating correlations between earlier sexual abuse and present mental health. These cases illustrate too that the TSC might be a very useful instrument in identifying the possibility of earlier, traumatic abuse, even when this is denied or repressed.

Table 6.3 indicates mean differences for the abuse categories between the major mental health indicators used (TSC-33, MHQ, SEI, and CES-D). In all cases, means for the 'short term abuse' group, although elevated, are closer to the means for the 'no abuse' group than to those for the 'long term abuse' group. This leads us to the conclusion that it is the long term abuse which is the most serious category — a similar conclusion to that reached by Sorrenti-Little et al. (1984) in operationalizing a definition of sexual abuse in terms of adult adjustment outcomes as indicated by the Tennessee Self Concept Scale.

Table 6.4 presents results of a comparison of clinical and demographic variables, using the t-test method of comparison. The demographic comparisons indicate that those from rural backgrounds, those with less education and currently lower income, had higher prevalence rates for sexual abuse. Younger women (aged 18 through 19) had significantly lower prevalence rates than did older women (20 through 27). Separation from a parent is a key variable distinguishing the short and long term abuse groups. Differences in religious background are interesting, but probably reflect the ecological pattern of rural areas, where residents are much more likely to be Protestant.

Conclusions

While these results seem to indicate, on the basis of this sample, that the TSC-33 is the instrument of choice in community samples in screening for young adults with a prior history of sexual abuse (who are also at risk in terms of current mental health) problems of generalizing from this sample should be emphasized. While the population screened is quite large, the number of victims of serious sexual abuse in childhood ($N=51$) is relatively small.

A second issue is whether the prior abuse has caused the high scores on the TSC-33. This is an important issue, since therapists often assume that current psychological distress is related to earlier traumatic events. If sexual abuse does not have a direct, causal effect then there are, presumably intervening factors which mediate this link. Physical and emotional abuse, and long term separation from a parent are also factors which are known to be associated with long term mental health problems, and are also associated to a significant extent with long term sexual abuse. We have used multiple regression analysis in an attempt to priorize the importance of these various factors in other studies (Bagley and MacDonald, 1984; Bagley and Ramsay, 1986; Bagley and Young, 1987) and concluded that sexual abuse had the greatest potential for long term impairment of mental health; however, the combination of long term physical and sexual abuse had the greatest negative impact on mental health. Regression analysis with the present sample (table not shown) points to a similar conclusion. However, Briere (1988) has shown that such analysis has inherent unreliabilities when used with measures of unknown reliability; when control, predictor and criterion variables are intercorrelated; and when sample sizes are relatively small.

Another relevant issue concerns the ethics of intervention. Should we offer counselling and therapy to individuals who have moderate scores on the TSC-33, but elevated scores on other measures of distress? Obviously, yes: all distressed people should be eligible for counselling. Furthermore, since those elements of the TSC-33 which measure anxiety and depression do not do so more effectively than other available measures, it may be that the TSC's sub-scales measuring specific outcomes of trauma should be expanded.

An interesting but unresolved question in this research is why some individuals (about a third of all victims of long term abuse) do not develop serious mental health problems, despite severe or multiple trauma in childhood. Consider:

> Case 3: A 22-year-old women recalled a childhood marked by emotional coldness, neglect, parental strife, and excessive physical punishment. Over a six-month period, from age 12 to 13 she had to

submit to sexual intercourse by her father. Then her parents separated, and she lived with an aunt. She was raped at age 15 by a cousin, and again at age 17 by a boyfriend. She presented herself in the interview as a cheerful, extroverted individual with many friends. She had excellent self-esteem, no sign of depression or neurosis, and a TSC-33 score of four. The only factor we could adduce in her survival was a chronically cheerful and extroverted personality, and her ability to make many friends. Yet this is a post hoc interpretation, and exactly why she has survived psychologically is ultimately a mystery.

Research based on clinical populations alone will not answer these questions; however, longitudinal studies of community populations (particularly of children, both before and after abuse) may be able to provide more specific answers (c.f. Finkelhor et al., 1988). Establishing what makes some individuals invulnerable to sexual assault in childhood may give us clues which can assist in both prevention and therapy.

Finally, the dangers of over-generalization from these results must be stressed. The power of the clinical instruments used in identifying former victims of sexual abuse is well below 100 per cent; and it would wrong also to assume that the short term category of sexual assault always has mild repercussions for victims. Consider:

Case 4: This 25-year-old woman was assaulted by a neighbour when she was nine. In this one-time assault the man forced the girl to fellate him, and ingesting seminal fluid caused the girl to have severe nausea. She complained immediately to her parents. Police were informed, and she was interviewed and examined extensively. At criminal trial she was aggressively cross-examined, and the abuser was acquitted. She had to face the man's sneers and invitations to further sexual activity on the street almost every day. She became chronically morose and depressed. In adolescence she became severely anorexic, and made a number of suicidal gestures. When interviewed she had high scores on a number of clinical indicators including the suicidal ideation scale, and had a TSC-33 score of 32. She had few friends, and said she was terrified of relationships with men. Since the psychiatric therapy she had received was notably unsuccessful we referred her to a women's self-help group.

While the TSC-33 and other clinical measures are useful guides for beginning clinical intervention programs, ultimately each case has to be considered in terms of the individual profile of trauma, vulnerability, long term harm and preferred treatment model.

Table 6.1
Correlations between Trauma Symptom Checklist (TSC), aspects of sexual abuse in childhood and other mental health indicators in 750 adult women

	TSC total score	Disso-ciation	Anxiety	Depre-ssion	Post-traumatic stress	Sleep distur-bance
Duration of sexual abuse	0.40	0.35	0.30	0.35	0.31	0.30
Type of CSA (Fondling thru intercourse)	0.28	0.24	0.28	0.21	0.17	0.20
Abuser (peer thru close relative)	0.35	0.22	0.26	0.25	0.24	0.22
Separation from parent > 6 months	0.20	0.10	0.20	0.17	0.16	0.09
Physical/ emotional abuse	0.25	0.06	0.16	0.20	0.110	0.10
Suicidal ideas/action	0.43	0.31	0.33	0.35	0.20	0.24
CESD: Depression in past week	0.55	0.35	0.43	0.45	0.22	0.36
Self-esteem (hi to lo)	0.34	0.24	0.30	0.28	0.16	0.18
MHQ: Psycho-neurosis	0.59	0.34	0.41	0.45	0.20	0.22
Free-floating anxiety	0.50	0.25	0.57	0.45	0.45	0.27
Somatic anxiety	0.44	0.19	0.44	0.38	0.26	0.20
Depression	0.54	0.20	0.32	0.63	0.25	0.30

Note: With 749 degrees of freedom, correlations of 0.10 and over are significant at the 0.000 level.

Table 6.2
Utility of various indicators in identifying victims of sexual abuse in childhood

Indicator	Proportions identified with no CSA N=510	Proportions identified with CSA < 1 week N=189	Proportions identified with CSA > 1 week N=51
Trauma Symptom Checklist			
Score 20+	28.2%	40.2%	92.1%
Score 30+	8.2%	23.8%	72.5%
Score 40+	5.9%	12.7%	45.1%
Middlesex Hospital Questionnaire			
Above median	44.1%	58.2%	88.2%
Above 3rd quartile	21.6%	30.2%	41.2%
Above 90th percentile	7.8%	12.2%	23.5%
CESD depression scale			
Score 31+	9.6%	25.9%	35.3%
Coopersmith SEI: Low Self-Esteem			
Score above 3rd quartile	22.0%	26.9%	49.0%
Suicide plans/DSH in past 6 months	6.7%	14.3%	27.4%

Table 6.3
Mental health indicator means within categories of child sexual abuse

	No abuse N=510	Short term abuse N=189	Long term abuse N=51	Eta
Trauma Symptom Checklist (TSC-33)	17.21	19.01	32.18	0.40
TSC Dissociation + PSAT-h + Sleep sub-scales	8.61	9.13	19.03	0.38
CESD Depression Scale	15.14	18.04	26.23	0.33
MHQ Psychoneurosis Measure	42.50	47.13	64.72	0.33
Coopersmith Self- Esteem Inventory	27.44	37.21	44.25	0.30

Note: Eta is a measure of association derived from the analysis of variance of the dependent measures across the categories of sexual abuse. For formula see Nie et al. (1976).

Table 6.4
T-test analysis for variables which distinguish between no abuse and any abuse; and between short and long term abuse

Variable	No abuse vs any abuse (510 vs 240) t-value	p	Short versus long term abuse (189 vs 51) t-value	p
Age: 18 - 29	-2.20	0.001	1.41	ns
Education: less to more	-2.19	0.005	-2.34	0.000
Income: less to more	-2.20	0.001	-2.00	0.05
Separation from a parent, > 6 months	1.58	ns	3.14	0.000
Residence in childhood: rural thru urban	2.01	0.05	1.34	ns
Religion in childhood: RC thru United Church thru None thru Other Protestant	-2.13	0.05	-1.43	ns
Number of sibs	2.44	0.000	1.45	ns
Suicidal ideas/behaviour in past 6 months	1.76	ns	2.76	0.000
CESD depression scale	3.10	0.000	3.92	0.000
Coopersmith self-esteem inventory	3.89	0.000	3.24	0.000
Measure of physical & emotional abuse or neglect	2.22	0.001	3.81	0.000
MHQ Psychoneurosis scale	3.24	0.000	4.16	0.000
TSC-33	4.22	0.000	5.18	0.000

Note: ns = not statistically significant, at the 0.05 level.

7 Victim to abuser: Mental health and behavioural sequels of child sexual abuse in a community survey of young adult males

Abstract

Respondents in a stratified random sample of 750 males aged 18 to 27 in Calgary, Canada were asked to recall unwanted sexual contacts occurring before their 17th birthday: 117 (15.6 per cent) had experienced one or more unwanted sexual contacts. Those recalling multiple events of abuse (52 individuals, 6.9 per cent of all respondents) were distinguished from other respondents at a statistically significant level on the following indicators: emotional abuse in childhood, higher rates of current or recent depression, anxiety, suicidal feelings and behaviour, and current sexual interest in or actual behaviour involving minors. The combination of emotional abuse in the respondent's childhood with multiple events of sexual abuse was a relatively good predictor of both poor mental health, and later sexual interest in or sexual contact with children. Eight apparently active paedophiles were identified, using a computer response system which assured anonymity. This study underscores the need for preventive measures, and the prompt identification and treatment of victims before they enter the victim-to-abuser cycle.

Introduction

The aim of this chapter is to overview briefly some of the reasons why individuals who have been victims of sexual abuse may themselves become, as adolescents and young adults, perpetrators of sexual abuse; and to report the results of a study designed to explore factors involved in this transition from abused child to abusive adult in a random sample of young Canadian

males. The research also documents various long term mental health sequels in young adult males of unwanted sexual contacts in childhood.

Research in Canada and the United States using a variety of methodologies and questionnaires has established that between two and 16 per cent of males in the general population will have experienced unwanted or abusive sexual contact before the age of 16 or 18. The variation of estimates can be accounted for by differences in region of the study, sampling methods used, the age of the respondents when questioned, the manner of questioning, and the wording and range of the questions asked (Finkelhor, 1984; Rison and Koss, 1987; Genuis, Thomlison and Bagley, 1991; Finkelhor, Hotaling, Lewis and Smith, 1990).

Although it is now established that some males who were victims of child sexual abuse (almost always at the hands of men) become perpetrators of child sexual abuse, the circumstances, extent and psychological reasons for this victim-to-abuser cycle are still unclear (Lane, 1991). Most research is usually based on special populations (Bolton, Morris and MacEachron, 1989; Lane, 1991). Carter and Prentky (1990) showed for example, that 57 per cent of males in a treatment program for sex offenders against children were themselves sexually abused as children. This victim-to-abuser cycle is open to a variety of theoretical explanation (Finkelhor, 1984 and 1985; Steen and Monnette, 1989; Faller, 1989; Bagley and King, 1990; Meiselman, 1990; Bagley and Thomlison, 1991).

These include the impulse to overcome the victimization experience by identifying with the offender; fixated sexual arousal patterns; development of addictive sexual behaviours; cognitive distortions which prevent the development of empathy; intergenerational transmission of deviant behaviours; a pattern of violent offending in which rape and sexual offenses are but a part; social learning of certain sexual behaviours; and various psychodynamic theories. A further possibility has been identified by Alexander (1992) with regard to the attachment to parent figures of an abused child: atypical or dysfunctional types of attachment to a parent (who may or may not be the abuser) may account for the kinds of attachments (including sexual attachments to children) which the abused person makes as an adult.

There is partial support from empirical studies for a number of competing theories to explain the victim-to-abuser cycle in males (Finkelhor, 1984; Burgess, Hartman and McCormack, 1987; Duncan, 1990; Tzeng and Schwarzin, 1990; Meiselman, 1990; Kahn and Chambers, 1991; Wachtel and Scott, 1991; Barbaree and Marshall, 1991; Lane, 1991). However, this knowledge has contributed little to an understanding of the motivations of adult paedophiles outside of clinical treatment and criminal justice systems; nor does this literature offer many insights into practical methods of breaking the victim-to-offender cycle in those who have not yet been

apprehended. The lack of such knowledge is one area identified as a high priority in research on child sexual abuse (Finkelhor, Hotaling and Yllo, 1988).

In addition, although knowledge is now accumulating on the long term psychological sequels of the sexual abuse of girls (Wyatt and Powell, 1988; Bagley and King, 1990), research findings on the long term (effects on boys are of more recent date, and provide less comprehensive knowledge (e.g. Bolton, Morris and MacEachron, 1989; Bagley and Sewchuk-Dann, 1991). It appears from recent work however that males as well as females who have been sexually abused do often suffer long term mental health problems. Some of these problems are similar to those experienced by female victims (Fromuth and Burkhart, 1989), but other modes of adjustment may be unique to male psychology (Grubman-Black, 1990; Doll, Joy, Bartolow, Harrison, Bolan, Douglas, Moss and Delgado, 1992).

Langevin (1982 and 1985) has reported on a large sample of adult males treated at the Clarke Institute of Psychiatry, Toronto following conviction for sexual assault against children. Langevin (1982) concluded that paedophiles appear to be generally similar to non-paedophiles (including 'normals') on many psychological profiles: the psychological character of paedophiles is elusive. These negative findings have been partially replicated in another Canadian study (Valliant and Blasutti, 1992), with the exception that a greater amount of chronic anxiety in incestuous offenders was found. In the United States too, psychological research has largely failed to find any clear-cut psychological factors (for example, on the MMPI) which could differentiate detected paedophiles from other criminals, and from non-criminal controls (Hall, 1989; Johnston, French, Schouweiler and Johnston, 1992).

These findings imply some difficulty in using psychological test data in trying to predict which victims of childhood sexual assault may be at risk for becoming offenders themselves. If, as Bernard and Bernard (1984) argue, the detected male abuser frequently attempts to deny the psychological reality of his offence as well as trying to manipulate and deceive those making assessments, then psychological data given anonymously by individuals who are at risk of offending, or at an early stage in a paedophile career, might offer insights into paedophile motivation which previous researchers have found elusive.

No available study has been able to explain why the majority of male victims do not go on to become adult offenders. Individual case histories from counselling practice indicate that some victims are able to empathize on the basis of their own victimization, with children whom they are tempted to exploit sexually (Bagley and King, 1990). This sub-group of males can be successfully counselled in becoming more aware of the hurt that their actions cause to children. Yet it is also clear from our clinical

124

practice that these approaches (grounded in rational — emotive therapy — of Ellis, 1990) fail to have any impact on the majority of adult abusers who were themselves abused as children.

Most of the available studies of paedophile motivations and desires in 'normal' populations have studies male college students. Thus Briere and Runtz (1989) in a study of 193 Canadian university males devised questions measuring the degree to which respondents were 'sexually attracted to small children'; had 'fantasies about sex with a child'; masturbated 'during fantasies about sex with a child' and 'hypothetical likelihood of sex with a child.' The actual age and sex of 'the child' in these questions was not specified. Nine per cent had on some occasion had fantasies about sex with a child, though only one per cent said that this had occurred often or very often. Similarly, one per cent often or very often masturbated to sex fantasies involving a child. The upper limit of serious paedophile activity according to this survey is about three per cent. Two questions asked about 'negative early sexual experiences,' and this measure was significantly related (p < 0.011) to the likelihood of sex with a child.

Another Canadian study, of 200 university males (Bagley and Genuis, 1991; Violato and Genuis, 1991) found that six per cent were 'interested or very interested' in sex with a male and/or a female child younger than adolescence. This sexual preference was significantly related (r = 0.22, p < 0.01) to the males' own history of sexual victimization, as well as to their own history of emotional abuse in childhood (r = 0.30, p < 0.01). A combination of sexual and emotional abuse in the respondents' childhood correlated 0.36 (p < 0.001) with current paedophile motivation.

This Canadian study developed a new technique for eliciting information on highly sensitive issues such as prior sexual abuse, and current sexual motivations and actions: an interactive program was developed for a portable computer, which allowed respondents to identify particular responses by means of a 'mouse' or track-ball. In this way complete anonymity was ensured, since the mode of data storage was specifically programmed to make it impossible for any individual to be identified. This research (Bagley and Genuis, 1991) showed that the computerized assessment technique elicited significantly more recollections of childhood sexual abuse than did conventional paper and pencil questionnaires.

In the United States, Fromuth, Burkhart and Webb-Jones (1991) surveyed 582 first year college men, and reported that three per cent (16 individuals) admitted that they had sexually abused one or more children. Four of these men had been multiple perpetrators during their adolescent years, each having abused at least two children. Seven of the 16 child abusers in this survey had themselves been abused as children; this proportion was significantly higher (p < 0.05) than in those not admitting sexual abuse of others. The abusers were not differentiated from the non-abusers on the

Symptom Check List; but they did show significantly more non-empathetic responses to potential victims on the Rape Myth Acceptance Scale (Fromuth et al., 1991).

Briere, Henschel and Smiljanich (1992) studied 212 college students (106 of them male) in southern California. Responses to a newly-devised Attitudes toward Sexual Abuse scale (ATSA) indicated that there was indeed some normative or attitudinal support for sexual exploitation of children and adolescents by young adults (particularly, amongst male respondents). However, "Sexual abuse history . . . was not related to ATSA scores, suggesting the link between sexually abusive behaviour and childhood sexual victimization may reflect less socially mediated (perhaps more 'clinical') processes." (Briere et al., 1992, p. 403). Another problem in interpreting responses to the ATSA is that it covers a range of hypothetical victim ages and types of sexual relationship, including those of individuals aged 13, 14 and 17 with an adult. The ATSA is not a measure of potential for paedophile behaviours per se; rather, it is an omnibus scale measuring a range of sexual attitudes, and tolerance for certain sexual behaviours involving minors. In addition, combining data for males and females may have obscured the relationship between early victimization and current attitudes to sexual exploitation of minors.

The available literature points both to accumulating knowledge, as well as to a number of gaps in understanding how and why individuals who have been sexually exploited in childhood become sexually abusive adults. As Briere et al. (1992) imply, it may be important to examine clinical variables in trying to explain why this transition from victim to abuser defines only a minority (and sometimes an elusive minority) of abuse victims. Briere (1992) argues cogently that research on special populations (including college students) should be extended to individuals in the general population.[1] What is needed is a research design using a clinical approach to understanding the victim-to-abuser cycle, in a random sample of community adults for whom histories of sexual abuse of themselves and others can be recorded in manner which will not inhibit honest and frank responses.

Aims and hypotheses

The present study aims first of all, to replicate a study of young, adult females randomly sampled from the population of Calgary, Alberta (Bagley, 1991a) through the study of a similar number of males aged 18 to 27, sampled in a similar manner. The same measures and questions were asked of males, with some additional instruments and questions. The mental health measures chosen are known to be valid and reliable, and have been

126

used in a number of previous studies of long term sequels of child sexual abuse in Britain and Canada (Bagley, 1991c).

The second aim was to try and estimate the incidence of sexual assaults against minors (aged less than 17) by young adult males in the community sample, as well as identifying social and psychological factors which might be linked to such patterns of sexual desire, and sexual offending.

The third aim was to examine the relative contributions of developmental factors, abuse history, and current stressors to variations in psychological adjustment; and the relative contribution of a similar range of factors to the degree of sexual interest in minors on the part of the sample of young adult males. Hypotheses for the study are broad rather than specific, given the tentative findings from previous studies:

1   There will be statistically significant links between an individual's experience of unwanted sexual activity in childhood and adolescence, and current mental health impairment.

2   As in the parallel study of 750 women in a community mental health survey (Bagley, 1991a), unwanted sexual contacts which continue for more than a single day (and which may involve months or years of entrapment in the abuse situation) will have the highest proportion of mental health problems as young adults. Parallel to this, it is also expected that the most serious aspect of male-on-male sexual contact (involving repeated acts of anal intercourse upon the child or adolescent) will have serious long term mental health implications for the individual, as Metcalfe, Oppenheimer, Dignon, and Palmer (1990) have suggested.

3   There will be statistically significant links between prior abuse history, some indicators of attachment patterns during the abuse, recent social stress, current mental health, and paedophile interest and activity.

Research methods: Methods and instruments

Child sexual abuse

As in previous surveys of sexual abuse or unwanted sexual acts in childhood and adolescence, questions about sexual events and sexuality were not asked until the very end of the questionnaire (Bagley and Ramsay, 1986; Bagley, 1991a). This was done in order to avoid possible influence on responses to mental health measures by feelings triggered by the recall of earlier sexual

abuse, abuse which was likely not revealed to anyone at the time (Bagley, 1991b).

After experience in using Finkelhor's (1979) method of establishing whether sexual abuse had taken place with a cohort of Canadian college students (Sorrenti-Little, Bagley and Robertson, 1984) we decided to use a simpler and more straightforward way of establishing whether abuse had taken place before the respondent's 17th birthday, by adapting the questions used in a national Canadian survey of the prevalence of child sexual abuse (Bagley, 1989b). This measure combines both the element of unwantedness in the sexual relationship as well as its duration; its seriousness in terms of bodily contact and penetration; and the relationship of the victim to the abuser.

This questionnaire (Bagley, 1990a and b) asks only about 'unwanted' sexual acts imposed on respondents before the age of 17, regardless of the age of the other person involved. Problems in trying to infer sexual abuse from differences in age between the participants are illustrated, inter alia in the study of Doll et al. (1992). Their study used a complex array of age differences, types of sexual contact, and use of verbal threat, physical force or weapon to achieve this contact. According to their criteria a sexual relationship between a 12-year-old and a 17-year-old (both males) would not be considered 'abusive' if no actual force or threat was used, even though anal penetration did take place. In our own classification, such a relationship would be classed as abusive if the younger person declared after mature reflection, that the sexual relationship had been 'unwanted.' It is likely that the criterion of 'unwantedness' in the prior sexual relationship will identify those who have experienced the most long term psychological trauma (Bagley and King, 1990).

The actual types of physical contact during the unwanted sexual contacts were classified according to the schema presented by Reinhart (1987) who studied types of abuse experienced by 189 boys referred for clinical investigation of sexual abuse. This was done in order to enable a comparison to be made of the type and severity of abuse experiences between community and clinical samples.

Emotional and physical abuse

This was measured by a factorially derived scale drawn from the European work of Arrindell, Emmelkamp, Monsma and Brilman (1983), and has been validated in a number of community mental health surveys in Canada (Ramsay and Bagley, 1985; Bagley and Young, 1990). This measure has an alpha value of 0.90 (reflecting the high loadings of items on the factorially-based scale), and test-retest reliability of 0.60 over one year (Bagley and Ramsay, 1986). The instrument includes such questions as:

'Could you seek comfort from your parents if you were sad?' and 'Did you get punished by your parents without having done anything?' As with the measure of child sexual abuse, we had no criteria of external validity for the scale in this study. However, some validity for the scale was obtained in an earlier British study in which social work records of child abuse were compared with respondents' own accounts of childhood neglect and abuse on scale items (Bagley and MacDonald, 1984).

Demographic and relationship questions

These questions were similar to those included in the parallel survey of women (Bagley, 1991a). They include questions about family structure when the individual was growing up, parental separation and divorce, presence of unrelated males in the household; the age and status of individuals perpetrating sexual abuse; and the individuals feelings about the perpetrator, including feelings of affection for this person. While this concept may seem contradictory (how could an individual be fond of an abuse perpetrator?) it is clear from many studies reviewed by Bagley and King (1990) that it is possible for victims to have positive emotional ties with an abuser, especially when that person is a member of the individuals household. This attachment to an abuser may complicate an individual's emotional reaction to the abuse, and could make it more difficult to achieve therapeutic resolution. It might also be one reason why some victims become perpetrators. No direct or well-validated measure of prior attachments was used in this study, although one question did ask about attachment to the person engaged in the sexual relationship with the young person.

Recent social stress

The measure of stress within the previous six months was developed by Ramsay and Bagley (1985) in a study of the antecedents of suicidal ideas and behaviour. The instrument asks about the presence or absence of events occurring in the previous six months which are potentially stressful for young adult males (loss of job/unable to find work following educational course; exam failure in educational course; death of close relative; permanent break with sexual partner or spouse; eviction from home; injury at work or in automobile, impairing ability to work; any condition causing chronic pain; any injury or illness impairing work capacity; crime victim — fraud, robbery or assault; unable to pay off debt of $5,000 or more; charged with/convicted of criminal offence). Each event was rated from 0 = not present, 1 = 'didn't bother me at all' through 5 'caused me a lot of stress.'

Research using medical examiner records for Alberta has indicated that there is growing sub-group of completed male suicides who have histories of family disruption, often accompanied by neglect and abuse in childhood. When faced with what seem major stressors these men sometimes commit suicide (Bagley 1989c and 1992a). For the present study we reasoned that recent stress might precipitate both mental health problems in vulnerable individuals (including suicidal feelings, gestures and attempts), as well as a regression towards earlier sexual interests and behaviour; there is evidence from previous studies which make this seem a viable proposition (Bagley and King, 1990).

Current sexual interests and activities

These questions are derived from a measure of sexual interests and behaviours developed by Langevin (1982) for the assessment of men referred for investigation and treatment following conviction for sexual offences. The full instrument contains 225 questions about all possible aspects of sexuality. Only those items referring to sexual contact with someone aged 13 to 16 (adolescents), and someone aged less than 13 of either sex; and to various kinds of homosexual contact with a man of any age were included.[2]

Three sub-scales were derived from this measure: a paedophile interest and activity scale asking questions about sex with a boy or girl under age 13, with the responses 'idea repulsive,' ranked 0; 'not interested,' 1; 'unsure,' 2; 'quite interested,' 3; 'very interested,' 4; actual sexual contact with someone under 13, ranked 5. These interests and contacts were those involving the respondent after his 18th birthday. A deviance with males sub-scale asked about sexual interests or contact with a male under age 16, and was scored in a similar way. A deviance with females sub-scale pertained to sexual contact with a female aged under 16, and was similarly scored. For regression analyses (in Tables 7.6 and 7.7) two of the scales, (sexual interest/activity involving children under 13, and males 13 to 15) were combined, since they had a similar range of correlations. Additional ad hoc questions were asked about reasons for not engaging in deviant sexual behaviours which were the subject of fantasy or desire.

No evidence of validity for these scales is available; we had no way of knowing in a community survey in which respondents were guaranteed anonymity whether the reports of deviant sexual behaviour were actually true, or whether any sexual interests and behaviours were concealed.

Mental health questionnaire

This measure was originally developed by Crowne and Crisp (1981) as the Middlesex Hospital Questionnaire. While the measure has been used principally in work in medical psychology and psychosomatic medicine, it has also had wide use in a variety of populations, and in various cultures outside of England where it was originally developed. The version used in the present study was developed by Bagley (1980) and although factorially shortened includes measures of depression and anxiety, as well as a general factor measuring psychoneurosis (a mix of neurotic symptoms including signs of depression, free-floating and somatic anxiety, and obsessionality). The questions relate to 'thoughts and feelings' in the previous six months.

The CESD Depression Scale

This widely-used instrument has known reliability, validity and has been used in a variety of cultures. The measure was used in a parallel study of parenting in relation to abuse history in a study of young mothers (Bagley and Young, 1990). In Canadian studies a score of 28 on the CESD scale has been shown to be a more efficient cut-off point for identifying serious, clinical depression (Barnes and Prosen, 1984; Devins, Orme, Costello and Binik, 1988) than the cut-off of 31 indicated by Radloff (1977) in her initial validation studies for the scale in the United States. The CESD scale asks about feelings and behaviour in the past week, and so covers a much more recent period that the Middlesex Hospital Questionnaire.

Suicidal ideas and behaviour

These questions were developed or used in earlier community mental health surveys (Ramsay and Bagley, 1985; Bagley and Ramsay 1993). The suicidal ideation questionnaire measures any thoughts and intentions about self-killing in the previous six months (scored as 1); planning for a suicide attempt (scored 2) during the same period; making a suicidal gesture involving deliberate self-harm in the individuals, lifetime (scored 3); and having ever made a failed attempt at suicide at any time (scored 4). A suicidal gesture is defined as an act of deliberate self-harm in which there is no clear intention to die, and a lethal method is not used. Attempted suicide involves either a clear intention to die, use of a potentially lethal method, or both.

This measure (the TSC) was developed by Briere (1989) as a screening instrument for long term trauma suffered by victims of child sexual abuse. This 33-item measure covers areas of post-traumatic stress, dissociative symptoms, depression, anxiety, and sleep disturbance. Respondents were asked to indicate the degree to which they had experienced the items identified in the previous six months. Validity is not well-established for this new scale, although in the community mental health study of 750 young adult females, the TSC total score was the most powerful instrument of any deployed, in identifying women who had experienced unwanted sexual contact in childhood (Bagley, 1991a).

Dissociative Experiences Scale

This was designed by Bernstein and Putnam (1986) to measure a dysfunctional state which sometimes follows severe childhood trauma, and involves dissociative psychological experiences (involving in extreme cases a multiple personality). There is some evidence of the scale's validity (Chu and Dill, 1989), although there are few published studies of the scale's use with normal, male populations. However, there is no theoretical reason for supposing that some traumatized males do not also suffer long term dissociative personality disorders.

Research methods: Sampling procedures

This study of young adult males was designed to parallel a study of a sample of 750 females aged 18 to 27 (Bagley, 1991a). Systematic sampling of populations of defined age can show in a series of comparisons at different points in time whether the actual incidence of recent sexual abuse recalled by young adults is actually decreasing, in parallel with a variety of prevention programs (Bagley, 1990c; Bagley and Thomlison, 1991). An additional reason for sampling younger individuals is that they are probably more able to respond frankly to questions about sexual exploitation in their childhood than older people, probably because they are more able to be frank about what was previously a taboo subject (Bagley and Ramsay, 1986; Bagley and King, 1990). Although the psychological impact of childhood abuse might be long-lasting for all individuals, young adults may have particular problems of psychosexual adjustment arising from recent abuse.

The sampling frame for this research was the 'reverse' telephone directory for the Calgary, a prosperous city in western Canada. This city has seen rapid population increase in the past two decades due to oil and

natural gas discoveries, with immigration from many parts of Canada and the United States, as well as Europe and Asia.[3] The reverse directory lists numbers by neighbourhood, rather than alphabetically by individual subscriber. This makes stratified random sampling of particular neighbourhoods fairly easy.

The neighbourhoods selected were similar to those in the study of females (Bagley, 1991a); all had a relatively high proportion of young adults. Cluster analysis of census data identified three types of neighbourhood containing high proportions of young adults: (1) middle class, with many young families living in detached or town-houses; (2) high proportion of apartments, with many unmarried young adults, usually with white collar jobs; (3) high proportion of low rent and public housing, and many young adults who were single, married or cohabiting. Two neighbourhoods (defined by postcodes) within these three strata were randomly selected. Random sampling was then undertaken within these six neighbourhoods.

Potential respondents were first contacted by telephone in order to establish that they were male, and in the required age range (18 to 27). If they were, we requested co-operation in a study of 'childhood events, current adjustment and current outlook on life.' Sampling continued until the requisite number of 18 to 23 year-old, was obtained, with approximately equal numbers in each of the 10 age categories aged 18 through 27. Of those contacted who were in the target age groups, 72.9 per cent agreed to participate. One-third of those who declined to participate said they had no time; another one-third were hostile or indifferent; six per cent had problems with English; five per cent agreed, but could not be located at the address listed; the remainder gave a variety of reasons including the low level of payment ($20) offered for participation. Sixteen individuals began the interactive computer program but declined to continue at some stage. The program took from 40 minutes to 1.5 hours to complete, and was administered in the respondent's home setting.

Respondents were advised that no record of their identity would be retained, and they were urged to answer the questions which would appear on the screen of the portable computer as honestly as possible. The research assistants introducing the interactive computer program were male, casually dressed, and in the same age range as the respondents. While the respondent completed the interactive program, the research assistant read a book, or watched TV, and declined (for reasons outlined below) to answer any specific questions about the response system.

Some ethical issues

A researcher in the field of sexual abuse has to meet a number of institutional, professional and legal requirements. An institutional ethics committee has to be assured that respondents give informed consent to the research; that they will not be harmed in any way by the research; and that distressed individuals encountered by the researchers should be appropriately, referred.

In addition, professional standards and legal obligations in most Provinces and States in North America require that individuals (and human service professionals in particular) must report any reasonable suspicion of child abuse to a relevant legal authority. This latter obligation imposes a profound dilemma for researchers on child sexual abuse. If we began the research with the informed consent statement 'We will ask you questions about your sexual interests and activities involving children and adolescents. If you do give such information however, we are obliged to make a report of this activity to a legal authority', the research design would be hopelessly compromised. Our solution to this dilemma has been to guarantee respondents complete anonymity in the completion of a questionnaire requiring the movement of a 'mouse' to select the appropriate response in one of the boxes appearing on the screen of a portable computer. The program ensured that no information could be retrieved until the responses of at least 20 individuals were stored on hard disk. Random ordering of data for each case meant that the researchers had no way of identifying the responses of any particular individual.

While such systematic ignorance does involve some ethical dilemmas, we attempted to compensate for this by giving on-screen messages through the interactive program advising respondents of the potential for harm which sexuality imposed upon a child could engender. In addition, telephone numbers were given on-screen of various counselling agencies who had agreed to respond to any calls.

Results

Initial results indicated that 117 of the 750 males (15.5 per cent) had experienced <u>unwanted</u> sexual contact involving at least the touching of the respondent's genitals or anus before the age of 17 (Table 7.1). There are clear differences in the incidence of types of sexual contact between those who were assaulted on one occasion only, and those assaulted more frequently (10 individuals were assaulted over a period of three years or more). Those assaulted more than once were much more likely than those experiencing single assaults to have experienced anal contact, and anal

penetration. With regard to this most serious type of assault upon a male child, our group of long term victims are quite similar in their abuse characteristics to Reinhart's (1987) clinical sample. Differences in proportions experiencing oral genital contact and anal contact without penetration are likely due to the fact that the clinical group were classified according to the most serious abuse experienced, whereas data from our own sample are presented on the basis of all of the kinds of abuse experienced.

Table 7.1 also indicates that the 52 long term victims were significantly more likely to occupy blue-collar jobs, or were unemployed; and their mothers had achieved fewer years of education. (Data on fathers has too many missing cases to be of use in these comparisons, because of the number of absent fathers). Significantly more fathers were absent for three or more years before respondent was aged 16, in the group who experienced prolonged abuse. The finding that male victims of sexual abuse come from somewhat disadvantaged backgrounds is consistent with the results of the national survey of child sexual abuse in Canada (Bagley, 1989b). The significant difference in age for the long term abuse group cannot be explained.

Table 7.2 indicates that the abuse of the long-duration group began earlier and was more likely to involve a parental figure (not, usually the biological father) and/or a neighbourhood adult. Three of the long term cases may have been abused in a ritual or satanic-type setting. Each of these three was abused over a period of more than three years. Individuals within the family setting accounted for 29 per cent of those who abused the one-time assault group, and 63 per cent of those in the long-duration group. Female assailants were involved in only five per cent of the abuse situations, while male authority figures (e.g. youth leaders, priests or ministers) were involved as abusers with 14 per cent of the victims.

As in the parallel study of 750 females resident in the same areas of the city, most of the victims had never told anyone about the unwanted sexual acts. Even when an adult was told, no intervention led to the prosecution of the abuser (Table 7.2). The long-duration group were significantly more likely to that they felt too ashamed, felt partly responsible, were scared of the abuser, or were too attached to the abuser as reasons for not reporting the abuse. Fifty per cent of the short-duration abuse respondents positively endorsed the items 'It didn't bother me,' and/or 'I could handle it myself' as reasons for not reporting the abuse at the time.

In Table 7.3 we present the results of comparing the three abuse groups (none; single episode; multiple episodes) according to the means of the psychological measures used. In all comparisons the multiple-episode group have significantly higher scores (p < 0.01) than the no abuse and single-episode (short term abuse) groups combined, according to a Scheffe post-hoc

135

analysis of mean scores. A fifth of the multiple-episode group had scores on the CESD depression scale of 28 or more, the cut-off point which implies a potential for diagnosis of a major depression (Devins et al., 1988). Furthermore, 26 per cent of the multiple-episode group had made a suicidal gesture or attempt during their lifetime. Respondents were invited by the interactive program to enter on 10 lines of free format the events precipitating a suicidal gesture or attempt. Two of the single-episode respondents entered the fact of being sexually abused as a precipitant, while 12 of the 63 multiple-episode respondents specified sexual abuse as an immediate or long term precipitant of the gesture or attempt.

The multiple episode group contained significantly more individuals who had made more than one suicidal gesture, and more individuals making a suicide attempt (involving either a life-threatening method, a clear intention to die, or both).

Table 7.4 presents the relationships between an individual's own sexual history and his current sexual interests and behaviours. This analysis indicates that the men who experienced multiple events of sexual abuse in their own childhood were those most likely to have, according to their self reports, recent or ongoing sexual contact with an under-aged person.

The correlations presented in Table 7.5 show a fairly strong link between a history of sexual abuse and emotional abuse (often accompanied by excessive physical punishment) in the childhood of our respondents. Both sexual abuse and emotional abuse have statistically significant links with a number of indicators of current mental health. The strongest correlations are with depression, anxiety, suicidal feelings and behaviour, psychoneurosis, post-traumatic stress, and dissociative experiences.

The combination of sexual and emotional abuse in childhood is the strongest predictor of sexual interest and activity involving male adolescents, and younger children of either sex. Those who report sexual interest and/or activities involving children tend to be more depressed and anxious and have more suicidal feelings and behaviours than those without such interests.

The regression analysis presented in Table 7.6 is an attempt to assess the relative strengths of the various predictors of sexual interests and activities involving children. Given the pattern of correlations presented in Table 7.5, the two scales representing sexual interest in males age 13 to 15, and males and females less than 13 have been combined. (Few of the mental health indicators are successful in predicting levels of sexual interest and activity involving females aged 13 to 15). A history of sexual abuse, and emotional abuse in respondent's own childhood were ordered to enter the regression analysis last, in test of the null hypothesis that when other relevant factors were controlled, there would be no significant links between abuse history, and current sexual interests.

136

The analysis in Table 7.6 disconfirms this hypothesis: even when the influence of paternal absence, mother's educational level, and history of emotional abuse are controlled for, sexual abuse history (none=0; single-episode=1; multiple-episode=2, normalized by a z-transformation) remains a statistically significant correlate or predictor of current sexual interest in children and male adolescents. Age of respondent was entered first into the regression analyses because there is a significant correlation of older age and unwanted sexual contacts (see Table 7.1). However, controlling for the effects of age at the onset of abuse did not influence the significant correlations of the other variables in the regression equations.

Table 7.7 presents a regression analysis which partials out the relative effects of selected variables in predicting scores on the measure of suicidal ideas and behaviour, including years of life at risk. Again, the fact of having been sexually abused in childhood was entered at the last step in the regression analysis; again, it remains a statistically significant predictor of suicidal ideas and behaviour (and by association, measures of anxiety, depression, post-traumatic stress, and dissociative emotional and cognitive responses).

The variables which had significant correlations with the combined sexual interest and activity with minors scale following regression analysis (Table 7.6) have been entered into a discriminant function analysis (Table 7.8) to examine the extent to which the known correlates of sexual interest and activity could correctly assign individuals with any history of sexual interest or activity involving minors. There are relatively few false positives (individuals wrongly assigned to the abuser group on the basis of developmental and psychological variables); but a third of those admitting sexual interests and behaviours involving minors were missed by this analysis. Nevertheless, two-thirds of these deviant individuals were correctly identified by the discriminant analysis.

Finally, in Table 7.9 we present reasons given by individuals who although 'interested' or 'very interested' in sex with an males and females aged less than 16, for not actually having had sexual contact with anyone in this age group. The responses imply that at least a third of the 71 individuals involved would not feel guilty about such an act, were not concerned about the harm which sexual contact might cause the child, and would not empathize with the potential victim, notwithstanding their own history of being abuse victims. Overall, about a half of those having sexual interests in children aged below 13 recorded that they did want help with sexual problems.

Discussion of research findings

The limitations of the present research must be stressed. First of all, the number of respondents actually admitting to sexual activities involving children under 13 is small — four individuals admitting to sexual activities involving females, three admitting to such activities involving males, and one individual being sexually involved with both male and female children under 13. Nevertheless, these presumed paedophiles are likely at an early stage in their hypothetical 'careers' involving sexual offending. Five of these eight individuals said that they offended against more than one child; one individual had sexually assaulted nine children of both sexes.

We should compare these findings with the research of Weinrott and Saylor (1991) who found in a study of convicted offenders that these 99 men '. . . admitted to over 8,000 sexual contacts with 959 children. The number ranged from 1 to 200, with a median of 7' (p. 291). The point is that identification and intervention with even a few actual and potential offenders at an early stage might well prevent literally hundreds of children suffering sexual assault. At present professional workers are faced with an ethical dilemma — if a client admits to even one sexual assault against a minor in the recent past, the worker is legally obliged to report such knowledge to a relevant authority. Yet such reporting is likely to undermine any counselling relationship. Knowledge of such reporting requirements may also inhibit potential and actual offenders from seeking professional help.

Another limitation of the present study concerns the unknown validity of the information elicited through the computerized response technique: while we had no way of establishing the validity of the personal reports of prior unwanted acts, and current sexual activities and interests, it should be noted that other workers do indicate some validity for self-report measures for adult offenders (Marshall, Barbaree and Eccles, 1991; Weinrott and Saylor, 1991). It is assumed however that measurement errors will err in the direction of understatement and concealment, a bias working against the establishment of statistical significance.

It is also acknowledged that sampling stable populations will miss some of those who have been particularly traumatized by earlier abuse, and are now leading unstable or institutionalized lives. Studies of the homeless, street people, and institutionalized male populations (e.g. in prisons, psychiatric hospitals, child care institutions) indicate that such individuals have much higher rates of sexual abuse in childhood than expected from general population surveys (Bagley, Burrows and Yaworksi, 1990).

A further methodological problem is the tendency for some victims of extreme and prolonged abuse beginning before the age of five or six to mentally dissociate themselves from traumatic experiences to the extent that they may lose conscious memory of the abuse, but nevertheless often

manifest some dysfunctional feelings and behaviours (Dunn, 1992). The presentation of self by such individuals is likely to be fragmented or fractured (Putnam, 1990), and although psychiatric symptoms are often present (Chu and Dill, 1989; Putnam, 1993) the memory of the abuse which caused these dissociative personality traits is not accessible until after some weeks or months of therapy (Bliss, 1986). It is likely however that dissociative personality features can be measured along a continuum, with some abuse victims displaying various forms of dissociative thinking (such as flashbacks, spacing out, forgetting hours of activity the previous day, sleep disturbances and nightmares) which fall short of actual amnesia, or multiple personality.

The findings of our community survey indicate that dissociative thinking is correlated at a modest but statistically significant level ($r = 0.29$, $p < 0.01$) with unwanted sexual contact in childhood, in the entire sample. The correlation within the multiple abuse group between age when abuse was first thought to occur is -0.46 ($p < 0.01$), indicating that early-onset sexual abuse was most likely to be associated with high scores on Bernstein and Putnam's (1986) measure of dissociative experiences. Within the 65 single-episode sexual contact cases the correlation between age at which abuse was experienced and dissociative experiences scale was close to zero.

Despite the various methodological problems, there does appear to be support for the hypotheses presented earlier:

1   Experiencing unwanted sexual activity before the age of 17 has a statistically significant link with various indicators of poor mental health, including depression, anxiety, post-traumatic stress, dissociative thinking, and a history of suicidal ideas and behaviour. Nearly a fifth of those experiencing long term abuse were seriously depressed at the time of the interview, and a third of these 52 individuals had made a suicidal gesture or attempt during their lifetime. This association between suicidal ideas and behaviour remained significant when years of life at risk, and various socioeconomic and developmental factors were controlled for, including emotional abuse in childhood, and recent stress.

2   Although the 750 women in the parallel survey (Chapter 7) were more likely than males to recall unwanted sexual contact before age 17 (32 per cent versus 16 per cent in males) the numbers recalling multiple episodes of abuse were similar between men and women (52 individuals or 6.9 per cent in men; 51 individuals or 6.8 per cent in women). This is an interesting finding, and if replicated has important implications for understanding the epidemiological findings on links between mental health, and child sexual abuse (c.f. Finkelhor, 1993).

The finding that, as in the female sample, single-episode assaults have much fewer adverse sequelae in terms of mental health impairment supports the clinical insights of Kempe and Kempe (1984, p. 188). The Kempes' idea that male victims of child sexual abuse may often have poorer psychological outcomes than female victims (Kempe and Kempe, 1984, p. 190) also finds support from our data: in comparison with our female sample (Bagley, 1991a) male victims of long term or multiple events of sexual abuse in childhood were particularly likely to manifest psychological problems, especially those taking the form of internalizing disorders, manifested as depression and suicidal behaviour.

Finkelhor's (1993) conclusion from a review of the literature on the epidemiology of child sexual abuse is also supported by our data: although there are some specific socio-economic correlates of sexual victimization of males, these correlations although statistically significant, do not explain very much of the variance in the rates of abuse. Child sexual abuse of males in our stratified samples is found in all types of family, regardless of family structure and social class levels. While the risk in economically poor and socially disorganized families is somewhat greater, the risk in 'normal,' middle class families is not negligible.

3   As hypothesized, there are statistically significant links between a history of abuse (particularly, multiple-episode sexual abuse) and current sexual interest or activity involving minors. This effect seems to be mediated by mental health problems in that those with current paedophile interests do have somewhat poorer mental health. These individuals may have had attachment problems too, since attachment to the abuser is an independent predictor of current paedophile interest and activity. However, these correlations although statistically significant explain only a small amount of the variance in the paedophile interests and activities measure. At least a half of those experiencing multiple-episode abuse did not admit to sexual interests in children and adolescents. However, a combination of current mental health problems, current social stress, prior emotional abuse, and attachment to the original abuser correctly identifies two-thirds of those with current interest in or activity with minors (males and females less than 13, and males aged 13 to 15). In the absence of a longitudinal design it is difficult to undertake causal modelling with these data. The hypothesis that one set of factors in the transition from victim to abuser involves prior attachment to the adult male abuser in individuals whose own families provide inadequate emotional support must be explored

in various ways in subsequent research studies. It is likely too that there are various pathways to different kinds of adult sexual identity involving idiosyncratic 'sexual scripts' as Plummer (1990) terms them.

It is noteworthy that none of those who were sexually abused but who were not emotionally abused as well (score below the median on the measure of emotional abuse in childhood for the whole sample) identified themselves as having sexual interests or activity involving children under 13. The hypothetical model of risk for one sub-type of potential offender involves an emotionally abused or neglected boy who develops some kind of attachment to a male who also sexually exploits him over a period of months or even years. This attachment hypothetically involves an internalization of the role of the abuser, as a means of fragile ego integrity. These ideas will have to be explored in future clinical studies: the important theoretical integration of Bowlby's ideas an attachment with research findings on outcomes for sexually abused children by Alexander (1992) was published after our Canadian research was completed. Alexander argues that current modes of attachment in adults (which imply in some cases a risk for sexual abuse perpetration) reflect childhood attachments, including attachments imposed by abusive adults. She concludes however (p. 192) that these hypotheses can only be fully elucidated by longitudinal studies of child victims. Such studies involve profound ethical dilemmas and logistic challenges (see Bagley and MacDonald, 1984 for an example of longitudinal research with child sexual abuse victims).

Our data do suggest some possibilities for prevention programs, in that the resolution of feelings of guilt, self-doubt and inappropriate attachments and identification with an abuser could be addressed therapeutically, as part of programs of tertiary prevention with adult male survivors (Bagley, 1991b). The poor mental health, including depression, anxiety, feelings of guilt, and suicidal ideas and behaviour of the men who express sexual interest in children, deserve comment. Their problems (of anxiety, depression and guilt) may reflect what Finkelhor (1984) describes as the struggle in former victims to find 'emotional congruence.' In Finkelhor's four-factor model of preconditions for child sexual abuse there must not only be motivation to sexually abuse; there must also be an attempt to find internal emotional congruence facilitating such an act (as well as sexual arousal, and opportunity or ability, to overcome at child's resistance). It could be that the potential paedophiles we have identified are not in a state of conventional emotional congruence, or ego integration. They have, in Finkelhor's terms (1984, p. 56) 'arrested emotional development; a need to feel powerful and controlling; to re-enact childhood trauma to undo the hurt; and narcissistic identification with self as a young child.'

One of Finkelhor's (1984) preconditions of actual sexual contact with children is the fact of having access to children. Ten individuals in our survey who reported actual or strongly desired sexual contact with children under 13 had direct contact with children, including step-siblings, stepchildren, or children whom they were connected with professionally, or in volunteer roles. This finding underscores the urgent need to find ways of intervening with male victims who are also potential abusers.

Our results suggest that the psychological processes which might be involved in the development of paedophilia cannot explain sexual interest in adolescent females (aged 13 to 15). These men do not appear to manifest the guilt, poor mental health or abusive childhoods which mark many of those with sexual interests in younger children, and in male adolescents. As argued elsewhere (Bagley and King, 1990), for these individuals motivation may reflect sexist, normative standards rather than personal pathology. Sex with an adolescent female is simply 'fair game' in the libidinous careers of many young, sexist males. Addressing this problem implies programs (probably school-based) which involve normative and value change with regard to relations between the sexes.[4]

It is possible that those males with a deviant sexual interest in children and young people who have not acted upon such interest might do so later (despite feelings of guilt and shame at such acts) in the face of new stressors such as failed marriage, onset or worsening of a drinking problem, or employment reverses. These stressors might cause some individuals to regress to earlier patterns of psychosexual relationships, including the awakening of latent or unresolved sexual interest in children (the 'regressed' offender — see Simon, Sales, Kaszniak and Kahn, 1992). That current social stressors can play a role in the emergence of patterns of sexual interest in children is supported to some extent by the regression analyses reported above in Tables 7.6 and 7.7.

Clinically, we would advocate that the potential of former victims for becoming offenders should be made much more explicit in community health information systems; men at risk of becoming offenders should be invited to join self-support groups or seek individual counselling which would help prevent them from sexually exploited children when they are tempted or motivated to do so. Such approaches could be incorporated into special community-based programs which focus on men's and women's personal development, gender relationships, and support of family life.

The most cost effective form of prevention in our view lies in school-based programs which screen and offer help to young victims during their early adolescent years (Bagley, 1991b). A survey of schools in rural Alberta has shown that young people are willing to report various kinds of stress, including physical, emotional and sexual abuse, and articulate the

need for help and support in areas of stress and crisis in their lives (Bagley, 1992b).

In the survey of young adult males in Calgary more than half of the men with paedophile motivation responded positively to the question 'I wish someone could help me with my sexual problems' indicating that preventive counselling could be a valuable community resource. Finally, we are impressed with the degree to which the community sample responded co-operatively and comprehensively to the computerized response techniques. Such techniques could be built into a wide range of child abuse investigations, including those of victims and of adult survivors and potential perpetrators. Computerized response systems are just as accurate in diagnosing non-psychotic psychiatric illnesses as are live psychiatrists (Lewis, Pelosi, Glover, Wilkinson, Stansfield, Williams and Shepherd, 1988).

Notes

1. A national survey of U.S. adults by Janus and Janus (1993) indicates that about two per cent of adult males have had sexual relations with a child or young adolescent. The estimates of the extent of adult male sexual interest in children from studies of college students in Canada and the U.S.A. are compatible with a life-time incidence figure of two per cent for males who sexually exploit children.

2. Our results indicate that one sequel of unwanted sexual experiences with an older male was current commitment to a gay sexual partner who was much older than the respondent. This subgroup indicated no particular sexual interest in individuals younger than themselves. These data will be reported in more detail in a subsequent paper. The findings are consonant with some previous work, indicating possible connections between being gay as an adult, and having been singled out for unwanted sexual advances as a youth (Plummer, 1990; Doll et al., 1992).

3. Ethnicity and racial characteristics, measured in a variety of ways, had no statistically significant associations with the variables analyzed in this study.

4. Such programs need to address not only normative and value change, but also the personality and self-esteem problems which inform particular value choices. In a report on a large-scale program intended to reduce the amount of inter-ethnic prejudice in junior high school students we found that self-esteem levels, as well as scholastic failure, and various personality problems were both correlated with hostile attitudes to ethnic minorities, and also prevented some individuals from benefitting from curriculum programs designed to reduce prejudice (Bagley, Verma, Mallick and Young, 1979). Similarly, school-based programs designed to diminish sexist attitudes, and the potentials for sexually assaultive behaviors need

143

to address the personality problems of individual students in parallel to curriculum innovations.

Table 7.1
Respondent characteristics, and types of unwanted sexual acts experienced before age 17 in a community survey

Frequency of unwanted sexual contact	N	Mean age at interview	% Current job: blue collar/ jobless	Mother: education beyond high school	Father: absent 3+ yrs before respondent aged 16
No unwanted act recalled	633	22.6 yrs	30.3%	25.1%	12.0%
Single unwanted act	65	22.1 yrs	32.3%	23.1%	14.3%
Multiple unwanted acts	52	24.1 yrs[b]	55.8%[b]	11.5%[b]	34.6%[b]

Type of Act	One-Time Assault (N=65)	Multiple Assaults (N=52)	U.S. Clinical Referrals[a] (N=189)
Oral genital contact	23%	60%[b]	35%
Non-oral genital contact (fondling, manipulation)	77%	75%	33%
Anal contact (without penetration)	18%	52%[b]	10%
Anal penetration	3%	38%	40%
Digital	1%	17%	8%
Penile	1%	21%	29%
Object	0%	2%	4%

[a] Data from (Reinhart, 1987)
[b] Differences between types of sexual act in one-time assault respondents, and multiple-assault respondents significant at the five per cent level (Fisher's *t*-test for proportions). The Reinhart (1988) classification is based on the most serious type of assault experienced. Our own data classify <u>all</u> types actions occurring during the unwanted sexual contacts.

Table 7.2
Perpetrator, duration and report status of unwanted sex acts

	Single Act (N=65)		Multiple Acts (N=52)	
Mean age at onset (range)	11.5 (5 to 15)		8.2 (3 to 16)[b]	
Mean duration (range)	-		3.5 weeks (2 days to 5.3 yrs)	
Perpetrator:				
Biological or adoptive father	0		2	(3.8%)
Step-father/mother's cohabitee	8	(12.3%)	14	(26.9%)[a]
Biological relative (grandfather, uncle or aunt, cousin, sibling)	10	(15.4%)	9	(17.3%)
Unrelated family friend	10	(15.4%)	10	(19.2%)
Neighbourhood adult	9	(13.8%)	15	(28.8%)
Non-adult (< 18) in neighbourhood, school, club, peer group	10	(15.4%)	6	(11.5%)
Authority figure (teacher, community worker, youth worker, priest, minister)	13	(20.0%)	7	(13.0%)
Stranger	6	(9.21)	0	
Female assailant	1	(1.6%)	5	(9.6%)
Unwanted sex act in ritual setting	0		3	(5.8%)
Confided in or reported unwanted act to:				
No-one	50	(76.9%)	44	(84.6%)
Adult - parent, relative, neighbour	5	(7.7%)	4	(7.7%)
Friend, sibling or peer	6	(9.2%)	3	(5.8%)
Teacher, social worker, Minister, police told by respondent, or indirectly	5	(7.7%)	3	(5.8%)
Respondent received help or counselling following report to authority	0		3	(5.8%)
Offender prosecuted	0		0	
Reason for not reporting:				
Felt too ashamed	10	(15.4%)	23	(44.2%)[b]
Felt partly responsible	4	(6.1%)	30	(57.7%)[b]

Table 7.2 (Continued)

	Single Act (N=65)		Multiple Acts (N=52)	
Scared of how others would react	26	(40.0%)	21	(40.4%)
Scared of person who did it	14	(21.5%)	17	(32.7%)[a]
Didn't want person who did it to be prosecuted/was too attached to the person	10	(15.4%)	23	(44.2%)[b]
Didn't bother me and/or I could handle it myself	33	(50.7%)	14	(26.9%)[b]

Note: Number of assailants in 'Multiple Acts' group is more than the number of victims, since some individuals were assaulted by different kinds of individuals, at different points in time.

Some individuals told more than one person; and some gave more than one reason for not reporting the act at the time.

[a]   Indicates differences between means or proportions significant at the five per cent level.

[b]   Indicates differences between means or proportions significant at the one per cent level or beyond. Fisher's (1944) t-tests for comparing means and proportions were used for these calculations.

Table 7.3
Mental health indicator means within categories of child sexual abuse

	No abuse N = 633	Short term abuse N = 65	Long term abuse N = 52	Eta[a]
Trauma Symptom Checklist (TSC-33)	15.77 (3.8)	18.47 (5.5)	25.14 (7.2)	0.34 -
CESD Depression Scale	14.31 (3.4)	16.82 (5.1)	25.58 (7.1)	0.32 -
MHQ Psychoneurosis Measure	37.11 (6.4)	44.69 (8.9)	61.10 (14.7)	0.35 -
Suicidal ideas & behaviour scale	0.71 (1.3)	1.63 (2.7)	2.36 (2.9)	0.39 -
Percent seriously depressed (28+ score on the CESD depression scale)	6.0%	7.9%	19.2%[b]	-
Percent making suicidal gesture in lifetime	4.1%	7.9%	30.8%[b]	-
Percent attempting suicide in lifetime	0.3%	1.6%	9.6%[b]	-

[a] Eta is a measure of association derived from the analysis variance of the dependent measure across the categories of sexual abuse (Nie et al., 1976). Figures in brackets are standard deviations. All values of Eta are significant at the one per cent level or beyond.

[b] Significance testing of percentages calculated by combining no abuse and single-episode groups versus the multiple-episode groups. All comparisons are significant at the one per cent level or beyond, according to Fisher's *t*-test for proportions.

Table 7.4
Associations between sexual activity and interest in minors, and respondent's own history of unwanted sexual contact in childhood

	No unwanted sex contact in own childhood N = 633	Single event of unwanted sex contact N = 65	Multiple events of sex contact N = 52
No interest/unsure	623 (98.4)	61 (93.8%)	41 (78.8%)
Currently - sexual interest in female < 13 years old	9 (1.4%)	4 (6.1%)	7 (13.4%)
Sexual contact (after age 18, with female < 13 years	1 (0.2%)	0	4 (7.7%)
	Chi-squared, 2 df, 17.3, $p < .001$*		
No interest/unsure	629 (99.4%)	61 (93.8%)	42 (80.8%)
Currently - sexual interest in males < 13 years old	4 (0.6%)	4 (6.1%)	6 (11.5%)
Sexual contact (after age 18) with male < 13 years old	0	0	4 (7.7%)
	Chi-squared, 2 df, 15.1, $p < .000$*		
No interest/unsure	621 (98.1%)	61 (93.8%)	30 (57.7%)
Currently - sexual interest in males aged 13 to 15	10 (1.6%)	2 (3.1%)	12 (23.1%)
Sexual contact (after age 18) with male aged 13 to 15	2 (0.3%)	2 (3.1%)	10 (19.2%)
	Chi-squared, 2 df, 40.1, $p < .000$.*		

Table 7.4 (Continued)

	No unwanted sex contact in own childhood N = 633	Single event of unwanted sex contact N = 65	Multiple events of sex contact N = 52
No interest/unsure	542 (85.6%)	54 (83.1%)	48 (92.3%)
Currently - sexual interest in females aged 13 to 15	55 (8.7%)	5 (7.7%)	3 (5.8%)
Sexual contact (after age 18) with females aged 13 to 15	36 (5.7%)	6 (9.2%)	1 (1.9%)

Chi-squared, 2 *df*, 2.5, N.S.[*]

Note: Respondents were asked to specify their sexual contacts and interests since their 18th birthday. 'Sexual contact' defined as any form of sexual contact with the unclothed body (including sexual contact under clothing) of the respondent or of the other person involved.

[*] Chi-squared calculated across the categories types of unwanted sexual contact (none; single; prolonged) and two categories of sexual interest or contact with minors (1 = idea repulsive, not interested, or unsure; 2 = interested or very interested or actual contact). In order to control for the numbers of cells with less than five cases, Yates' correlation (Siegel and Castellan, 1988) has been applied.

Table 7.5

Correlations of paedophilia and sexual deviance sub-scales with prior sexual abuse in childhood and adolescence, prior emotional abuse, and current mental health in 750 males aged 18 to 27

	Own sexual abuse < 16	Own emotional abuse < 16	Sexual activity & interests:		
			Sex with children < 13 subscale	Sex with males 13 - 15 subscale	Sex with females 13 - 15 subscale
Sexual abuse before age 16	-	0.41	0.20	0.29	0.09
Emotional abuse before age 16	0.41	-	0.23	0.25	0.05
Sexual abuse and emotional abuse before age 16	-	-	0.31	0.36	0.09
Trauma Symptom Check-List (TSC):					
Total score	0.33	0.18	0.24	0.20	0.12
Post-traumatic stress	0.37	0.26	0.25	0.21	0.07
Sleep disorder	0.30	0.18	0.21	0.18	0.01
Depression	0.35	0.29	0.24	0.17	0.19
Anxiety	0.33	0.19	0.25	0.22	0.08
Dissociation	0.24	0.19	0.17	0.11	0.05

151

Table 7.5 (Continued)

| | Own sexual abuse < 16 | Own emotional abuse < 16 | Sexual activity & interests: | | |
			Sex with children < 13 subscale	Sex with males 13 - 15 subscale	Sex with females 13 - 15 subscale
Dissociative Experiences Scale (Bernstein & Putnam)	0.29	0.20	0.20	0.16	0.08
Middlesex Hospital Questionnaire:					
Total score	0.21	0.18	0.17	0.15	0.02
Depression	0.27	0.21	0.23	0.19	0.12
Somatic anxiety	0.26	0.20	0.20	0.16	0.03
Free-floating anxiety	0.29	0.25	0.23	0.25	0.02
Obsessionality	0.12	0.07	0.06	0.09	0.01
Suicidal ideas & behaviour scale	0.37	0.20	0.25	0.20	0.09

Note: Correlations of 0.1 and above are significant at the one per cent level or beyond.

Table 7.6
Multiple regression analysis of score on measure of sexual interests and activities involving males aged 13-15, and children of both sexes aged less than 12, of 750 males aged 18-27

Variable	Dependent variable: sexual interests/ activities involving minors	
	Correlation before multiple regression	Correlation after multiple regression (partial correlation)
Respondent's age	0.13	0.13
Stress in previous 6 months	0.15	0.17
Trauma Symptom Check List	0.23	0.22
Suicidal ideas & behaviour	0.23	0.18
CESD Depression scale	0.20	0.14
Dissociative Experiences Scale	0.19	0.12
Psychoneurosis (Middlesex Hospital Questionnaire)	0.15	0.02
Amount of social stress in previous 6 months	0.15	0.11
Emotional abuse before age 16	0.23	0.07
Duration of any sexual abuse before age 16	0.25	0.14
Severity of sexual abuse	0.30	0.03
Victim "too attached to abuser" to report	0.19	0.11
Multiple correlation	-	0.45

Note: Correlations of 0.1 and above are significant at the five per cent level or beyond. Variables entered into the regression analyses in the order above. Calculations by SPSS (Nie et al., 1976).

153

Table 7.7
Multiple regression analysis of variables predicting suicidal ideas and behaviour in lifetime of 750 males aged 18 to 27

Variable	Dependent Variable: Suicidal Ideas/Behaviour	
	Correlation before multiple regression	Correlation after multiple regression (partial correlation)
Respondent's age	0.15	0.15
Stress in previous 6 months	0.23	0.17
Parental absence (>3 yrs before age 16)	0.19	0.22
Currently: blue collar worker/unemployed	0.15	0.08
Mother: years of education	0.15	0.01
Emotional abuse	0.20	0.17
Duration of any sexual abuse (0=none; 1=single event; 2 to n weeks of abuse duration)	0.24	0.18
Severity of sexual abuse (0=none; 1=touching; 3=oral sex; 4=anal penetration)	0.29	0.18
Abuser was 'trusted' adult: 0=no; 1=yes	0.22	0.09
Victim 'too attached to abuser' to report	0.18	0.12
Victim didn't report abuse because of threats	0.15	0.07
Victim didn't report abuse because 'It didn't bother me'	-0.15	-0.21
Multiple correlation	-	0.46

Note: Correlations of 0.1 and above are significant at the five per cent level or beyond. Variables entered into the regression analyses in the order above. Calculations by SPSS (Nie at al., 1976).

154

Table 7.8
Classification of individuals interested in or having had sexual contact with males under 16, and males and females under 13 by discriminant analysis

Known Groups	N	Predicted Group I	Predicted Group II
A. No sexual interest/contact with minors	707	697 (99%)	10 (1%)
B. Sexual interest/contact with minors	43	15 (35%)	28 (65%)

Note: Variables used in this classification analysis are those which remained statistically significant predictors of sexual interest/activities with minors, following regression analysis (Table 7.7): Trauma Symptom Check List; Suicidal Ideas & Behaviour; Depression Scale; Dissociative Experience Scale; Paternal Absence in Childhood; Recent Social Stress; Emotional Abuse; Duration and Severity of Sexual Abuse; Attachment to Sexual Abuser; Abuse 'Didn't bother me.'
Discriminant analysis by SPSS (Nie et al., 1976).

Table 7.9
Responses given by young adult males interested or very interested in sex with a minor to questions on potential for completing the abuse

	Interest in males < 13	Interest in females < 13	Interest in males 13 to 15	Interest in females 13 to 15
	N = 14	N = 20	N = 24	N = 63
Responding 'Yes' to:				
'I've had no opportunity'	28.6%	45.0%	16.7%	38.1%
'It's just fantasy - I'd never really do it'	42.8%	55.0%	29.2%	55.5%
'Having been a victim of unwanted sex myself, prevents me'	14.3%	0.0%	16.7%	4.8%
'I feel guilty, and this holds me back'	50.0%	55.0%	29.2%	19.0%
'I have someone in mind - I will have sex with them if I can'	21.4%	5.0%	8.3%	15.9%
'I'm afraid of being found out'	78.6%	40.0%	33.3%	19.0%
'I worry about the harm I could do to the kid'	14.3%	40.0%	29.2%	7.9%

156

Table 7.9 (Continued)

	Interest in males < 13	Interest in females < 13	Interest in males 13 to 15	Interest in females 13 to 15
	N = 14	N = 20	N = 24	N = 63
'I only have this problem (or it gets worse) when I drink too much alcohol'	7.1%	10.0%	12.5%	15.9%
'When I get close to a child or adolescent in private, I can hardly control myself	14.3%	10.0%	4.2%	1.6%
'I think of having sex with a child or adolescent every day'	28.6%	15.0%	12.5%	4.8%
'I wish someone could help me with my sexual problems'	85.7%	35.0%	41.7%	6.3%

Note: In addition to the above figures (which concern 71 individuals, since a number of respondents fell into more than 'interest' category) 3 of the 5 individuals who actually had sexual contact with a female under 13 desired such help; 3 of the 4 individuals admitting to sexual contact with a male under 13; 5 of the 14 individuals admitting sexual contact with a male 13 to 15; and 11 of the 43 individuals admitting to sex with a female aged 13 to 15 wanted help with a sexual problems.

8 Sexual and physical child abuse and the development of dissociative personality traits: Canadian and British evidence from adolescent child welfare and child care populations

Abstract

An attempt was made to construct a measure of dissociative personality traits from file review of 61 Canadian adolescents with a known history of sexual abuse before the age of six. The study was then extended to 55 British adolescents in residential care and therapy centres. Between 18 per cent and 29 per cent of adolescents displayed several features of dissociative personality, implying the possibility of multiple personality disorder. Those with two or more indicators of dissociative personality style tended to have more problematic behavioural histories, including a particularly high prevalence of deliberate self-harm. In the UK group the Dissociative Experiences Scale (Bernstein and Putnam, 1986) completed by 55 adolescents correlated 0.67 with the dissociative personality trait index constructed from case file review. Implications for treatment of abused children are discussed.

Introduction

There is growing evidence that suggests a link between severe abuse early in a child's life, and the development in some of these child victims of dissociative and multiple personality states (Putnam, 1989; Ross, 1989; Ross, Norton and Wozney, 1989). While severe and prolonged sexual and physical abuse beginning before the child is six may in an unknown minority of cases, lead to the development of multiple personality disorder, it is also true that a number of the dissociative mental mechanisms associated with multiple personality may occur to a lesser degree as a sequel of severe and

traumatic abuse occurring after the age of six (Kluft, 1985; Chu and Dill, 1989; Ross et al., 1989; Bagley, 1991a; Bagley, Wood and Young, 1994).

Cases of multiple personality are spectacular, alarming to the popular media, and of great interest for clinicians since they illustrate complex processes of mental organization which have challenged conventional thinking about social learning, consciousness, emotional life and the determinants of behaviour (Dunn, 1992). What appears to happen is that a young child who is subjected to intolerable levels of physical abuse, pain, or sadistic sexual intrusion may create an alter ego, another person within the self, who accepts the pain and degradation. The ego is sometimes split into several selves each addressing the pain in different ways including a 'bad' child who suffers the abuse, as well as different selves or egos who are tied in complex ways to different aspects of the abuse, sometimes with different alter egos addressing abuse occurring at different times.

As the child grows and the abuse lessens, ceases or becomes different in nature, the alternative selves who have protected the child from pain still remain in the unconscious so that the child experiences them only in dreams or nightmares, or in waking trance like-states which cannot be remembered or recognized by a master self, or integrative ego.

Despite Freud's denial of his early finding that childhood sexual abuse was responsible for much adult neurosis (Rush, 1980), ego psychology derived from psychodynamic theory is still helpful in understanding the mechanisms of dissociation and multiple personality: there is a splitting of the ego in some victims of early, severe abuse, together with repression, and unconscious terror and guilt which continues into adulthood. These indicators of post-traumatic stress may without treatment last a lifetime. Individuals with chronic dissociative personality styles are probably at elevated risk for the development of major mental illness, and suicidal behaviour (Bagley et al., 1994).

Ross (1985 and 1989) has argued from his clinical experience of treating several hundred cases of multiple personality disorder that MPD is far more common than originally thought: many individuals diagnosed as having borderline personality or psychotic disorder manifest the dissociative experiences which are particularly marked in MPD individuals. Dissociative disorders are manifested on a continuum of increasingly large amounts of ego dissociation:

At one end of the spectrum would be psychogenic amnesia in its most transient forms. At the other extreme would be the most fully developed MPD. Fugue states and depersonalization would occupy intermediate positions depending on their severity, but would never be as severe as MPD or as benign as a brief isolated amnesia . . . Partial forms of MPD would occupy an intermediate point of the spectrum

159

somewhere in the region of fugue states and depersonalization. (Ross, 1985, pp. 935–36)

Ross (1985) suggests that three criteria are essential for identifying a partial MPD or dissociative mental state: the existence within the individual of two or more distinct personalities, each of which is predominant at a particular time; the personality that is dominant at any particular time determines the individual's behaviour; the secondary personality exists in a transient form and does not develop independent social relationships (it may only emerge in psychotherapy). Autobiographies of individuals who have been treated for MPD give valuable insights into the condition — for example, Truddi Chase's *When Rabbit Howls* (1987), and Sylvia Fraser's *My Father's House: A Memoir of Incest and Healing* (1987). An excellent account of the development, course and treatment of multiple personality is given by Watkins and Johnson (1982), a book collaboratively written by a therapist and client.

Putnam (1989) in a review of case material from the United States indicates that 'pathological dissociation' in childhood (often a reflection of serious early abuse and pain) is not uncommon. These dissociative states are marked by (a) amnesias; (b) disturbances in sense of self; (c) trance-like states; (d) rapid shifts in mood and behaviour; (e) perplexing shifts in access to knowledge, memory and skills; (f) auditory and visual hallucinations; and (g) vivid imaginary companionship in children and adolescents. Normal children sometimes display a few of these traits, which disappear with the onset of adolescence. Children who retain these mental mechanisms through adolescence and beyond are particularly likely to have suffered severe, early abuse. The mental mechanisms of dissociation, once protective of the ego, become severely dysfunctional.

There are several underlying processes influencing the development of dissociative or multiple personality traits in a child: dissociation of self from noxious stimuli, a defence mechanism which initially protects the child from trauma; transfer of upsetting experience from self to alter egos; and attack on or attempts to modify the ego by the 'victims' within the multiple personality framework when the cries of pain (or the howls of Truddi Chase's murdered rabbit) become too loud to ignore. Sometimes these imaginary others attack the mind, body and free will of their host (in terms of frequent and unexplained physical pain; as eating disorders; as self-mutilation and deliberate self-harm; as psychotic-like episodes; or as attacks on others while in fugue or trance-like states).

In order to measure the continuum of measurement of dissociative experiences, Bernstein and Putnam (1986) devised a dissociation scale, for which there is some evidence of criterion validity: groups hypothesized to have dissociative experiences have significantly higher scores on the scale

than 'normal' individuals (e.g. Ross and Norton, 1988; Ross et al., 1989; Sandberg and Lynn, 1992). This Dissociation Scale was used in one of the studies of adolescents, reported below. The dissociation sub-scale in Briere's (1989b) Trauma Symptom Check List was also completed by the U.K. subjects.

A new measure, the Dissociative Disorders Interview Schedule appears to have promise. Details of this scale became available only after the research reported below was completed; it is interesting to note however that in a Canadian city (in the same city as our own child welfare sample, reported below) this scale had clear validity (Anderson, Yasenik and Ross, 1993). The study by Anderson and colleagues of young adult women showed that 88 per cent of those with a history of child sexual abuse had a dissociative disorder of some type, while 55 per cent had indications of multiple personality disorder, as well as high rates of depression, borderline personality, substance abuse, somatic symptoms, suicide attempts.

Assumptions and methods

The authors of the present study work in the field of child welfare and child care: we wished to explore the idea (rather than test the hypothesis) that adolescents with a history of severe abuse beginning in early childhood would as adolescents often manifest a number of the classical dissociative signs; and the idea that adolescents displaying a number of these signs would have particularly troublesome adjustment problems. An initial screening of the case records of Canadian adolescents who were known to have been sexually abused, and whose files had been closed (because of age, or transfer to other facilities) indicated that there was evidence on file of sexual abuse occurring before the age of six (a previously identified criterion for the development of dissociative disorder) in about a third of these adolescents (Rodberg, Bagley and Wellings, 1990).

Encouraged by this pilot work, we extended the review of case files until 61 adolescents were identified who had been sexually abused before (and often after) their sixth birthday. It should be stressed that although case file review can identify a mass of interesting reports on the child's experiences and development, these reports are often not systematic in a clinical sense, and are usually responses to the need for processing, treatment and referral within the child welfare system. We were unable to conduct personal interviews with any of the adolescents in the Canadian study, but were able to interview personally the adolescents in residential care and treatment institutions in Britain.

In the British study we were able to compare raters' assessments of the same case material; but in the Canadian study we had no such checks on

161

reliability. In neither the Canadian nor the British studies were raters 'blind' to the hypotheses being tested, so the possibility of bias in producing the research material must be borne in mind. However, since the understanding of dissociative and multiple personality was quite limited amongst psychiatrists and psychologists before 1990, none of the records assessed gave any indication that checking for dissociative personality traits had been undertaken at the time. No therapist or assessing psychiatrist, or psychological report we reviewed had even tentatively suggested the possibility of MPD or dissociative disorders.

In the absence of direct access to the adolescents in question we devised a 'Dissociative Personality Traits' (DPT measure), on which the presence or absence of dissociative personality traits identified in the clinical literature (Putnam, 1989; Ross, 1989) was recorded. A binary scoring method was used: present or probably present versus probably not present, or no salient information. Since the adolescents studied had long histories within child welfare and child care systems and in many cases had several psychological or psychiatric investigations on file, as well as written observations on behaviour by child care workers, we assumed that failure to mention any particular behavioural trait implied that it was not present. Cases which in the raters' opinion did not contain sufficient information (e.g. no clinical assessment was on file) on which to complete the dissociative personality profiles were excluded from analysis.

Thus, we have seemingly complete information on history of child sexual abuse and clinical history, although there is often considerable missing data on other aspects of the case (e.g. data on the background of the abuser). To the extent that the adolescents studied were identified as 'false negatives' (the dissociative personality trait existed, but no-one observed or recorded it) our study is biased against producing statistically significant results.

Using the concepts and measures generated in the Canadian work, a second study was carried out in the United Kingdom in four residential care and treatment centres, in London and the North of England. Records of current adolescent residents were screened, and those with fairly complete records on which to make ratings of current and past behaviours and abuse histories were selected for study. Inter-rater reliability was established in the case file review study in Britain by comparing assessments of three researchers for the same 10 cases. Differences in interpretation were discussed after the first five cases; following standardization of concepts of interpretation, the average overall agreement of the raters for five further cases was 86 per cent. In addition, the three raters randomly assigned themselves to read separate parts of the case file; this strategy might reduce 'halo' effects in rating. The adolescents themselves were personally interviewed, and sometimes were able to corroborate the occurrence of traumatic life events.

The adolescents also completed the Dissociative Experiences Scale (DES) of Bernstein and Putnam (1986) and Briere's (1989b) Trauma Symptom Check List. The case file raters were blind to the personal interviews and assessments.

In this exploratory study, more variables have been compared across different groups than would be the case in a hypothesis-testing study. Comparing a large number of variables across relatively small research populations can lead to a spurious excess of statistically significant results. For this reason, we interpret or discuss only those variables which indicate a difference across various categories which is significant at the one per cent level (i.e. one in 100 probability of chance occurrence).

Results

Table 8.1 indicates that for all of the dissociative traits measured, the British adolescents had lower prevalence than the Canadian adolescents. When the traits are combined, the numbers of individuals in whom a high number of the dissociative personality traits coexist (five or more traits recorded) is 29.5 per cent in the Canadian adolescents, and 18.1 per cent in the British adolescents.

The 10 dissociative personality traits are intercorrelated to a statistically significant extent, yielding a fairly high internal reliability measures (alpha = 0.74 in Canadian adolescents, and 0.62 in the British adolescent sample). The most frequently mentioned traits in both cultures were time lapses or blank memory for recent events; observed bizarre behaviours not recalled by child; persistent dreams and nightmares; trance-like states; and polarized behaviour changes over short periods.

Table 8.1 indicates that 49 per cent of the Canadian adolescents had two or more of the dissociative personality traits present. This cut-off point has also been applied to the British adolescents in order to ensure some comparability between the two samples: 29 per cent of the British group had high DPT scores. These differences are probably due to the fact that proportionately fewer of the British adolescents had on the evidence available, experienced sexual abuse before the age of six. Since we did not have access to the full casework records of the British adolescents we were only able to make judgements about the presence or absence of early sexual abuse in 31 of the 55 cases.

An important validator of the reconstruction of the dissociative personality trait indicators from case files is available for the British adolescents: all of the high DPT group had scores on the Dissociative Experiences Scale which were above the median. The product moment correlation between the two measures is 0.67 (p < .00) providing some evidence of construct validity

163

for the DPT measure. These adolescents also completed Briere's (1989b) Trauma Symptom Check List. The dissociative experiences sub-scale in this instrument correlated 0.58 (p < .01) with the DPT, and 0.76 (p < .00) with the Bernstein and Putnam DES.

The Dissociative Personality Traits (DPT) measure derived from summing indicators of presence or absence of the traits listed in Table 8.1 has been used to indicate high (above the median) and low scorers in the Canadian and British samples (Tables 8.2 and 8.3). Comparison between high and low scoring groups indicates a number of statistically significant differences (p < .01). All of the Canadian adolescents had (by definition) been sexually abused before the age of six; but many had been physically abused and severely neglected as well. The combination of early physical and sexual abuse in the Canadian sample identified 87 per cent of the high scorers on the DPT measure.

In the British adolescents high scorers on the DPT measure (identified by the median test — Siegel and Castellan, 1988) experienced more sexual abuse than low scorers occurring after their sixth birthday. In both national groups, high DPT profiles were associated with more prolonged and frequent sexual abuse either both before and/or after the age of six; more within-family abuse (including abuse by groups of family members); more sexual abuse by different people on separate occasions; in the Canadian group, more sexual abuse of siblings as well as the victim; and more abuse by an individual who had themselves been abused as a child. The high dissociative traits group had in one or both of the Canadian and British populations, more physical symptoms; more self-mutilation and deliberate self-harm; more violent assault on others; and more drug and alcohol abuse.

The high dissociative traits group in Canada were also more likely to have run from home; to be referred for psychiatric assessment and treatment; and to be treated or cared for in a residential setting.

Both high DPT groups (in Canada and Britain) had more suicidal behaviour, and drug and alcohol abuse than the contrast groups. However, the British DPT group were not distinguished by an excess of conduct disorder, delinquency or assaults on others. The British adolescents were somewhat more likely than the Canadian group to be described as extremely withdrawn, 'living in a world of fantasy.' Six of the British adolescents had been diagnosed as psychotic (including one male with complex seizures and fugue states said to arise from temporal lobe epilepsy).

Discussion and conclusions

The limitations of this study should be stressed. First of all, it is an exploratory rather than a hypothesis-testing study, and has been undertaken

in a new area of child abuse research in which methodologies and instruments are not well developed. This was not a carefully designed cross-cultural study, but one based on opportunist access to samples of adolescents in the two cultures. No 'normal' comparison groups were available at the time of the study, and none of the raters was blind to the ideas being explored. Case files are not the best source of data, and even the most comprehensive record contains irritating gaps. Our assumption that failure to mention what are assumed to be salient behaviour traits implies that these have likely not occurred, could involve a conservative bias against finding significant differences.

While some statistical comparison between the Canadian and British groups has been made, it should stress that we examined case files kept by different kinds of professionals, often for different purposes. Standards of clinical judgment and assessment may also differ between the two cultures, in unknown ways. One of the difficulties of research on the validity and antecedents of dissociative behaviour traits is that the actual mechanisms of dissociation mean that events of traumatic abuse are often precluded from conscious memory. The interviews with British adolescents bore this out: about half of the events of early abuse recorded in case files could not be recalled by the adolescents themselves.

It is possible that the link between dissociative personality traits and problematic behaviours has an element of tautology: the most disturbed individuals were those receiving the fullest and most frequent psychological investigation and reports. Since these reports were the source of information on both the dissociative traits and the existence of disturbed behaviour, the statistical association between the two may be artifactual. This source of bias, if it exists, is not fatal for our research, but does imply that disturbed behaviours and dissociative personality traits are often intimately linked in many individuals with a prior history of abuse.

Another clinical problem concerns the differential diagnosis of dissociative personality disorder: there is considerable discussion amongst clinicians on whether borderline psychosis, schizophrenia, various psychosomatic conditions, and complex partial epileptic seizures are diagnostically separable from dissociative states and multiple personality disorder (Ross, 1985, 1989; Ross and Norton, 1988; Ross et al., 1989; Ross, Heber, Norton and Anderson, 1989b; Richards and Persinger, 1991). Six of the British adolescents had a diagnosis of psychosis (including two with schizophrenia, and one with temporal lobe epilepsy). We suspect from reading the case material on these individuals that they were wrongly diagnosed, but have no definite proof of this.

Assuming our findings have validity, they have implications for the assessment and treatment of young people in child welfare caseloads, and in residential treatment. Conventional behavioural therapy and

psychological therapies are unlikely to be successful when the presenting problems involve reactions to repressed trauma which become manifest only in fugue or trance states, or in disturbing dreams.

With these limitations in mind, we conclude that this review of case files for adolescents in child welfare caseloads and child care facilities has indicated that between 18 and 29 per cent had marked indicators of dissociative personality style, indicating the possibility of the existence of multiple personalities within the psyche. The evidence from both the Canadian and British samples indicates that sexual and physical abuse occurring early in life (both before and after the age of six) may be an important antecedent of the development of dissociative personality traits.

We are unable to provide reliable figures on prevalence of dissociative disorder in child welfare and child care populations. What we can conclude however, is that there is sufficient likelihood of underlying multiple personality or dissociative personality traits in adolescents in social work and child care systems to justify further study of these populations, using a more formal methodology within the framework of clinical epidemiology, including the use of personal interviews with both clinical and control groups.

The MPD phenomenon is likely to occur in severely abused children in all countries, even though local factors may influence the actual form that separate personalities take (Aldridge-Morris, 1990). Cultural factors too may influence how multiple and dissociative personalities are assessed or tolerated by the community (e.g. Adityanjee, Raju and Khandelwal, 1989's study of MPD in India). Our current work in Hong Kong confirms earlier findings (Yap, 1960): multiple personality does exist in oriental populations, but may be presented somewhat differently than in the west. Putnam (1989) also points to case evidence suggesting that many Cambodian children who experienced prolonged imprisonment, torture and genocidal threats during that country's civil war have manifested dissociative personality traits.

There is a growing literature on the treatment of dissociative and multiple personality phenomena (Putnam, 1989; Ross, 1989; Dunn, 1992). One therapy used with dissociative individuals is hypnotherapy (Bliss, 1986). Susceptibility to hypnotic suggestion (which varies considerably between individuals) is probably a necessary but not sufficient cause of the development of dissociative personality traits. Hypnotherapy is often used in beginning treatment with dissociative or MPD individuals (Ross, 1989; Frankel, 1990). Simple revelation to the conscious mind of the existence of multiple voices addressing, guiding or criticizing the actor is the first step in therapeutic resolution: but much careful, supportive psychotherapy must continue for several months or years after this revelation (Putnam, 1989; Bagley and King, 1990). One issue that remains controversial is how an alternate self which has aggressively defended the core personality can be

adapted so that this element of protective psychological functioning can be retained (e.g. Ross, 1984).

Finally, we cannot tell from our Canadian and British case material if or how many of the adolescents actually had multiple personality syndrome; nevertheless, there is a good case for screening all very disturbed adolescents for both dissociative personality traits, and evidence of early physical and sexual abuse. Further research should be based on standardized protocol and assessment criteria for disturbed children and adolescents seen by child welfare systems.

Table 8.1
Possible indicators of dissociative personality traits in 61 Canadian adolescents in a child welfare caseload; and in 55 British adolescents in residential care

	Clearly present in:	
	Canadian adolescents N = 61	British adolescents N = 55
1. Reports of time lapses, distorted memory of recent events, blank memory for recent past	29.5%	18.2%
2. Complains of hearing voices of people who are not there	13.1%	9.1%
3. Reports of marked changes of behaviour, during which child calls self by a different name/refers to self in third person	19.7%	9.1%
4. Episodes of disturbed or bizarre behaviours observed by others, but not recalled by child	26.2%	14.5%
5. Has talked of being possessed by sprits or having body taken over by someone else	21.3%	10.9%
6. Child has reported that he/she looks in mirror, sees someone else	3.3%	3.6%
7. Reliable observer indicates that child's voice changes radically at times of behavioural change	19.7%	9.1%

Table 8.1 (Continued)

	Clearly present in:	
	Canadian adolescents N = 61	British adolescents N = 55
8. Child reports disturbed dreams or nightmares which are persistent, recurring and contain common themes	39.3%	33.3%
9. Reports of child going into trance-like states, switching off and staring into space for long periods	29.5%	5.4%
10. Polarized behaviour changes within one day (puritanical-promiscuous; passive-aggressive; very happy-very sad; radical changes of dress style)	47.5%	40.0%
Total number of above traits	Percent in Canada	Percent in U.K
Two or more of (1) to (10) clearly present	49.2%	29.1%
Three or more clearly present	37.7%	25.4%
Four or more clearly present	23.0%	18.2%
Five or more clearly present	16.4%	14.5%
Six or more clearly present	9.8%	3.6%
Alpha coefficient of internal reliability for DPT measure	0.74	0.62

Table 8.2

Demographic, clinical and child welfare processing variables differentiating Canadian and British adolescents with high and low scores on Dissociative Personality Traits (DPT) measure

Variable		DPT Measure		Phi	P
		Low Score CDN: N=31 UK: N=39 (or less)	High Score N=30 N=16 (or less)		
Adolescent Profiles and Abuse History					
Female	CDN: 44/61	21 (67.7%)	23 (76.7%)	0.01	0.40
	UK: 33/55	21 (53.8%)	12 (75.0%)	0.15	0.30
Age 15+ when interviewed/	CDN: 30/61	14 (45.2%)	16 (53.3%)	0.08	0.30
case reviewed	UK: 22/55	16 (41.1%)	6 (37.5%)	0.03	0.50
Physical abuse when aged	CDN: 41/61	15 (48.4%)	26 (87.7%)	0.40	0.01
< age 6	UK: 10/31	2 (10.0%)	8 (72.7%)	0.57	0.01
Sexual abuse when aged	CDN: 61/61	31 (100.0%)	30(100.0%)	-	-
< age 6	UK: 7/31	2 (10.0%)	5 (45.4%)	0.31	0.10

Table 8.2 (Continued)

Variable		DPT Measure		Phi	P
		Low Score CDN: N=31 UK: N=39 (or less)	High Score N=30 N=16 (or less)		
Physical and sexual abuse < age 6	CDN: 33/61 UK: 5/31	7 (22.6%) 0	26 (86.7%) 5 (45.4%)	0.64 0.50	0.00 0.00
Extreme physical neglect < age 6	CDN: 24/50 UK: 7/31	7 (26.9%) 4 (20.0%)	17 (70.8%) 3 (27.7%)	0.40 0.10	0.01 0.60
Sexual abuse at age 6 or older	CDN: 30/59 UK: 25/55	12 (40.0%) 9 (23.7%)	18 (62.1%) 16 (94.1%)	0.22 0.62	0.10 0.00
Sexual abuse duration > 2 years	CDN: 25/60 UK: 16/55	8 (26.7%) 4 (10.2%)	17 (56.7%) 12 (75.0%)	0.35 0.56	0.01 0.00
Sexual abuse frequency 10 + times	CDN: 44/61 UK: 19/55	17 (54.8%) 4 (10.2%)	27 (90.0%) 15 (93.7%)	0.35 0.75	0.00 0.00
Sexual abuse: vaginal and/or anal penetration	CDN: 25/56 UK: 14/55	9 (36.0%) 4 (10.2%)	16 (57.7%) 10 (62.5%)	0.28 0.50	0.05 0.00

171

Table 8.2 (Continued)

Variable		DPT Measure		Phi	P
		Low Score CDN: N=31 UK: N=39 (or less)	High Score N=30 N=16 (or less)		
Sexual Abuse Perpetrator					
1st sexual abuse perpetrator: father/father figure	CDN: 29/59	7 (23.3%)	22 (75.9%)	0.46	0.00
	UK: 13/55	5 (16.6%)	8 (50.0%)	0.38	0.01
Father joined by other family members in sexual abuse	CDN: 9/59	2 (6.7%)	7 (24.1%)	0.22	0.10
	UK: 2/55	0	2 (12.5%)	-	-
Sexual abuse by 2 + people, separately	CDN: 30/55	6 (21.4%)	24 (88.9%)	0.64	0.00
	UK: 7/55	2 (5.1%)	5 (31.2%)	0.30	0.05
Other sexual abuse victims in family	CDN: 22/48	9 (37.5%)	13 (54.2%)	0.17	0.20
	UK: -	-	-	-	-
1st sexual abuse perpetrator aged < 18	CDN: 9/57	5 (17.2%)	4 (14.3%)	0.00	0.99
	UK: 5/55	3 (7.7%)	2 (12.5%)	0.01	0.90

Table 8.2 (Continued)

Variable		DPT Measure			
		Low Score CDN: N=31 UK: N=39 (or less)	High Score N=30 N=16 (or less)	Phi	P
History of drug use/alcoholism by abuser	CDN: 16/24 UK: -	3 (13.6%) -	13 (59.1%) -	0.46 -	0.03 -
Abuser: sexual/physical abuse in childhood	CDN: 13/20 UK: -	2 (22.2%) -	11(100.0%) -	0.60 -	0.01 -
Abuser: female	CDN: 4/61 UK: 0	1 (3.2%) -	3 (10.0%) -	0.07 -	0.60 -
Mother: alcohol abuse and/or mental illness	CDN: 20/37 UK: -	6 (35.3%) -	14 (73.7%) -	0.37 -	0.05 -

173

Table 8.2 (Continued)

Variable		DPT Measure		Phi	P
		Low Score CDN: N=31 UK: N=39 (or less)	High Score N=30 N=16 (or less)		

Referral and Processing by Child Welfare and Child Care System

Presenting/referral problem:

Variable		Low Score	High Score	Phi	P
Sexual abuse	CDN: 22/59	13 (43.3%)	9 (31.0%)	0.15	0.20
	UK: 12/55	7 (17.9%)	5 (31.2%)	0.15	0.30
Physical abuse or neglect	CDN: 14/59	7 (23.3%)	7 (24.0%)	0.00	0.99
	UK: 11/55	7 (17.9%)	4 (25.0%)	0.03	0.80
Behaviour problems	CDN: 14/59	3 (10.0%)	11 (28.9%)	0.31	0.05
	UK: 40/55	28 (71.8%)	12 (75.0%)	0.03	0.80
Sexual abuse investigated by police	CDN: 33/60	27 (90.0%)	6 (20.0%)	0.68	0.00
	UK: -	-	-	-	-

Table 8.2 (Continued)

Variable		DPT Measure			
		Low Score CDN: N=31 UK: N=39 (or less)	High Score N=30 N=16 (or less)	Phi	P
Child removed from/ran from home	CDN: 44/61	14 (45.2%)	30(100.0%)	0.56	0.00
	UK: 55/55	-	-	-	-
Child referred for psychiatric assessment/treatment	CDN: 44/61	17 (54.8%)	27 (87.1%)	0.35	0.01
	UK: 55/55	-	-	-	-
Child treated in residential setting	CDN: 25/61	6 (19.3%)	19 (63.3%)	0.45	0.00
	UK: 55/55	-	-	-	-
Child in 5 or more separate child care placements	CDN: 14/59	3 (10.0%)	11 (37.9%)	0.28	0.05
	UK: 4/55	0	4 (25.0%)	-	-

Note: CDN = Canadian. UK = British.

Percentages calculated vertically.

Phi is a measure of relationship for data in a 2 x 2 table, and has a range of values from 0 to 1, calculated by the formula: square root of (Chi-squared divided by N). In calculating Chi-squared, Yates' correction was applied where numbers in any cell were less than five (Siegel and Castellan, 1988).

P indicates probability of chance occurrence.

175

Table 8.3

Behavioural problems in adolescence compared by high and low scores on Dissociative Personality Traits Measure

Variable		DPT Measure			Phi	P
		Low Score CDN: N=31 UK: N=39 (or less)		High Score CDN: N=30 N=16 (or less)		
Erratic learning style	CDN: 30/57	11	(37.9%)	19 (67.9%)	0.30	0.05
	UK: 19/55	13	(33.3%)	6 (37.5%)	0.04	0.80
Frequent/severe headaches	CDN: 19/61	8	(25.8%)	11 (36.7%)	0.12	0.30
	UK: 12/55	7	(17.9%)	5 (31.2%)	0.15	0.30
Abdominal/gynaecological pain	CDN: 19/61	5	(16.1%)	14 (46.7%)	0.33	0.02
	UK: 21/55	9	(23.1%)	12 (75.0%)	0.44	0.01
Anorexia/bulimia/obesity	CDN: 11/61	3	(9.7%)	8 (27.7%)	0.18	0.20
	UK: 7/55	4	10.3%	3 (18.7%)	0.06	0.70
Self-mutilation/suicidal gesture/attempt	CDN: 16/61	5	(16.1%)	11 (35.5%)	0.26	0.05
	UK: 28/55	13	(33.3%)	15 (94.0%)	0.51	0.00

Table 8.3 (Continued)

Variable		DPT Measure		Phi	P
		Low Score CDN: N=31 UK: N=39 (or less)	High Score N=30 N=16 (or less)		
Severe conduct disorder/very aggressive	CDN: 23/61	7 (22.6%)	16 (52.6%)	0.32	0.02
	UK: 27/55	19 (48.7%)	8 (50.0%)	0.01	0.90
Convicted of robbery/theft/assault/other	CDN: 34/61	11 (35.5%)	23 (76.7%)	0.42	0.01
	UK: 20/55	14 (39.5%)	7 (43.7%)	0.07	0.60
Physical/sexual assaults on younger children	CDN: 32/61	12 (38.7%)	20 (66.7%)	0.28	0.03
	UK: 19/55	12 (30.7%)	16 (43.7%)	0.12	0.40
Drug/solvent/alcohol abuse	CDN: 17/61	6 (19.3%)	11 (36.7%)	0.19	0.20
	UK: 20/55	9 (23.1%)	11 (68.7%)	0.43	0.01
Lives in fantasy world	CDN: 13/61	3 (9.7%)	10 (33.3%)	0.50	0.01
	UK: 17/55	5 (12.8%)	12 (75.0%)	0.57	0.00
Psychotic or borderline states	CDN: 0	-	-	-	-
	UK: 6/55	1 (2.6%)	5 (31.2%)	0.35	0.01

Table 8.3 (Continued)

Variable		DPT Measure		Phi	P
		Low Score CDN: N=31 UK: N=39 (or less)	High Score N=30 N=16 (or less)		
Bernstein & Putnam's Dissociative Experiences Scale (above median)	UK: 27/55	11 (28.2%)	16(100.0%)	0.60	0.00

Note: CDN = Canadian. UK = British.
Percentages calculated vertically.
Phi is a measure of relationship for data in a 2 x 2 table, and has a range of values from 0 to 1, calculated by the formula: square root of (Chi-squared divided by N). In calculating Chi-squared, Yates' correction was applied where numbers in any cell were less than five (Siegel and Castellan, 1988).
P indicates probability of chance occurrence.

9 Early sexual experience and sexual victimization of children and adolescents: Review and summary

The world experienced (otherwise called the 'field of consciousness') comes at all times with our body as its center of vision, center of action, center of interest. Where the body is, is 'here'; when the body acts is 'now'; what the body touches is 'this'; all other things are 'there' and 'then' and 'that'. These words of emphasized position imply a systematization of things with reference to a focus of action and interest which lies in the body . . . The body is the storm center, the origin of coordinates, the constant place of stress in all that experience-train. Everything circles round it, and is felt from its point of view. The word 'I', then, is primarily a noun of position, just like 'this' and 'here.' (James, 1890, pp. 154-155)

It is the thesis of this chapter that prolonged and intrusive sexual abuse imposed on the physically immature body and developmentally immature psyche of a child frequently creates an adolescent who cannot find adequate solutions to the dilemmas of identity development defined by Erikson (1980); as a result, the adolescent is extremely vulnerable to stress, and may develop in extreme form a number of the psychological disorders (for example, suicidal ideas and behaviour, depression, eating disorders, alienation from school and peers, sexual problems, acting out behaviours, and substance abuse) which have an increasing prevalence amongst adolescents (Olmstead, O'Malley and Bentler, 1991, Garrison, McKeown, Valois and Vincent, 1993).

The body of the sexually abused child has been violated, and his or her integrity stolen. The victims of prolonged sexual abuse often have profound problems in finding an integrated sense of self in which bodily consciousness, feelings and emotions are integrated. Instead, the body is feared, loathed and punished in a variety of ways: through eating disorders,

179

sexual problems, self mutilation and suicidal behaviour, somatic symptoms, somatic and free-floating anxiety, impaired self-esteem, and profound, long term depression which have all been identified as common, long term sequels of long term, within-family sexual abuse (Bagley and King, 1990).

Defining child sexual abuse: Distinctions between childhood sexuality, sexual victimization, and incestuous abuse

The decade of the 1970s was a period of revelation and rethinking for professionals working with children and adolescents: our assumptions that sexual abuse of children was rare and perhaps even harmless (Bagley, 1969) were subjected to radical criticism. First of all, feminist writers began to publish authentic and persuasive accounts of the harm wrought by adult sexual abuse and exploitation of girls and adolescent women (e.g. Armstrong, 1978; Brady, 1979; Allen, 1980). These pioneering writers were joined by feminist-oriented scholars who began to map the nature of child sexual abuse, its prevalence, and the short and long term consequences (Meiselman, 1978; Finkelhor, 1979; Renovoize, 1982). In 1980 the historian, Florence Rush, published a landmark book which described how all societies (and all major religions) had since the beginning of recorded history sexually exploited and abused children. Rush made the important point that the taboo on incest was not violated by the sexual abuse of daughters; rather, the property rights which fathers held over children allowed them to sexually exploit children before puberty (see too Vander May, 1992). When the child reached sexual maturity, her father exercised a different kind of control over sexual access in approving a particular son-in-law. Children could be 'given away' in marriage very early: in traditional Catholic canon law a female child can be given in marriage as young as 12 (for example in the Province of Quebec, Canada five 12-year-old females were married in 1980. All were pregnant).

Some researchers refer to all sexual abuse of children occurring within a nuclear family setting as 'incest.' Such an over inclusive definition is often unhelpful, however. Firstly, the crime of incest is defined in most criminal codes and relates to completed, heterosexual intercourse. Such individuals might in the case of adults, freely consent to such arrangements (for example, in the case of adult siblings separated at birth by adoption, and meeting for the first time as adults). The sexual exploitation of children by adult males within the family only atypically meets criminal code definitions — the sexual assault may be male on male, of a non-biological (adopted) child, or stop short of actual intercourse.

A second reason for keeping the definition of 'incest' separate from non-consummated sexual abuse by a close relative is that there are still powerful

normative controls inhibiting behaviour which is likely to render an individual pregnant by her father or brother (Fox, 1980). These controls need to be understood by anthropologists and policy makers in framing laws and policies for regulating and deterring sexual assaults within families. The earlier literature on the incest taboo, reviewed and summarized by Bagley (1969) shows that there are powerful normative arguments against the practice of incest, since it undermines patterns of care and socialization of vulnerable individuals, and indeed undermines the whole basis of the nuclear family system, which depends on new marital partners being recruited from other, unrelated families. The paradox of motives implied by 'incestuous abuse' which is not 'incest' may be solved by regarding the sexual misuse and humiliation of children as a form of socialization in which females learn to accept, without complaint, the role of lifelong subordination and service for men. If this supposition is true, then the sexual exploitation of male children by adult males is phenomenologically different from the sexual abuse of female children.

There are also some biological grounds for sanctions against incest (Bixler, 1992). Nevertheless, it is also true that the cultural values pertaining to incest have been framed by male lawmakers, in sexist terms (Adams, Trachtenberg and Fisher, 1992). It is not particularly helpful in framing programs of prevention and treatment to refer to all within-family sexual assaults as 'incest' (as for example Russell, 1986 does). I prefer the term 'incestuous assault' to cover sexual assaults on minors by other family members which stop short of actual intercourse, or which involve biologically unrelated individuals such as step-fathers.

Surveys of adult women such as those of Russell (1986), Wyatt, Guthrie and Notgrass (1992) and Bagley and Ramsay (1986) have all indicated a greatly elevated risk (about seven-fold) of incestuous abuse when the father figure in the household is not the child's biological father. This is an important finding, since it implies that there are normative and perhaps biological factors which often deter or prevent men from sexually abusing their daughters. Epidemiological studies using adult recall of childhood events as the data source indicate that sexual assault by fathers on their biological daughters is relatively rare, and occurs in less than one per cent of all families. The changing role of the father in North American society implies that he is moving towards a role defined more by nurturance and mutual bonding, and away from a role defined by the values of traditional patriarchy (Chesnais, 1981). A study by Parker and Parker (1986) provides an insight into these changing values. This study compared men found guilty of sexual assaulting their biological daughters with non-assaultive controls who also had daughters of the same age. The men who incestuously abused their child were significantly more likely than controls to have been separated from their child for most of her first five years of

181

life, for various reasons including job-related absences. Fathers who were present in these crucial development years were likely to share in the intimate care of their child, including feeding, bathing, dressing etc. Such interactions proved to be a powerful inhibitor of any sexual interest in their child, perhaps because such close and tender interaction provides some hormonal or biological inhibition against sexual interest. It's also true than men prepared to enter into nurturing roles are much less likely to express sexual dominance and exploitation of their daughters.

Another important debate on defining child sexual abuse stems from the pioneering work of David Finkelhor (1979). Finkelhor was the first scholar to use the technique of adult recall in estimating the prevalence of child sexual abuse. His important research has however led to some methodological confusion in deciding what sexual relationships are actually abusive. Finkelhor's questionnaire was completed by a large sample of college students, and asked about all kinds of sexual relationship in which the child had engaged, from earliest memory until late 'teens. This research and its replications (e.g. Sorrenti-Little, Bagley and Robertson, 1984; Kilpatrick, 1992) generates a huge amount of data, since around 60 per cent of children and adolescents will have had some kind of sexual contact with a peer, older child, or an adult.

Finkelhor defines sexual abuse broadly, to include exhibitionism and verbal threats and overtures as well as a range of physical contacts. Sexual abuse occurs, in Finkelhor's definition when either force or threat is used in the sexual contact, or there was a significant age difference (the other party being an adult, or five years older than a child, or 10 years older than an adolescent). This definition is complex, difficult to apply in practice, and is an imperfect instrument in detecting need for intervention, without additional psychological test data (Sorrenti-Little et al., 1984).

The problem with Finkelhor's definition of sexual abuse is that it fails to address the manner in which children and adolescents themselves react to and interpret sexual activities. Finkelhor argues that sexual activities involving a child and an older person are morally wrong because the child cannot give informed consent to such a relationship. There are two problems with this argument: young people are judged to be legally or psychologically competent in several different areas in giving informed consent (e.g. in choosing to have a termination of pregnancy or other surgery, even when parents object; and in choosing to live with one parent rather than another following parental separation). Children of twelve and above are also deemed competent in many jurisdictions to stand trial for a criminal offence. Adolescents frequently engage in sexual relations with close-in-age peers. In Canada for instance recent legislation on sexual exploitation declares that a 12-year-old may freely consent to a sexual relationship with a 14-year-old (Wells, 1990).

We have argued (Bagley and King, 1990) that sexual intercourse involving an older person is wrong not because of problems of giving informed consent, but because the child is immature in both a physical and psychological sense; this immaturity means that the sexual relationship may do great harm to the child's developing psychosexual identity. At least a quarter of children (i.e. those under 17) who engage in a long term sexual relationship with someone of any age who imposes the relationship by force or threat will suffer long term psychological harm as a result (Bagley and King, 1990; Bagley, 1991a; Bagley et al., 1994). In some 10 per cent of cases the harm will be profound and result in long-lasting psychiatric disability. Since it is difficult to know at the outset who will be harmed and who will not, any sexual relationship imposed by an older upon a younger person is ipso facto wrong. Employing this idea of psychological harm, we showed using Finkelhor's questionnaire that those sexual relationships which were achieved through the use of coercion, threat or manipulation (typically, by a person in authority over the child) were indeed strongly correlated with long term negative mental health profiles (Sorrenti-Little et al., 1984).

We also found (like other researchers) that many sexual relationships which the child entered into voluntarily with an older person who had no authoritarian control over the child, had benign psychological outcomes. Indeed, as Kilpatrick (1992) has shown in her American work, age differences between the child and the other participant in the sexual relationship are not by themselves statistically significant predictors of long term psychosexual impairment. However, no researcher has established with any certainty how to predict long term outcomes for any particular child (Kilpatrick, 1992). For these reasons alone, we argue that any sexual relationship between an adult and a child is unwise, and should be deterred by legal sanctions.

In seeking to define child sexual abuse and to identify psychological sequels of such events we have developed a different definition than that used by Finkelhor (1979). In our usage, child sexual abuse occurs when the child (i.e. someone under the age of 17) experiences an unwanted sexual contact with another person, of any age (Bagley, 1989b and 1991e). Sexual contact is defined as any unwanted physical contact by the other person upon the child's breast, genital or anal areas; and/or any unwanted contact by the child with the sexual parts of the other persons body. All contacts in this conservative definition, are made on the unclothed sexual areas (including contact under clothing) of the body of the child, and/or the assailant. These definitions have the advantage of adding a phenomenological element to the measurement of child sexual abuse, and a humanist dimension in that we are fundamentally concerned with how the victim (rather than any other person) perceives and interprets the sexual activity. Another advantage of questions enquiring about 'unwanted' sexual activities is that they are much simpler

to ask than those in other measures (e.g. Finkelhor, 1979), and can easily be adapted for use by clinical and lay workers screening for prior abuse in various child populations (Bagley, 1992b).

The conservative estimate of sexual abuse which results from asking only about unwanted, physical-contact sexual activity also implies a greater efficiency in identifying individuals who have been psychologically traumatized by the abuse.

Issues in prevalence of child sexual abuse: Long term versus single-event abuse

Recent epidemiological studies of community samples of young adults (1,500 men and women aged 18 to 27) have shown the importance of the distinction between single-event and multiple-event sexual abuse in childhood (Bagley, 1991a; Bagley et al., 1994). While the amount of single-event sexual abuse before age 17 in these samples was higher in women (32 per cent in females versus 15.6 per cent in males) the amount of multiple-event abuse (i.e. continuing for more than a day, and sometimes for several years) was similar (6.8 per cent in females, and 6.9 per cent in males).

While a single event of traumatic sexual abuse (e.g. a brutal rape) can create profound problems for long term adjustment, evidence indicates that the large majority of never-repeated unwanted sexual acts imposed on children (both male and female) cause less long term psychological harm which continues into adulthood (Bagley and King, 1990). Consider the following case:

> A, a 10-year-girl was assaulted by a 15-year-old cousin, who tried to insert fingers into her vagina, and ordered her to fellate him. A escaped, running immediately to her mother to tell her of the incident. A was a normal child before the assault, had good relationships with her parents, and had good self-esteem. A's parents acted immediately to prevent any repetition of the abuse, and comforted their child. A's parents sought psychological assessment for their daughter, which rapidly established that she remained psychologically normal, without need for prolonged therapy. At follow-up five years later A's emotional and cognitive profiles were essentially normal. A had good ego strength prior to the assault; her excellent self-esteem, based on a warm and trusting relationship with both parents had enabled her to seek help immediately. This same ego-strength, reinforced by the calm and sympathetic reaction of her significant others, enabled her to

184

overcome any trauma created by the incident. (Case from series reported by Bagley and Ramsay, 1986)

Contrast A's situation with that of B, sexually assaulted for the first time by her step-father when she was 10.

B's biological father left the family when she was five, and mother remarried when B was eight. According to school reports, B lacked confidence in social relationships. Her stepfather manipulated his authority, forcing B to keep silent about the abuse. He told her that she was wicked and dirty, and no-one would believe her if she told others about the assault. By the age of 12 B had to endure vaginal and anal intercourse at least weekly. She ran from home, and by the age of 14 was a juvenile prostitute. She had devastated self-esteem, regular drug use, and a recent history of suicide attempts. (Case from series reported by Bagley and Young, 1987)

The crucial difference between these two cases at the onset of the abuse was the contrast between them in terms of ego-strength, warm and trusting relationships with mother, and self-esteem prior to the abuse. B had poor self-esteem at the onset of the abuse, and this impaired her ability to seek help from others, or to resist the threats of her step-father. Feelings of guilt, loneliness and terror were imposed on an already vulnerable child who was then deeply traumatized by the continued assaults.

This case illustrates the probability which several researchers have identified, that long term sexual abuse of female children is most likely to occur in disrupted or dysfunctional families, and will often involve victims whose mental health has been impaired by psychological abuse and neglect, and often times physical abuse or harsh punishment as well. Studies which identify a range of types of child abuse point to the fact that the combination of physical abuse, sexual abuse and emotional abuse or neglect is particularly likely to be associated with long term impairment of mental health (Bagley and King, 1990).

Clinical identification of victims of child sexual abuse

Adult recall studies have been valuable in giving us some estimates of the prevalence of child sexual abuse (CSA), and the long term damage it may impose on the victim. This knowledge has had a political impact, and the much greater awareness of the problem of CSA has resulted in the development of methods of screening for victims (e.g. by presentations in schools), and the development of specialized teams for the protection, assessment and treatment of victims (Bagley and King, 1990). The adult

recall studies of prevalence have enabled us to show historical trends in abuse rates: these appeared to be steady throughout the century until the early 1950s — e.g. women aged 30 to 39 recalled about the same amount of CSA in their childhoods as did women aged 60 to 69. However, women born after 1950 report much higher rates of CSA (Bagley, 1990b). This was the time when divorce rates began to increase, and when the expression of adult sexuality became less inhibited.

The adult recall studies suggest that many women were put at risk of CSA when their biological fathers separated from the family because of divorce, and new adults males entered the family setting. These adults were not inhibited or deterred by the taboo on incest, and recent epidemiological data suggest that about 10 per cent of step-fathers or cohabitees impose sexual assault on female children in these reconstituted families. The recall studies show too that these victims were rarely able to tell adults about the ongoing abuse. With increasing awareness of the impact of child sexual abuse in the 1970s and 1980s, many victims (both past and current) were identified, and presented child protection and child and adolescent therapy programs with challenges in terms of procedures required, and the professional personnel required to provide support and treatment.

For a while, in the early 1980s 'worst case' scenarios often occurred, with an abused adolescent being removed from home when abuse was revealed: the victim was then placed in an emergency youth shelter, along with runaways and delinquents. No treatment for the CSA was available, and the girl would drift through a series of group and foster homes into the life of the street, and eventually into drug abuse and prostitution (Bagley, 1985b; Bagley and Young, 1987; Bagley, Burrows and Yaworksi, 1990b).

The quality of professional practice in child protection across Europe and North America is uneven, particularly in rural areas. Most major cities in North America and Northern Europe now have integrated protection and treatment programs, with established protocol for schools in recognizing and referring suspected cases of CSA (Thomlison and Bagley, 1992). Aspects of treatment programs are discussed below.

The effects of child sexual abuse: Clinical studies

The child who comes to a treatment agency following child sexual abuse is atypical of the population of abused children. The abuse will have been discovered (sometimes because the child asked for help from a professional — often a teacher); but we know (from adult recall studies) that only a minority of abused children reach even this first stage. The abuse will have been verified by the child protection team, and some decision taken about the child's future. Ideally, when the abuser lives in the child's household

186

that person should leave: but when the alleged abuser is hostile and denies the abuse, legal options are limited. The large majority of men who are convicted of sexual assault upon a child plead guilty (Stephens, Grinnell, Thomlison and Krysik, 1991): paradoxically, it is the hostile, arrogant or psychopathic abuser who is likely to escape prosecution.

Sexual abuse imposed upon a child can have paradoxical effects. The child may at first feel flattered, excited and physically aroused. But combination of sexual excitement simultaneously with shame and guilt often has powerfully negative influences upon psychosexual development, especially if the child is required to deceive her mother about the abuse, and has to collude with father or step-father in this wicked deceit. While Freud's recantation of his thesis that many of his female patients had been sexually abused in childhood, the psychic devastation wrought by child sexual abuse is compatible with Freud's theory of the incest taboo, and the emotional chaos which could result in individuals who violate this taboo (e.g. Stekel, 1926). Psychoanalysts have been fascinated by cases in which fathers imposed a sexual relationship on their daughters and have presented several hundred case reports in the clinical literature (reviewed in Bagley, 1969). The preponderance of this evidence indicates that if the sexual relationship is imposed in adolescence, crucial identity tasks for the child are disrupted, and latent oedipal desires flood consciousness, with a sequel in profound degrees of guilt, anxiety and depression. While there may have been a high degree of selection in such case reports, they do offer a theoretical model of why incestuous abuse (particularly that involving a father and daughter) are so damaging to the child's ego, in comparison with sexual abuse involving individuals who are unrelated. The post-Freudian, psychodynamic view of the psychological damage imposed by incestuous abuse is succinctly outlines by Levine (1990) and Wasserman and Rosenfeld (1992).

Child sexual abuse and the violation of self-systems

In the young child self-esteem is often fragmented, with pride and confidence in one area co-existing with doubts and uncertainty over other achievements or relationships. However, by the age of seven the child's self-esteem (evaluations of self characteristics) and self-concept (understanding of the roles and role performance required in interaction with significant others) begin to crystallize as the child enters the fourth stage of identity building ('industry versus inferiority' in Erikson's schema). The self-concept of the child becomes increasingly global, incorporating both knowledge of the roles to be performed, and evaluations of the quality of action in those roles involving interaction between self and others. In this

symbolic interaction framework the child absorbs (and sometimes rejects) the image of himself or herself created by others. Adolescence is a crucial stage in this process of self-appraisal and self-understanding, when the young person incorporates many more roles into an ego framework, and evaluates role performance in more comprehensive and complex ways. The ideal process is for a 'diffused identity' (Erikson, 1980) to be formed by mid-adolescence. Within this identity structure the individual holds a model of the nature of key roles required (in respect of parents, kin, peers, school and society); how those roles should be performed in terms of mastery and satisfaction (the beginning of what Maslow calls 'self actualization'); and how self-confidence in role performance (i.e. optimizing self-esteem) can be achieved. Important evidence from longitudinal studies indicates that identity and global self-esteem measured in the first years of junior high school can predict many of the problems which occur in later adolescence including scholastic failure and school dropout, deliberate self-harm, use of drugs, alcohol and tobacco, delinquency and runaway behaviour, and teenage pregnancies (Kaplan, 1980).

It follows that if child abuse (physical, emotional and sexual) impairs self-esteem and identity development then the child will be at special risk for the development of various kinds of deviant and problem behaviours in adolescence and adulthood. The evidence, unfortunately, indicates that child abuse (and especially prolonged sexual abuse combined with physical and emotional abuse) is powerfully detrimental to the development of adequate levels of self-esteem and identity development which could have buffered the child against new stressors, or could have prevented a drift into various forms of self-defeating or deviant behaviour.

Diminished self-esteem in CSA victims is a commonly observed short and long term sequel of abuse, especially if that abuse has continued for weeks, months or even years (Bukowski, 1992). The evidence is fairly consistent in suggesting that duration of the abuse (particularly that beginning in latency and extending into adolescence); the degree of physical imposition on the child (usually, penetration of the child's body); and the combination of sexual abuse with attachment and bonding failures, emotional abuse and neglect; and physical abuse — all are associated in combination or interaction, with diminished self-esteem in the child victim (Morrow and Sorell, 1989; Briere and Runtz, 1990; Jackson, Calhoun, Amick, Maddever and Habif, 1990; Bifulco, Brown and Adler, 1991; Hunter, 1991; Mannarino, Cohen, Smith and Moore-Motily, 1991; Alexander, 1992; Kilpatrick, 1992; Kendall-Tackett, Williams and Finkelhor, 1993; Wyatt et al., 1992; Brewin, Andrews and Gotlieb, 1993).

There is also evidence of impaired ego development in CSA survivors (Jennings and Armsworth, 1992), and of dissociation or splitting of self-characteristics (Cole and Putnam, 1992).

However, the thesis that impairment of self-esteem and of ego strength leading to greatly increased problems of identity development in CSA victims, is a core process in the vulnerability of survivors has found less universal support (Kendall-Tackett et al., 1993). Nevertheless, it is the argument of this chapter that prolonged CSA often impairs identity formation to the extent that the victim is vulnerable in many areas of development, including body image (e.g. as manifested in bulimia, anorexia, and induced obesity); presentation of the sexual self (e.g. as an unattractive, asexual person, or as a person who degrades the sexual self through promiscuity); as a person who enters helplessly into degrading relationships; and is vulnerable too as a person who symbolically degrades the self through self-mutilation, deliberate self-harm, and drug and alcohol abuse. The evidence for these propositions is reviewed by Bagley and Young (1990).

Why does incestuous abuse impair self-esteem and identity development to such a profound degree, in many victims of such abuse? There are several complementary explanations. Continued guilt and fear, and disruption of normal role obligations and expectations associated with the assaults mean that the child has many more identity tasks to perform than a normal adolescent, and has a much more complex and fractured self-concept and self-esteem. The abuse takes away from the child the satisfaction at knowing that there is progress, humanity and co-operation in most human relationships. As Gelinas (1983) puts it:

> Former victims show a profound impairment of self-esteem. The family relational imbalances have taught them that they literally have no rights, particularly to needs of their own; nothing is owned by them, inherently or because of their contributions, and they are allowed no claim to needs, reciprocity or even acknowledgment. With such fundamentally impaired self-esteem, incest victims tend to be extremely passive, to the point of paralysis. (p. 322)

Stigmatization, self-blame and chronically impaired self-esteem often occur together in abuse survivors, of both sexes. Chronic post-traumatic stress may also occur, with abundant amounts of free-floating and somatic anxiety, nightmares and sleep terrors, flashbacks of trauma, and dissociation of personality (Briere, 1989b). Young (1992) conceptualizes these common psychological sequels of sexual abuse as 'problems of embodiment,' a kind of self-loathing for the body which betrayed its owner. In identity terms, the adolescent and his or her developing body (which incorporates the sexual vision of the self) are profoundly dissociated. Chronic depression and suicidal ideation can also occur as a direct result of the sexual abuse, or as

an outcome of the combination of poor self-esteem and lack of ego buffering in the face of new stressors. This model of human development is supported by a quasi-experimental study of young women identified in a community mental health study (see Chapter 6 for a fuller account).

In the quotation which began this chapter I quoted the seminal work of William James (1890) on the crucial importance of a person's body as the centre and the essence of personal functioning. Prolonged sexual abuse can create a fundamental division between the child and his or her body, in a way which makes satisfactory achievement of the Eriksonian tasks of self-integration very difficult. Similarly, the stages of development described by Maslow are difficult to achieve. Maslow (1973) argues that violation of an early developmental need — the need for safety and security — makes it difficult for a child to master later stages of development, including identity integration and self-esteem maintenance. The child who is sexually abused in her home is betrayed: home should be a place of safety and trust, not of fear, terror and violation. Such violation of basic needs can lead to distorted patterns of development, including in extreme case dissociated and multiple personality (Putnam, 1989).

Dissociative personality traits and multiple personality: Special types of ego fragmentation

Although cases of multiple personality have been described in the psychiatric literature since the turn of the century it is only in the past 15 years that we have begun to understand both how prevalent this distortion of personality development is, and what are its fundamental causes (Putnam, 1989; Ross, 1989).

Some children who have to experience intolerable trauma (prolonged physical pain, physical abuse, sexual abuse, or combinations of these traumas) before the age of six may dissociate that part of themselves (in mind and body) which endures the pain and violent intrusion. This is an ego-protective strategy in that the child is able to create several alter egos who both endure the pain, and comfort and protect the child. However, by the onset of the latency period these alter egos enter into hidden areas of the child's psyche, sometimes emerging to dominate the ego in ways which direct the child into unanticipated behavioural paths. In these dissociated states the child or adolescent may injure themselves or others, engage in delinquent behaviours, or flee from customary surroundings.

There is a psychological continuum between normal dissociation (e.g. being unaware of immediate surroundings whilst driving) through dissociative abnormalities (e.g. rapid and contradictory changes of behaviour; inability to remember hours or days of one's recent existence; blocking out childhood memories covering a period of years; feelings of

possession by another person, or hearing directive voices; episodes of bizarre or disturbed behaviour observed by others, but not remembered by the child; and half remembered terrifying dreams, and frequent nightmares) through to complex multiple personalities in which the alter egos exercise complete domination over personality for short, or long periods (Ross, 1985).

In a review of child welfare and adolescent treatment files in Canada and Britain (see Chapter 8) we found that 15 per cent of those with history of sexual abuse before age six manifested five or more dissociative symptoms. These adolescents were much more likely than others to have histories of sexual abuse continuing into the latency period, multiple sexual and physical abuse occurring in disorganized families, and emotional abuse or neglect by mentally ill or alcoholic parents.

These findings are important for those who conduct adult recall studies of community populations (e.g. Bagley, 1991e) in order to discover the prevalence and long term psychological sequels of sexual abuse. An unknown proportion of those interviewed will have many symptoms of adverse mental health, but cannot recall the events of sexual abuse which caused these problems. Because of this, the adult recall studies reviewed by Bagley (1992c) will both underestimate the actual prevalence of CSA, as well as underestimating the psychological problems which are the long term sequels of CSA. This is a conservative bias, working against finding statistically significant correlates of CSA: because of this bias, those findings which actually are significant (e.g. the finding of increased rates of depression, anxiety, impaired self-esteem, and suicidal thoughts and behaviour in CSA populations) are especially important.

Child sexual abuse histories in special populations: Runaways, prostitutes, street people, prison and mental hospital inmates

The adult recall studies carried out by ourselves and others indicate that about six per cent of children of both sexes will have had to endure prolonged and unwanted sexual relations imposed upon them by an older person: at least half of these individuals (about three per cent of the population sampled) will have long term impairment of mental health as a result of these experiences. In addition, some child victims of a brutal rape which is not repeated will nevertheless suffer from post-traumatic stress: however, the psychological outcomes of the rape-victims are rather different from those experienced by victims of long term, incestuous abuse (Briere, 1989b). It is emphasized once again that these estimates of prevalence, and of psychological harm, are conservative ones.

One effect of incestuous abuse is rebellion by the child against family rules and values (which she rightly sees as hypocritical and meaningless, when the chief arbiter of family rules is also her sexual oppressor). Although she is psychologically incapable of denouncing her oppressor, nevertheless she acts with anger and despair at her fate. Often the victim is blamed for this disturbed behaviour, and the social systems with which the child must interact (the disciplinary procedures of school, juvenile court, and group homes) confirm the negative label imposed on her. She is likely to rebel against these sanctions, and the label has become self-confirming (Zingaro, 1987).

Special studies of juvenile prostitutes, street kids, delinquents, drug use populations, adolescent psychiatric inpatients, as well as adult mental hospital patients, adult prisoners, and homeless adults — all indicate greatly elevated rates of prolonged, within-family abuse (Bagley and King, 1990; Bagley et al., 1990b; Thomlison and Bagley, 1992).

In a comparison of juvenile prostitutes in America and Canada, it was found that at least two-thirds had suffered prolonged incestuous abuse in childhood (Silbert and Pines, 1983 and Chapter 4). Biographical analysis indicated a common sequence of events: the boy or girl rebelled against both the sexual abuse and the authority of the abuser, and either ran from home or was thrown out by his or her family; on the streets the struggle for survival involved various delinquencies, including drug pushing and drug use.

Absorption into prostitution often follows: in Canada, the <u>average</u> age of entry into prostitution is 15.5 years (Bagley, 1985b). Thus about half of all women who enter the sex trade industry will have become prostitutes before the age of 16. Adolescent males too are drawn into the web of prostitution, and often too they pair with an adolescent prostitute, supporting each other emotionally and financially (Bagley et al., 1990b). Society holds a negative view of the pimp, but often he is simply a young male victim of sexual abuse, trying to survive on the street.

Young people in child welfare caseloads and in residential care institutions often have histories of child sexual abuse. Frequently however these children and adolescents have been processed for reasons other than their earlier sexual abuse; rather, they were sent to residential care and treatment centres because of their acting out behaviour, runaway status, or delinquency. It is clear too from our extensive case file reviews that professionals in the past only atypically understood the significance of child sexual abuse, and often failed to check or record this information. It is crucial that all child welfare workers and child care professionals ask standard questions in their assessments about histories of unwanted sexual contacts, as well as questions which try and establish the temporal sequence of disturbed behaviours which may be sequels of that abuse.

192

It is technically quite simple to screen for such abuse (Bagley, 1990a and b). What is crucial too is that front-line workers have the training and skills to undertake initial counselling and assessment prior to referring CSA victims for fuller psychological assessments, which can identify which kind of treatment programme would be most effective. It is crucial too that social service delivery systems should actually have a range of treatment options available. While it is in the short run expensive to provide such specialized treatment, in the long run such interventions can be hugely cost effective in preventing the drift into street life, crime, chronic drug and alcohol abuse, and mental illness.

Another problem in using adult recall studies to estimate the prevalence of CSA is that since suicidal ideas and behaviour are known sequels of sexual abuse, those most severely damaged might have actually killed themselves, and are uncounted as victims by prevalence studies using conventional epidemiological methods. There is indeed some evidence that adolescents and young adults who complete suicide may have been victims of a type of sexual abuse which occurs together with family disorganization, as well as physical and emotional abuse and neglect. This evidence comes from a review of several thousand files of the Alberta Medical Examiner which identified a type of completed suicide in which childhood abuse and neglect was a precursor (Bagley, 1989c). Furthermore, it is this type of suicide which has accounted for the increase in youth suicide, particular amongst males (Bagley, 1992a). While it is difficult to know whether prior abuse was a direct precursor of suicide, this finding is consonant with community surveys indicating that sexually abused males have a greatly increased prevalence of suicidal ideas and behaviour, and depressive thinking (Bagley et al., 1994). Prior physical and sexual abuse and neglect are also precursors of 'careless death' including alcohol-related, reckless behaviour in adolescents and young adults (Bagley, Wood and Khumar, 1990b).

Who are the abusers? How shall we treat them?

Knowledge about the status and motivation of sexual offenders against children, and how they may be treated, deterred and perhaps reintegrated into society and family is imperfect. There are three clear research findings however: the large majority of those who sexually exploit male and female children (probably in excess of 95 per cent) are males; at least 80 per cent of those who assault children are known to the child, although only 20 per cent of male victims, and around a third of female victims will have been assaulted by someone in their immediate family; and a third of sexual offenders are themselves adolescents. The motivation to use children

193

sexually often develops in adolescence, which is also a crucial time for intervention and treatment (Bagley, 1992c).

Violations of the incest taboo

Rush (1980) and Chesnais (1981) stress in their historical accounts that adult males have rarely been deterred from sexually exploiting children simply because those children are physically immature, or in a state of vulnerable dependency. Children have in the past been protected to some extent from the sexuality of outsiders principally because they were the property of a protective nuclear family or extended kin. The price of this protection however was submission to the male-dominated ideal that the virgin adolescent could be given to (and perhaps traded with) another co-operative kin group.

The past 40 years in North America and Northern Europe have seen an unprecedented rise in divorce rates and single parenthood. This means that many of the men introduced into these families are biologically unrelated to the children for whom they become the father-figure. The incest taboo does not deter them, and some of these men seem to regard these female children as sexual extensions of their mother, to be used sexually when the whim occurs. The abuse perpetrated by these men seems almost casual in nature, without thought for the often fearful consequences that the children suffer. Several researchers have found that sexual abuse by non-biological father figures is the most serious in terms of length of occurrence, frequency, and intrusiveness (involving repeated penetrations of the child's body). As Young (1992) observes:

> There is growing evidence that the most serious long-term effects result from highly intrusive sexual abuse such as oral, anal, or vaginal penetration; abuse that is violent, forceful or sadistic in nature; abuse that continues over many years; and from intrafamilial abuse, particularly when the perpetrator is a parent, step-parent, or parent figure. (p. 89)

There is also evidence that some paedophiles (men with a fixation on children as sex objects, or a desire to achieve sexual relations with a child in preference to any other kind of sexual relationship) seek out single mothers as marriage partners with the intention of gaining sexual access to the children in that family (Bagley and King, 1990).

Studies of paedophile motivation (reviewed in Bagley et al., 1994) indicate that paedophiles can usually present themselves as 'normal' when presented with psychological tests (e.g. Rorschach, MMPI) customarily used in assessment. Moreover, such men may be manipulative liars. This makes inferences about causal factors in the developmental history of the offender

194

difficult to assess. Some sexual abusive males can however be diagnosed, after extensive observation and testing as manifesting 'sadistic personality disorder' (Spitzer, Feister, Gay and Pfohl, 1991). Such individuals frequently have histories of multiple abuse (sexual, physical and emotional) in their own childhoods.

A rather paradoxical sub-group of offenders against children do not have a paedophiliac fixation and are easier to detect, assess and treat. These are the so-called 'regressed' individuals, who for a variety of reasons have increasing difficulty in maintaining adequate psychosexual relationships with age peers, and turn to children for both emotional affection, and sexual outlet. These men usually feel great distress at their behaviour, and are often relieved when their actions are discovered. While these men will often have imposed great psychological distress on the child, nevertheless if their remorse is genuine and the child and the non-offending spouse so wishes, these men can be reintegrated into their family after comprehensive and prolonged therapy (using either the humanist model, or an adapted family therapy model, discussed below).

Almost certainly there are different types of offenders who need to be deterred and treated in different ways. All practitioners seem to be in agreement that the psychopathic individual, contemptuous of the sufferings of his child victims, and cunning in his methods of sexual access and concealment is a person who is both difficult to apprehend and to treat (Woody, McLellan, Luborksy and O'Brien, 1985). Indeed, the majority of men who plead guilty to sexual offenses against children (and who receive terms ranging from probation to lengthy imprisonment) are the regressed type of offender who would be unlikely to reoffend, even without specific treatment (Bagley and King, 1990). There is too a type of sexual assault against children and adolescents which is simply casual and sexist in nature, and is usually imposed on the child by relatives other than a parent, or by a family friend. This type of abuse although frequent, does not often come to the attention of those providing clinical treatment of victims, or processing of offenders. Indeed, clinical sources although often used to provide information on victim and offender profiles will be overweighed by cases of incestuous abuse, and abuse which seems to have done a great deal of psychological harm to the victim.

In an attempt to avoid the pitfalls of generalizing from the biased data sources available from treatment agencies, we studied the motivation to sexually assault children in a random community sample of 750 men aged 18 to 27 living in a large Canadian city (Bagley et al., 1994). Respondents were assured anonymity through the use of a computerized response system, and completed a number of validated mental health instruments, a questionnaire on their own unwanted childhood sexual experiences, and a

measure of their current sexual interests in and/or activities with children in various age and sex categories.

Fifty-two of these young men had experienced multiple, unwanted sexual contacts; 34 of these victims of sexual assault had experienced anal penetration, and all had experienced genital fondling or fellatio. These adult survivors had significantly poorer mental health than the 65 individuals experiencing only a single assault, and those who recalled no unwanted sexual contact before their 17th birthday. The measure of prolonged sexual abuse was highly correlated with current sexual interests and activities involving minors, both male and female. However, the majority of the sexual abuse victims did not declare any sexual interest or activities involving minors: 41 per cent of the prolonged abuse victims had paedophile interests, compared with two per cent of the non-victims. Regression analyses showed that combinations of physical and sexual abuse, emotional neglect or rejection within the boy's family, current poor mental health (particularly depression, low self-esteem, anxiety, dissociative personality traits, post-traumatic stress indicators, suicidal ideas and behaviour), and emotional attachment to the abuser were all independent, statistically significant predictors of paedophile interest. Combining these various indicators in a discriminant analysis successfully identified two-thirds of the young men with serious sexual interest in minors.

While this community survey suggests that only about three per cent of the adult male population living in stable conditions (i.e. excluding institutionalized individuals, highly mobile people and street dwellers) have strong motivations to involve children in sexuality, the fixated paedophile can nevertheless be of considerable danger in the community. For example, Weinrott and Saylor (1991) found in a study of convicted sexual offenders that these 99 men ' . . . admitted to over 8,000 sexual contacts with 959 children. The number ranged from 1 to 200, with a median of 7' (p. 291). Identification and intervention with even a few actual or potential offenders at an early stage might prevent literally hundreds of children from suffering sexual assault.

Much more research needs to be undertaken on various ways of identifying and treating male victims of abuse, and males who have entered the victim-to-abuser cycle.

Preventing child sexual abuse

Primary prevention involves various strategies, which include giving children the knowledge, skills and psychological strengths to recognize sexual exploitation, to resist it, and seek immediate help from a responsible adult. Research indicates that about a quarter of children who are

approached by an abuser who is known to them (usually, as a family member) are not able to resist such approaches, and are unable to get any immediate help from an adult (Bagley and King, 1990; Bagley, 1991d; Bagley et al., 1994). Special educational programs can be very helpful in this regard, and recent experience indicates that when children and adolescents are given adequate knowledge and skills concerning sexual abuse, then approaches by children to their teachers about recent and current sexual abuse increase significantly (Bagley, 1992b; Bagley and King, 1990).

One of the paradoxes of prevention programs (e.g. the 'Good Touch-Bad Touch' program extensively promulgated by the Canadian government — see Bagley and Thomlison, 1991) is that it purports to give children knowledge and skills about unwanted touching (the 'bad' touch) which will help them to resist sexually exploitive approaches. But logically if we ask children to reject 'bad touches,' they should have the right to resist all kinds of physical brutality and corporal punishment as well. However, as Straus, Gelles and Smith (1990) have amply demonstrated:

> Over 97% of American children experience physical punishment . . . such widespread use of ordinary physical punishment is one of the factors accounting for the high rate of child abuse and wife beating. . . . Victimization in the family starts in infancy and, for half of all American children, continues until they leave home. Moreover, for one out of seven children the violence is severe enough to be classified as child abuse. (p. 421)

In our view (elaborated in Bagley and King, 1990) the sexual exploitation of children and adolescents can be properly prevented only when society itself is to some degree healed, when the large majority of families are both caring of children and non-violent towards them. Epidemiological studies in Britain, Canada and the U.S.A. have shown that families in which a child is sexually abused are over-represented by families practising haphazard or systematic violence against a child, and by families who emotionally abuse or neglect their children. Children who have been cowed by physical punishments, whose self-confidence is sapped by emotional rejection or neglect have few ego resources left, and quite easily fall prey to the sexually abusive adult, both inside and outside of their families. For males, emotional attachment to the male abuser also puts the adolescent at risk for entering the victim-to-abuser cycle of sexual violence.

Since so many sexual abusers escape detection, the imposition of punitive sentences as a declaration of public morality is likely to have paradoxical impact. If the offender has the clear expectation of a long jail term if convicted he is likely to lie convincingly or cover his tracks in ways which make criminal convictions difficult. In the worst case when the penalty for

child rape may be as severe as that for murder, a rapist may kill his child victim in order not to have her testify.

The most successful kind of criminal justice program (outlined in Bagley and King, 1990) seems to be that in which the sexual offender knows that if he co-operates with those who treat the victim, he will receive a light or suspended sentence. In Canada jurisdictions which have such a policy have seen an increase in the number of men who plead guilty when charged with sexual assault on a child. Paradoxically this puts up the rate of convictions for child sexual assault, leading some to argue that deterrent sentences really are necessary. This view ignores the fact that offenders making court appearances are still the tip of the iceberg. Another strategy is to appeal to potential abusers through public service messages, advising them of the great harm wrought by sexual involvement with a child.

All of these strategies will be ineffective with the fixated paedophile who also has a sadistic or sociopathic personality style (Spitzer et al., 1991; Feister and Gay, 1991). Such men lie unscrupulously, and fabricate social and sexual histories (e.g. of abuse in their own childhood) in order to win sympathy from prosecutors, jurists and therapists. For such individuals there is little alternative to lengthy terms of imprisonment, not for any deterrent purpose but to keep these dangerous individuals out of the communities in which they render so much harm. Both chemical and physical castration has had limited effect, since the motivation to sexually assault for many sexual offenders lies in the psyche rather than in the hormonal system. The offender unable to gain erection can still do considerable harm in a sexual assault on a child.

Secondary Prevention involves the prompt, humane and efficient treatment of child sex abuse victims, once discovered. Primary prevention activities such as school programs on sexual abuse prevention also form a beginning stage of secondary prevention, when current victims seek help from a teacher. It is crucial for teachers to have a well-prepared protocol for handling such reports, with early involvement by child protection and law enforcement agencies. Child protection workers dealing with abuse allegations need to have special skills (including those required in co-operative work with police personnel with whom they will simultaneously investigate the abuse allegation). They need too, an adequate network of referral sources for medical examination, psychological assessment, and support for the child who must give evidence in court. Ideally when within-family abuse is suspected, the suspected offender should leave the home, rather than the child: removing her risks 'blaming the victim' reaction. Indeed, when child sexual abuse is seen by the community as a heinous offence, the child herself may become morally tainted by her victim-status, and can be rejected along with the offender.

198

Several well-developed models for the investigation and treatment of child and adolescent sexual abuse victims have emerged (O'Donohue and Elliott, 1992). These programs have different approaches, but common elements:

1   The primary focus must be on the recovery of self-esteem and mental health of the CSA victim, rather than on the welfare of adults, or of the family as a unit.

2   Individual therapy must begin with the victim, endeavouring to remove the sense of guilt and shame which has accompanied the guilt and its revelation, addressing as well symptoms of post-traumatic stress. This is an essential first step in rebuilding self-esteem. If the offender agrees he can assist this healing with an admission of his own responsibility for the assaults, together with an assurance to the victim that none of what happened was her fault.

Probably a range of counselling models and methods can work in the process of restoring the victim's self-respect; indeed, the commitment, warmth and empathy of the counsellor may be more important than the model of therapy used. Group therapy for victims can follow or coincide with individual therapy. Parallel groups of mothers are also valuable, as well as specific dyadic therapy, particularly that involving mother and daughter. Offenders can also be treated in groups by the agency treating the victim and her mother. This model, incorporating elements of the humanistic approach described by Giarretto (1982) is elaborated in Bagley and King (1990).

It is important that conventional family therapy should not be used in families in which a child has been sexually abused. Blaming a mythical 'family system' for abuse inevitably involves blaming of the victim, and will only depress her fragile feelings of self-worth yet further. However, a modified form of the family therapy approach has been developed by Larson and Maddock (1985) which avoids victim blaming. Careful screening (described by Babins-Wagner, 1991) can admit the offender into family therapy groups after individual assessment and counselling if it is established that he is not a fixated, paedophile offender, and he also is clearly remorseful in ways which can help to heal both the victim, and her family.

A number of other potentially valuable approaches to therapy of the child and adolescent victim have been described (Friedrich, 1990; James, 1989; Kilpatrick, 1992; Mandell and Damon, 1989; Meiselman, 1990; Trepper and Barrett, 1989). What is much needed now is research on the optimization and evaluation of these various programs, and investigation of the ways in which different programs and kinds of therapy can be tailored

to fit the individual needs of the victim (Downing, Jenkins and Fisher, 1988; O'Donohue and Elliott, 1992; Walker, 1992).

Another challenge to therapists is treatment of male victims who as adolescents have begun a pattern of sexual offenses against others (Bolton, Morris and MacEachron, 1989; Mezey and King, 1992; Ryan and Lane, 1991).

The complexities and potential success of an integrated approach to the treatment of child sexual abuse is illustrated by the following composite case, based on research and evaluation studies in Canada:

J was 12 years old when she complained to a teacher about her stepfather's sexual abuse. Two events precipitated this revelation: a presentation to her elementary school on sexual abuse by the local sexual assault centre; and her father's recently expressed sexual interest in her 10-year-old sister. The teacher consulted a guidance counsellor, who reassured J that she had done the right thing. In line with agreed protocol between the school board and social services, a specialized child protection worker arranged for J to be seen by a paediatric gynaecologist at the children's hospital. This forensic evidence was later produced later in court. Similar procedures were used in the case of J, the 10-year-old sister, and statements were taken from both girls by a detective who specialized in cases of abuse. Mother was disbelieving at first, but faced with the evidence from both her girls soon began to offer them support. Step-father denied the abuse. Mother and the girls left the home, to stay with mother's sister. Step-father was charged, but continued to deny the assaults. J was seen by counsellor specializing in the integrated therapy for abuse victims. J was depressed, had suicidal thoughts, and an eating disorder. S, her younger sister had no obvious psychological symptoms. After reassurance, mother joined a mother's group, and the younger daughter entered group therapy also. J entered another group later, when her immediate psychiatric crisis was resolved. Both S and J were supported by a Family Court Clinic which introduced them to the procedures used by the court, and reduced their anxiety about having to give evidence. In court they were allowed to give evidence from behind a screen. The stepfather was convicted, and received a four year jail term. At the time of sentence it was revealed that the man had a prior conviction for sexual assault of minors. Mother immediately began divorce proceedings, and moved back to the family home, which the step-father was required to leave as a condition of bail. S continued to receive individual therapy for a year, because of continuing mental health problems. At follow-up two years later both

girls had good mental health, recovered self-esteem, and were making good progress in school.

This case represents a 'best case' scenario — even though father denied responsibility, the mutually corroborating evidence from the two girls as well as forensic evidence was sufficient to enable a conviction to be made. The abused girls had good therapy and support during the crucial stages preceding the trial, as well as long term therapy. Mother too was supportive of her daughters.

It is still true however that 'worst case' scenarios exist, in which the abused child is blamed for making false accusations, is labelled and scapegoated, receives no help from counselling or social service agencies, runs from home, becomes involved in drug subcultures, and spends time in a youth detention centre. Services for sexually abused, runaway youth are not well developed; nor are foster parents well trained to cope with a behaviourally disturbed or sexually acting out teenager who has received no specific treatment for abuse (Raychaba, 1991). Sexualized behaviour is one of the sequels of sexual abuse of children (Friedrich, 1990), and unprepared foster parents and child care staff may be involved in further sexual assaults on a disturbed child whose sexualized behaviours seem to invite this.

Mother's role, and the feminist perspective

The role of the mother in supporting her daughter after within-family abuse has been discovered is crucial. Revelation of the abuse presents the mother with a potential mental health crisis, when she realizes that a man she loved and trusted has deceived her, and abused her daughter. In a study of mothers of sexually-abused children referred to child protection workers we found that less than 10 per cent had any suspicions or knowledge of the abuse (Chapter 5). This estimate agrees with that of other researchers (Johnston, 1992).

Mothers in families where a child had been abused had some unique features (in comparison with control families): at least half of the mothers with a sexually abused daughter had themselves suffered prolonged sexual abuse in childhood. Two-thirds had escaped from families marked by neglect and abuse by marriage when in their 'teens — a fifth married when they were aged 16 or less. Divorce and remarriage rates were high, but some of the men who married young teenagers went on to sexually molest their daughters, and it is probable that these men had paedophile impulses in marrying a young girl, and in later assaulting her daughters. A half of the women escaped first marriages marked by domination and physical abuse only to enter relationships with seemingly similar men: in these new relationships the step-father or cohabitee put the daughters (and sons) of the

201

woman at considerable risk of sexual abuse. Many of these women had entered a cycle of 'learned helplessness,' drifting hopelessly from one abusive relationship to the next, unable to provide a psychological climate in which children could appeal to their mother for protection. Nevertheless, these women rarely had any inkling about what was actually happening. Revelation of the abuse came as a profound shock, and many women began to relive the trauma of their own childhood abuse. Mental health interventions are crucially important for women at this stage, first as individual therapy and then in the: form of mother's groups which provide mutually support and shared insights. Many of these women recover self-esteem, and enter a phase of self-actualization in which they regroup their lives, and escape exploitation in family, work and social relationships (Bagley and Young, 1990).

The feminist perspective of child sexual abuse, which was so valuable in demonstrating the extent of child sexual abuse and the damage it imposed on victims, is also a relevant voice in providing mothers of victims with new strengths (Adams, Trachtenberg and Fisher, 1992). Feminist social and group work can support women in being psychologically independent of men, following the break-up of a first marriage. The normative pattern is still for a divorced women to enter a relationship with another male, sometimes with very negative consequences for her children. As well as sexual abuse these include a variety of forms of physical and emotional abuse: families in which a step-father 'adopts' the children of his new partner have high rates of disruption involving an acting-out child (Bagley and Young, 1993).

Conclusions: The paradoxes of child sexual abuse

I have referred frequently in this chapter to paradoxes — outcomes or events which seem contradictory but yet have logic in demonstrating the complexity of child sexual abuse, and the challenges offered to research, prevention, and therapy. By way of conclusion I offer the following paradoxes:

1   Child sexual abuse has existed at all times in recorded history, and yet its extent and potentially negative impact on the children and adolescents involved has only been fully recognized in the past two decades.

2   Recent research has established that about half of those children (i.e. those under the age of 17) who have a sexual relationship with an older person do not appear to suffer any long term harm as a result. Kilpatrick argues that:

Questions regarding the confusion of mores with actual harm done are raised by the finding that older partners are not found to be a significant factor in correlations with later adult functioning. This finding challenges the linear assumption that all children are victimized by any type of sexual experience with a person who is five or more years older than them. One must guard against making assumptions that have no empirical bases and against buttressing existing mores that may be actually harmful to children and adolescents. (p. 121)

Nevertheless unwanted sexual acts do cause severe long term psychological harm to a substantial minority of children. Paradoxically, when a child enters into a sexual relationship with an adult 'willingly' (despite difficulties for the child in giving informed consent to such a relationship) no significant long term impact on mental health can usually be detected (Kilpatrick, 1992).

I argue, nevertheless that adult sexual contact with children is morally wrong (as well as being in many cases illegal) because no-one can predict at the outset whether or not any particular child will in the long run, suffer psychological harm through the relationship. These potential risks for the child are far too grave for society to be tolerant about adult sexual involvement with children.

3   It is paradoxical that what many researchers and clinicians describe as 'incest' is not in fact incest in a legal or sociological sense. The incest taboo does to a large extent protect adolescents from being forced to have sexual intercourse with close relatives. However, incestuous abuse which stops short of heterosexual intercourse is quite common, especially that involving a stepfather or relatives outside of the nuclear family. While at least five per cent of both male and female children experience prolonged sexual assaults by an adult or older person, less than one per cent of all children are victims of incest, as defined by criminal law. We offer an alternative definition, 'incestuous abuse' to cover a wide spectrum of sexual assaults on children by a variety of relatives or family members, including step-fathers.

4   Freud has been rightly blamed for distorting his original findings of incestuous assault on children as a common precursor of adult neurosis. Nevertheless, analysts working within the Freudian tradition have provided valuable insight into why incestuous abuse can be so damaging for a child's psychosexual development. Ego psychologists who draw some inspiration from Freud, but who have significantly modified his paradigm offer a valuable model for therapists: failure to achieve a level of self-esteem which is adequate for coping with

various stressors, and the development of an identity which incorporates consciously or unconsciously the impact of past trauma, all combine to prevent adequate solution of identity tasks at various stages of child and adolescent development.

5   Paradoxically, a single act of rape perpetrated upon a child may be less traumatic than a more gradual seduction imposed by an older person. Often the child will receive support from her family, and from professionals after a single assault which the child is able to report to an adult. But the subtle and secret seduction of a child often imposes a psychologically corrupting burden which can gravely impair the young person's psychosocial development.

6   It is cruel paradox that those children least able to cope with the burden of sexual seduction are those most vulnerable to its effects. Children with good self-esteem, a trusting and confident relationship with an adult, and well developed ego strengths are likely to report any attempted or achieved sexual assault immediately. However, a child whose ego development has been undermined by loss of a parent, problematic attachments to adults, and depressed self-esteem because of emotional and physical abuse or neglect is particularly vulnerable, and is rarely able to prevent or report continuing sexual assaults. Unwanted, imposed sexuality (particularly, incestuous abuse) is likely to be gravely harmful to the child's identity development.

We need to have better information on both vulnerability and resilience of children faced by acute stress of the kind which sexual abuse may impose (c.f. Kolko, 1992). While my own ideas on pre-existing self-esteem and subsequent identity development as important factors predicting psychosocial outcomes for abused children are supported by evidence from various Canadian studies (Bagley, 1991a) replications and extensions of this thesis in other cultures (United States, Europe and Asia) are important (c.f. Kendall-Tackett et al., 1993).

7   Just as there are sub-types of victim reaction, so there are sub-types of men who sexually offend against children. It is an ironic paradox that the determined and manipulative paedophile can both find access to children and through psychological wiles escape detection or prosecution; but the regressed offender, in his pathetic retreat into the psychosexual relationships of childhood is the type of offender most likely to plead guilty when detected, and also the individual most likely to receive jail time. Another paradox of offending is that harsh sentences which reflect an attempt at deterrence, or a sense of

204

community outrage, rarely have their intended effect and may actually discourage the co-operation of abusers with those offering therapy to the child.

8   One group is defined by paradox: males having been victims of sexual abuse themselves become, in adolescence and adulthood, sexual abusers, sometimes with a paedophile fixation on young children. A variety of factors may explain this — trying to gain mastery over the earlier abuse by repeating it, but in a controlling manner; socially learned behaviour, reinforced by sexual stimuli; and attachment to the abuser, in a youth whose own families provided imperfect emotional attachments.

9   Some prevention programs aim to give children knowledge about 'bad touching,' and ways in which such touching may be avoided, or reported. Yet when the large majority of North American households impose physical pain on children as a means of control and socialization, prevention programs are unlikely to be fully effective until all bad touching is ended, including the beating, punching, kicking, caning and strapping of children by adult caretakers.

10   Even though we now have the skills, knowledge and experience to offer successful therapy programs for children and their families following sexual abuse, the number of current and former victims who need help in childhood, adolescence and young adulthood greatly exceed the resources of social service and counselling agencies. A child 'protected' after sexual abuse may drift through foster homes and youth facilities without receiving adequate help, even when the professional knowledge to offer such help has been developed.

11   Some youth act out in seemingly antisocial ways following sexual abuse: they are often blamed, processed and incarcerated for such behaviour, without the root causes being addressed. Blaming the victim may satisfy society's moral outrage, but in such condemnation there is no justice, and no healing.

References

Abel, G., Becker, J. and Skinner, L. (1980). Treatment of the violent sex offender. In L. Roth (ed.), *Clinical treatment of the violent person* (pp. 71–90). Washington: National Institute of Mental Health, Crime and Delinquency Monographs.

Able-Peterson, T. (1981). *Children of the evening.* New York: Putnam.

Adams, J., Trachtenberg, S. and Fisher, J. (1992). Feminist views of child sexual abuse. In W. O'Donohue and J. Geer (eds), *The sexual abuse of children: Theory and research* (pp. 359–96). Hillsdale: Lawrence Erlbaum.

Adityanjee, Raju, G. and Khandelwal, S. (1989). Current status of multiple personality disorder in India. *American Journal of Psychiatry,* 146, 1607–10.

Ageton, S. (1983). *Sexual assault among adolescents.* Toronto: Lexington Books.

Akins, F., Akins, D. and Mace, G. (1981). *Parent-child separation.* New York: Plenum Publishers.

Aldridge-Morris, R. (1990). *Multiple personality: An exercize in deception.* London: Lawrence Erlbaum.

Alexander, P. (1992). Application of attachment theory to the study of child sexual abuse. *Journal of Consulting and Clinical Psychology,* 60, 185–97.

Alexander, P. and Lupfer, S. (1987). Family characteristics and long-term consequences associated with child sexual abuse. *Archives of Sexual Behavior,* 16, 235–45.

Allen, C. (1980). *Daddy's girl: A very personal memoir.* Toronto: McLelland and Stewart.

Anderson, C. and Mayes, P. (1983). Treating family sexual abuse: The humanistic approach. *Journal of Child Care,* 2, 31–47.

Anderson, G., Yasenik, L. and Ross, C. (1993). Dissociative experiences and disorders among women who identify themselves as sexual abuse survivors. *Child Abuse & Neglect,* 17, 677–86.

Armstrong, L. (1978). *Kiss daddy goodnight.* New York: Pocket Books.

Arrindell, W., Emmelkamp, P., Monsma, A. and Brilman, E. (1983). The role of perceived parental rearing practices in the aetiology of phobic disorders. *British Journal of Psychiatry,* 143, 183–7.

Arrindell, W., Perris, C., Hjordis, P., Eisemann, M., Van der Ende, J. and Von Knorring, L. (1986). Cross-national in invariance of dimensions of parental rearing behaviour. *British Journal of Psychiatry,* 148, 305–09.

Babins-Wagner, R. (1991). Development and evaluation of a family systems approach to the treatment of child sexual abuse. *Journal of Child and Youth Care,* Fall Special Issue, 103–28.

Badgley, R. (1984a). *Report of the committee of enquiry into sexual offences against children and youth.* (Chaired by R. Badgley), Ottawa: Minister of Justice and Attorney General, and Minister of National Health and Welfare.

Badgley, R. (1984b). *Sexual offenses against children.* Ottawa: Ministry of Justice, Government of Canada.

Bagley, C. (1969). Incest behaviour and incest taboo. *Social Problems,* 16, 505–19.

Bagley, C. (1970). *Social structure and prejudice in five English boroughs.* London: Institute of Race Relations.

Bagley, C. (1973). *The Dutch plural society: A comparative study in race relations.* London: Oxford University Press.

Bagley, C. (1979). Social policy and development: The case of child welfare, health and nutritional services in India. *Plural Societies,* 10, 3–26.

Bagley, C. (1980). The factorial reliability of the Middlesex Hospital Questionnaire in normal subjects. *British Journal of Medical Psychology,* 53, 53–8.

Bagley, C. (1982). Child sexual abuse and childhood sexuality: A review of the monograph literature 1977 to 1981. *Journal of Child Care,* 3, 100–21.

Bagley, C. (1983a). Child sexual abuse: A bibliography of journal studies, 1978 to 1982. *Journal of Child Care,* 5, 81–6.

Bagley C. (1983b). The validity of a short version of the Middlesex Hospital Questionnaire for mental health assessment in a Canadian population. Unpublished manuscript, Faculty of Social Welfare, University of Calgary.

Bagley, C. (1983c). Alienation and identity in young West Indians in Britain and the Netherlands. In C. Bagley and G. Verma (eds),

Multicultural childhood. Aldershot: Gower Press.

Bagley, C. (1984a). Child sexual abuse: A child welfare perspective. In B. Wharf and K. Levitt (eds), *Child welfare: A textbook.* Vancouver: University of British Columbia.

Bagley, C. (1984b). Mental health and the sexual abuse of children and adolescents. *Canadian Mental Health,* June, 17–23.

Bagley, C. (1985a). *Child sexual abuse within the family: An account of studies 1978-1984.* Calgary: The University of Calgary Press. (Rehabilitation and Health Monographs, No. 12).

Bagley, C. (1985b). Child sexual abuse and juvenile prostitution. *Canadian Journal of Public Health,* 76, 65–6.

Bagley, C. (1986). Prevention of child sexual abuse and its sequels. *The Social Worker,* 54, 16–20.

Bagley, C. (1987). *Child sexual abuse and self-concept: A survey of 1,200 students.* Unpublished paper.

Bagley, C. (1988a). Daycare and child development. *Early Childhood Care, Health and Development,* 39, 139–61.

Bagley, C. (1988b). An experimental study of self-esteem enhancement and social support for women at risk of serious depression. *Paper present to International Congress for the Advancement of Counselling,* Calgary, July.

Bagley, C. (1988c). *Child sexual abuse in Canada: Further analysis of the 1983 national survey.* Ottawa: National Health and Welfare.

Bagley, C. (1988d). Self-concept and achievement in Canadian and British adolescents. In G. Verma (ed.), *Education for all: The Canadian dimension.* Brighton: The Falmer Press.

Bagley, C. (1988e). *Child sexual abuse in a national Canadian survey.* Ottawa: Department of Health and Welfare.

Bagley, C. (1989a). Development of a short self-esteem measure for use with adults in community mental health survey. *Psychological Reports,* 65, 13–14.

Bagley, C. (1989b). Prevalence and correlates of unwanted sexual acts in childhood in a national Canadian sample. *Canadian Journal of Public Health,* 80, 295–96.

Bagley, C. (1989c). Profiles of youthful suicide: Disrupted development and current stressors. *Psychological Reports,* 65, 234.

Bagley, C. (1990a). Validity of a short measure of child sexual abuse for use in adult mental health surveys. *Psychological Reports,* 66, 449–50.

Bagley, C. (1990b). Development of a measure of unwanted sexual contact in childhood, for use in community mental health surveys. *Psychological Reports,* 66, 401–02.

Bagley, C. (1990c). Is the prevalence of child sexual abuse decreasing?

Evidence from a random sample of 750 young adult women. *Psychological Reports,* 66, 1037-38.

Bagley, C. (1991a). The prevalence and mental health sequels of child sexual abuse in a community sample of women aged 18 to 27. *Canadian Journal of Community Mental Health,* 10, 103-16.

Bagley, C. (1991b). Preventing child sexual abuse: The state of knowledge, and future research. In C. Bagley and R. Thomlison (eds), *Child sexual abuse: Critical, perspectives on prevention, intervention and treatment* (pp. 9-26). Toronto: Wall and Emerson.

Bagley, C. (1991c). Long-term effects of child sexual abuse: The Canadian and British evidence. *Annals of Sex Research,* 4, 23-48.

Bagley, C. (1991d). Mental health and the sexual abuse of children and adolescents. In J. Veevers (ed.), *Community and change in marriage and the family* (pp. 314-25). Toronto: Holt.

Bagley, C. (1991e). Psychological sequels of child sexual abuse: Canadian and European studies. *Annals of Sex Research,* 4, 23-48.

Bagley, C. (1992a). Changing profiles of a typology of youth suicide in Canada. *Canadian Journal of Public Health,* 83, 169-70.

Bagley, C. (1992b). Development of an adolescent stress scale for use by school counsellors: Construct validity in terms of depression, self-esteem and suicidal ideation. *School Psychology International,* 13, 31-49.

Bagley, C. (1992c). Sexually assaultive children and adolescents. *Journal of Forensic Psychiatry,* 3, 299-311.

Bagley, C., Burrows, B. and Yaworksi, C. (1990a). Adolescent prostitution: A challenge for legal and social services. In N. Bala, J. Hornick and R. Vogl (eds), *Canadian child welfare law: Children families and the state.* Toronto: Carswell Legal Publications.

Bagley, C., Burrows, B. and Yaworski, C. (1990b). Street kids and adolescent prostitution: A challenge for legal and social services. In N. Bala, J. Hornick and R. Vogl (eds), *Canadian child welfare law: Children, families and the state* (pp. 109-31). Toronto: Thompson.

Bagley, C. and Dann, D. (1991). Characteristics of 61 children and adolescents with a history of sexual assault against others. *Journal of Child and Youth Care,* 9, 141-52.

Bagley, C. and Evan-Wong, L. (1975). Neuroticism and extraversion in responses to Coopersmith's self-esteem inventory. *Psychological Reports,* 36, 253-54.

Bagley, C. and Genuis, M. (1991). Sexual abuse recalled: Evaluation of a computerized questionnaire in a population of young adult males. *Perceptual and Motor Skills,* 72, 287-88.

Bagley, C. and Greer. S. (1972). Clinical and social predictors of repeated attempted suicide. *British Journal of Psychiatry,* 119, 515-22.

Bagley, C. and King, K. (1990). *Child sexual abuse: The search for healing*. London: Tavistock-Routledge.

Bagley, C. and McDonald, M. (1984). Adult mental health sequels of child sexual abuse, physical abuse and neglect in maternally separated children. *Canadian Journal of Community Mental Health, 3,* 15-26.

Bagley, C. and Ramsay, R. (1985). Psychosocial correlates of suicidal behaviour in an urban population. *Crisis: International Journal of Suicide Prevention,* 6, 63-77.

Bagley, C. and Ramsay, R. (1986). Sexual abuse in childhood: Psychosocial outcomes and implications for social work practice. *Journal of Social Work and Human Sexuality,* 4, 33-47.

Bagley, C. and Ramsay, R. (1993). Suicidal ideas and behavior in contrasted generations: Evidence from a community mental health survey. *Journal of Community Psychology,* 21, 26-34.

Bagley, C., Rodberg, G., Wellings, D., Moosa-Mitha, M. and Young, L. (1994). Physical and sexual child abuse and the development of dissociative personality traits: Canadian and British evidence from adolescent child welfare and child care populations. *Child Abuse Review,* in press.

Bagley, C. and Sewchuk-Dann, D. (1991). Characteristics of sexually abusive adolescents in residential care. *Journal of Child and Youth Care,* Special Issue on Child Sexual Abuse, 43-52.

Bagley, C. and Thomlison, R. (1991). *Child sexual abuse: Critical perspectives on prevention, intervention and treatment.* Toronto: Wall and Emerson.

Bagley, C. and Thurston, B. (1988). *Preventing child sexual abuse: A review.* Ottawa: National Health and Welfare.

Bagley, C. and Thurston, W. (1989). *Preventing child sexual abuse: Key Research.* Calgary: University of Calgary, Rehabilitation and Health Monograph Series, No. 18.

Bagley, C., Verma, G., Mallick, K. and Young, L. (1979). *Personality, self-esteem and prejudice.* Aldershot: Saxon House.

Bagley, C., Wood, M. and Khumar, H. (1990b). Suicide and careless death in an aboriginal population. *Canadian Journal of Community Mental Health,* 29, 127-42.

Bagley, C., Wood, M. and Young, L. (1994). Victim to abuser: Mental health and behavioural sequels of child sexual abuse in community survey of young adults. *Child Abuse and Neglect,* 18, 683-97.

Bagley, C. and Young, L. (1987). Juvenile prostitution and child sexual abuse: A controlled study. *Canadian Journal of Community Mental Health,* 6, 52-6.

Bagley, C. and Young, L. (1988). Depression, self-esteem and suicidal

behaviour as sequels of child sexual abuse: Research and treatment. In M. Jacobs (ed.), *Family violence*. Waterloo: Wilfrid Laurier University Press.

Bagley, C. and Young, L. (1990). Depression, self-esteem and suicidal behaviour as sequels of sexual abuse in childhood: Research and therapy. In M. Rothery and G. Cameron (eds), *Child maltreatment: Expanded conceptions of helping* (pp. 183–209). New York: Lawrence Erlbaum.

Bagley, C. and Young, L. (1993). *Transracial and international adoptions: A mental health perspective*. Aldershot: Ashgate.

Barbaree, H. and Marshall, W. (1991). Treatment of the adult child molester. In C. Bagley and R. Thomlison (eds), *Child sexual abuse: Critical perspectives on prevention intervention, and treatment* (pp. 217–55). Toronto: Wall and Emerson.

Barnard, G., Fuller, A., Robbins, L. and Sliaiv, I. (1989). *The child molester: An integrated approach to evaluation*. New York: Brunner Mazel.

Barnes, G. and Prosen, H. (1984). Depression in Canadian general practice attenders. *Canadian Journal of Psychiatry, 29*, 2–10.

Benedek, E. and Schetky, D. (1987). Problems of validating allegations of sexual abuse. *Journal of the American Academy of Child Psychiatry, 26*, 912–21.

Benjamin, M. (1985). *Juvenile prostitution: A portrait of "the life"*. Toronto: Ontario Ministry of Community and Social Services.

Bernard, J. and Bernard, M. (1984). The abusive male seeking treatment: Jekyll and Hyde. *Family Relations, 33*, 543–47.

Bernstein, E. and Putman, F. (1986). Development, reliability and validity of a dissociation scale. *Journal of Nervous and Mental Disease, 174*, 727–35.

Bifulco, A., Brown, G. and Adler, Z. (1991). Early sexual abuse and clinical depression in adult life. *British Journal of Psychiatry, 159*, 115–22.

Billings, A., Cronkite, R. and Moos, R. (1983). Social environmental factors in unipolar depression: Comparisons of depressed patients and nondepressed controls. *Journal of Abnormal Psychology, 92*, 119–33.

Bixler, R. (1992). Do we/should we behave like animals? In W. O'Donohue and J. Geer (eds), *The sexual abuse of children: Theory and research* (pp. 81–107). Hillsdale: Lawrence Erlbaum.

Bliss, E. (1986). *Multiple personality, allied disorder and hypnosis*. London: Oxford University Press.

Bolton, F., Morris, L. and MacEachron, A. (1989). *Males at risk: The other side of child sexual abuse*. Newbury Park: Sage.

Bowlby, J. (1951). *Maternal care and mental health*. Geneva: World

Health Organization.

Brady, K. (1979). *Father's days: A true story of incest.* New York: Dell.

Brewin, C., Andrews, B. and Gotlieb, I. (1993). *Psychological Bulletin,* 113, 82–98.

Briere, J. (1988a). The long-term clinical correlates of childhood sexual victimization. *Annals of the New York Academy of Sciences,* 528, 327–34.

Briere, J. (1988b). Controlling for family variables in abuse effects research. *Journal of Interpersonal Violence,* 3, 80–89.

Briere, J. (1989a). *Therapy with adult survivors of child sexual abuse.* New York: Guilford Press.

Briere, J. (1989b). *Therapy for adults molested as children: Beyond survival.* New York: Springer.

Briere, J. (1992). Methodological issues in the study of sexual abuse effects. *Journal of Consulting and Clinical Psychology,* 60, 196–203.

Briere, J., Henschel, D. and Smiljanich, K. (1992). Attitude toward sexual abuse: Sex differences and construct validity. *Journal of Research in Personality,* 26, 398–406.

Briere, J. and Runtz, M. (1987). Post-sexual abuse trauma: Data and implications for clinical practice. *Journal of Interpersonal Violence,* 2, 367–79.

Briere, J. and Runtz, M. (1988a). *The Trauma Symptom Checklist (TSC-33).* Unpublished.

Briere, J. and Runtz, M. (1988b). Symptomatology associated with childhood sexual victimization in a non-clinical adult sample. *Child Abuse and Neglect,* 12, 51–9.

Briere, J. and Runtz, M. (1988c). Multivariate correlates of childhood psychological and physical maltreatment among university women. *Child Abuse and Neglect,* 12, 331–41.

Briere, J. and Runtz, M. (1989). University males' sexual interest in children: Predicting potential indices of 'paedophilia' in a non forensic sample. *Child Abuse and Neglect,* 13, 65–75.

Briere, J. and Runtz, M. (1990). Differential adult symptomatology associated with three types of child abuse histories. *Child Abuse and Neglect,* 14, 357–63.

Brown, G. and Harris, T. (1979). *Social origins of depression: A study of psychiatric disorder in women.* London: Tavistock.

Bukowski, W. (1992). Sexual abuse and maladjustment considered from the perspective of normal development processes. In W. O'Donohue and J. Geer (eds), *The sexual abuse of children theory and research* (pp. 261–82). Hillsdale: Lawrence Erlbaum.

Burgess, A., Hartman, S. and McCormack, A. (1987). Abused to abuser:

Antecedents of socially deviant behaviors. *American Journal of Psychiatry*, 144, 1431–36.

Carter, D. and Prentky, R. (1990). Overview of the program at the Massachusetts treatment centre. In D. Weisstaub (ed.), *Law and mental health: International perspectives* (pp. 104–19). New York: Pergamon Press.

Chase, T. (1987). *When rabbit howls: The troops for Trudi Chase*. New York: Jove Books.

Chesnais, J.P. (1981). *A history of violence in the west*. Paris: The National Research Institute.

Chu, J. and Dill, D. (1989). Dissociative symptoms in relation to childhood physical and sexual abuse. *American Journal of Psychiatry*, 147, 887–92.

Cole, P. and Putnam, F. (1992). Effect of incest on self and social functioning: A developmental psychopathology perspective. *Journal of Consulting and Clinical Psychology*, 60, 174–80.

Cooper, I. and Cormier, B. (1982). Inter-generational transmission of incest. *Canadian Journal of Psychiatry*, 27, 231–35.

Coopersmith, C. (1981). *Manual for the self-esteem inventories*. Palo Alto: Consulting Psychologists.

Crisp. A., Jones, M. and Slater, P. (1979). The Middlesex Hospital Questionnaire: A validity study. *British Journal of Medical Psychology*, 51, 269–79.

Crook, N. (1984). *A report on prostitution in the Atlantic Provinces*. Ottawa: Policy, Programs and Research Branch, Government of Canada.

Crowne, S. and Crisp, A. (1970). *Manual of the Middlesex Hospital Questionnaire*. Branstaple: Psychological Test Publications.

Crowne, S. and Crisp, S. (1981). *The Crowne-Crisp experiential index: The Middlesex Hospital Questionnaire*. London: Hodder and Stoughton.

Cunningham, J. (1988). Contributions to the history of psychology: 1) French historical views of the acceptability of evidence regarding child sexual abuse. *Psychological Reports*, 63, 343–53.

Dawson, R. (1987). Child sexual abuse, juvenile prostitution and child pornography: The Federal response. *Journal of Child Care*, 3, 19–51.

De Jong, A. (1988a). Childhood sexual abuse precipitating maternal hospitalization. *Child Abuse and Neglect*, 10, 551–53.

De Jong, A. (1988b). Maternal responses to the sexual abuse of their children. *Pediatrics*, 81, 14–21.

De Mause, L. (1974). *The history of childhood: The untold story of child abuse*. New York: Peter Bedrick Books.

Devins, G., Orme, C., Costello, C. and Binik, Y. (1988). Measuring depressive symptoms in illness populations: Psychometric properties of

the CESD depression scale. *Psychology and Health,* 2, 139–56.

DeYoung, M. (1994a). Women as mothers and wives in paternally incestuous families: Coping with role conflict. *Child Abuse and Neglect,* 18, 83–5.

DeYoung, M. (1994b). Immediate maternal reactions to the disclosure or discovery of incest. *Journal of Family Violence,* 9, 21–33.

Doll, L., Joy, D., Bartolow, B., Harrison, J., Bolan, G., Douglas, J., Saltzman, L., Moss, P. and Delgado, W. (1992). Self-reported childhood and adolescent sexual abuse among adult homosexual and bisexual men. *Child Abuse and Neglect,* 16, 855–64.

Downing, J., Jenkins, S. and Fisher, G. (1988). A comparison of psychodynamic and reinforcement treatment with sexually abused children. *Elementary School Guidance and Counselling,* 22, 291–98.

Duncan, D. (1990). Prevalence of sexual assault victimization among heterosexual and gay/lesbian university students. *Psychological Reports,* 66, 65–6.

Dunn, G. (1992). Multiple personality disorder: A new challenge for psychology. *Professional Psychology: Research and Practice,* 23, 18–23.

Eichler, M. (1983). *Families in Canada today.* Toronto: Gage Publishing Limited.

Ellis, A. (1990). Commentary on the status of sex research: An assessment of the sexual revolution. *Journal of Psychology and Human Sexuality,* 3, 5–16.

Erikson, E. (1980). *Identity and the life cycle.* New York: Norton.

Everson, M., Hunter, W., Runyon, D., Edelsohn, G. and Coulter, M. (1989). Maternal support following disclosure of incest. *American Journal of Orthopsychiatry,* 59, 197–207.

Faller, K. (1989). Why sexual abuse? An exploration of the intergenerational hypothesis. *Child Abuse and Neglect,* 13, 543–48

Feister, S. and Gay, M. (1991). Sadistic personality disorder: Review of data and recommendations for DSM-IV. *Journal of Personality Disorders,* 5, 376–85.

Finkelhor, D. (1979). *Sexually victimized children.* New York: Free Press.

Finkelhor, D. (1984). *Child sexual abuse: New theory and research.* New York: Free Press.

Finkelhor, D. (1985). Sexual abuse of boys. In A. Burgess (ed.), *Rape and sexual assault: A research handbook* (pp. 97–109). New York: Garland Publishing.

Finkelhor, D. (1993). Epidemiological factors in the clinical identification of child sexual abuse. *Child Abuse and Neglect,* 17, 67–70.

Finkelhor, D. (1994). The international epidemiology of child sexual abuse. *Child Abuse and Neglect,* 18, 409–17.

Finkelhor, D. and Associates. (1986). *A source book on child sexual abuse.* London: Sage Publications.

Finkelhor, D. and Hotaling, G. (1984). Sexual abuse in the national incidence study of child abuse and neglect: An appraisal. *Child Abuse and Neglect, 8.*

Finkelhor, D., Hotaling, G., Uwis, I. and Smith, C. (1990). Sexual abuse in a national survey of adult men and women: Prevalence, characteristics, and risk factors. *Child Abuse and Neglect, 14,* 19–28.

Finkelhor, D., Hotaling, G. and Yllo, K. (1988). *Stopping family violence: Research priorities for the coming decade.* London: Sage Publications.

Fisher, R. (1944). *Statistical methods for research workers.* Edinburgh: Oliver and Boyd.

Fleischman, J. (1984). *A report on prostitution in Ontario.* Ottawa: Policy, Programs and Research Branch, Government of Canada.

Fox, R. (1980). *The red lamp of incest.* New York: Hutchison.

Frankel, F. (1990). Hypnotizability and dissociation. *American Journal of Psychiatry, 147,* 823–42.

Fraser, P. (1985). *Pornography and prostitution in Canada.* Ottawa: Government of Canada.

Fraser, S. (1987). *My father's house: A memoir of incest and healing.* Toronto: Doubleday.

Freud, S. (1977). *On sexuality.* London: Penguin books.

Friedrich, W. (1990). *Psychotherapy for sexually abused children and their families.* New York: Norton.

Fromuth, M. (1986). The relationship of childhood sexual abuse with later psychological and sexual adjustment in a sample of college women. *Child Abuse and Neglect, 10,* 5–15.

Fromuth, M. and Burkhart, B. (1989). Long-term psychological correlates of childhood sexual abuse in two samples of college men. *Child Abuse and Neglect, 13,* 533–42.

Fromuth, M., Burkhart, B. and Webb-Jones, C. (1991). Hidden child molestation: An investigation of adolescent perpetrators in a nonclinical sample. *Journal of Interpersonal Violence, 1991,* 6, 376–84.

Garrison, C., McKeown, R., Valois, R. and Vincent, M. (1993). Aggression, substance use, and suicidal behaviors in high school students. *American Journal of Public Health, 83,* 179–84.

Gavey, N., Florence, J., Pezaro, S. and Tan, J. (1990). Mother-blaming, the perfect alibi: Family therapy and the mothers of incest survivors. *Journal of Feminist Family Therapy, 2,* 1–25.

Geisser, R. (1979). *Hidden victims: The sexual abuse of children.* Boston: Beacon Press.

Gelinas, D. (1983). The persisting negative effects of incest. *Psychiatry,*

46, 312–32.

Gemme, R., Murphy, A., Bourque, Nemeh, M. and Payment, N. (1984). *A report on prostitution in Quebec.* Ottawa: Policy, Programs and Research Branch, Government of Canada.

Genuis, M., Thomlison, B. and Bagley, C. (1991). Male victims of child sexual abuse: A brief overview of pertinent findings. *Journal of Child and Youth Care,* Special Issue, 1–6.

Giarretto, H. (1982). *Integrated treatment of child sexual abuse: A treatment and training manual.* Palo Alto: Science and Behavior Books.

Glick, I. and Kessler, D. (1980). *Marital and family therapy.* New York: Grune and Stralton.

Gold, E. (1986). Long-term effects of sexual victimization in childhood: An attributional approach. *Journal of Consulting and Clinical Psychology,* 54, 471–5.

Goodwin, J. McCarthy, T. and DiVasto, P. (1981). Prior incest in mothers of abused children. *Child Abuse and Neglect,* 5, 87–95.

Greaves, G. (1980). Multiple personality 165 years after Mary Reynolds. *Journal of Nervous and Mental Diseases,* 168, 577–96.

Greer, S. and Gunn, J. (1966). Attempted suicides from intact and broken homes. *British Medical Journal,* 2 , 1344–57.

Groth, N. (1979). Sexual traumas in the life histories of rapists and child molesters. *Victimology,* 4, 10–16.

Grubman-Black, S. (1990). *Broken boys/mending men: Recovery from childhood sexual abuse.* Blue Ridge Summit: TAB Books.

Hall, G. (1989). WAIS-R and MMPI profiles of men who have sexually assaulted children: Evidence of limited utility. *Journal of Personality Assessment,* 53, 404–12.

Herman, J. (1981). *Father-daughter incest.* Cambridge: Harvard University Press.

Hoinville, G. and Jowell, R. (1978). *Survey research practice.* London: Heinemann.

Hudson, W. (1981). Index of sexual satisfaction. In W. Hudson, D. Harrison and P. Crosscup (eds), A short-form scale to measure sexual discord in dyadic relationships. *Journal of Sex Research,* 17, 157–74.

Hunter, J. (1991). A comparison of the psychosocial maladjustment of adult males and females sexually molested as children. *Journal of Interpersonal Violence,* 6, 205–17.

Jackson, J., Calhoun, K., Amick, A., Maddever, H. and Habif, V. (1990). Young adult women who report childhood intrafamilial sexual abuse: Subsequent adjustment. *Archives of Sexual Behavior,* 19, 211–21.

James, B. (1989). *Treating traumatized children: New insights and creative interventions.* Lexington: Lexington Books.

216

James, W. (1890). The Principles of Psychology. In H. Thayer (ed.), *Pragmatism: The classic writings* (pp. 135-79). New York: New American Library.

James, J. and Meyerding, J. (1978). Early sexual experience as a factor in prostitution. *Archives of Sexual Behavior, 7,* 31-42.

Janus, S. and Janus, C. (1993). *The Janus report on sexual behavior.* New York: Wiley.

Jennings, A. and Armsworth, M. (1992). Ego development in women with histories of sexual abuse. *Child Abuse and Neglect, 16,* 553-65.

Johnston, J. (1992). *Mothers of incest survivors: Another side of the story.* Bloomington: Indiana University Press.

Johnston, S., French, A., Schouweiler, W. and Johnston, F. (1992). Naivete and need for affection among pedophiles. *Journal of Clinical Psychology, 48,* 620-27.

Kahn, T. and Chambers, H. (1991). Assessing reoffense risk with juvenile offenders. *Child Welfare, 70,* 333-45.

Kaplan, H. (1980). *Deviant behavior in defense of self.* New York: Academic Press.

Kelly, R. and Scott, M. (1986). Sociocultural considerations in child sexual abuse. In K. MacFarlane (ed.), *Sexual abuse of young children: Evaluation and treatment.* New York: The Guilford Press.

Kempe, R. and Kempe, C. (1984). *The common secret: Sexual abuse of children and adolescents.* New York: Freeman.

Kendall-Tackett, K., Williams, L. and Finkelhor, D. (1993). Impact of sexual abuse on children: A review and synthesis of recent empirical studies. *Psychological Bulletin, 113,* 164-80.

Kercher, G. and McShane, M. (1984). The prevalence of child sexual abuse victimization in an adult sample of Texas residents. *Child Abuse and Neglect, 8,* 495-501.

Kiedrowski, J. and Van Dijk, J. (1984). *Pornography and prostitution in Denmark, France, The Netherlands and Sweden.* Ottawa: Policy, Programs and Research Branch, Government of Canada.

Kilpatrick, A. (1986). Some correlates of women's childhood sexual experiences: A retrospective study. *Journal of Sex Research, 22,* 221-42.

Kilpatrick, A. (1992). *Long-Range effects of child and adolescent sexual experiences: Myths, mores and menaces.* Hillsdale: Erlbaum.

Kluft, R. (1985). *Childhood antecedents of multiple personality.* Washington: American Psychiatric Press.

Kolko, D. (1992). Characteristics of child victims of physical violence: Research findings and clinical implications. *Journal of Interpersonal Violence, 7,* 244-76.

Lane, S. (1991). The sexual abuse cycle. In G. Ryan and S. Lane (eds), *Juvenile sexual offending: Causes, consequences and correction* (pp. 103–42). Lexington: D.C. Heath.

Langevin, R. (1982). Heterosexual and homosexual paedophilia. In R. Langevin (ed.), *Sexual strands. Understanding and treating sexual anomalies in men* (pp. 263–300). Hillsdale: Lawrence Erlbaum.

Langevin, R. (1985). *Erotic preferences, gender identity and aggression in men.* Hillsdale: Lawrence Erlbaum.

Larson, N. and Maddock, J. (1985). Structural and functional variables in incest family systems. In T. Trepper and M. Barrett (eds), *Assessment and treatment of intrafamilial sexual abuse* (pp. 104–28). New York: Haworth Press.

Lautt, M. (1984). *A report on prostitution in the prairies.* Ottawa: Policy, Programs and Research Branch, Government of Canada.

Levine, H. (1990). *Adult analysis of child sexual abuse.* Hillsdale: Analytic Press.

Lewis, G., Pelosi, A., Glover, E., Wilkinson, G., Stansfield, S., Williams, P. and Shepherd, M. (1988). The development of a computerized assessment for minor psychiatric disorder. *British Journal of Psychiatry,* 18, 727–45.

Linedecker, C. (1981). *Children in chains.* New York: Everest House.

Lowman, J. (1984). *Vancouver field study of prostitution.* Ottawa: Policy, Programs and Research Branch, Government of Canada.

Mandell, J. and Damon, L. (1989). *Group treatment for sexually abused children.* New York: Guildford Press.

Mannarino, A., Cohen, J., Smith, J. and Moore-Motily, S. (1991). Six and twelve-month follow-up of sexually abused girls. *Journal of Interpersonal Violence,* 6, 494–511.

Marshall, W., Barbaree, H. and Eccles, A. (1991). Early onset and deviant sexuality in child molesters. *Journal of Interpersonal Violence,* 6, 323–36.

Maslow, A. (1973). *Dominance, self-esteem and self-actualization.* California: Brooks-Cole.

Mayhew, P. (1990). *Crime in 14 cultures: Survey findings.* London: The Home Office.

McCormack, A., Rokous, F., Hazelwood, R. and Burgess, A. (1992). An exploration of incest in the childhood development of serial rapists. *Journal of Family Violence,* 7, 219–28.

McFarlane, K. (ed.) (1986). *Sexual abuse of young children: Evaluation and treatment.* New York: The Guilford Press.

McIntyre, K. (1981). Role of mothers in father-daughter incest: A feminist analysis. *Social Work,* 26, 426–66.

Meiselmann, K. (1978). *Incest.* San Francisco: Jossey Bass.

Meiselman, K. (1990). *Resolving the trauma of incest.* San Francisco: Jossey-Bass.

Meites, K., Lovallo, W. and Pishkin, V. (1980). A comparison of four scales of anxiety, depression and neuroticism. *Journal of Clinical Psychology,* 36, 427-32.

Metcalfe, M., Oppenheimer, R., Dignon, A. and Palmer, R. (1990). Childhood sexual experiences reported by male psychiatric patients. *British Journal of Psychiatry,* 20, 925-29.

Mezey, G. and King, M. (1992). *Male victims of sexual assault.* New York: Oxford University Press.

Morrow, G. and Sorell, G. (1989). Factors affecting self-esteem, depression, and negative behaviors in sexually abused female adolescents. *Journal of Marriage and the Family,* 51, 677-86.

Mrazek, R. Lynch, M. and Bentovim, A. (1983). Sexual abuse of children in the United Kingdom. *Child Abuse & Neglect,* 7, 147-53.

Muram, D., Rosenthal, T. and Beck, K. (1994). Personality profiles of mothers of sexual abuse victims and their daughters. *Child Abuse and Neglect,* 18, 419-23.

Naspini, O. (1988). *Mothers and child sexual abuse.* Calgary: M.S.W. thesis, University of Calgary.

Nie, N., Hull, C., Jenkins, J., Steinbrenner, K. and Bent, D. (1975). *Statistical package for the social sciences.* New York: McGraw-Hill.

O'Brien, S. (1983). *Child pornography.* Dubuque: Kendall-Hunt Publishing.

O'Donohue, W. and Elliott, A. (1992). Treatment of the sexually abused child: A review. *Journal of Clinical Psychology,* 21, 218-28.

Oliver, J. and Cox, J. (1973). A family kindred with ill-used children: The burden on the community. *British Journal of Psychiatry,* 123, 81-90.

Olmstead, R., O'Malley, P. and Bentler, P. (1991). Longitudinal assessment of the relationship between self-esteem, fatalism, loneliness, and substance abuse. *Journal of Social Behavior and Personality,* 6, 749-70.

Otis, L. (1985). *Prostitution in medieval society.* Chicago: University of Chicago Press.

Painter, S. (1986). Research on the prevalence of child sexual abuse: New directions. *Canadian Journal of Behavioural Science,* 18, 323-39.

Parker, H. and Parker, S. (1986). Father-daughter sexual abuse: An emerging perspective. *American Journal of Orthopsychiatry,* 56, 531-47.

Perris, C., Jacobson, L., Linstrom, H., Van Knorring, L. and Perris, H. (1980). Development of a new inventory for assessing memories of parental rearing behavior. *Acta Psychiatrica Scandinavica,* 61, 265-75.

219

Peters, S., Wyatt, G. and Finkelhor, D. (1986). The prevalence of child sexual abuse: Reviewing the evidence. In D. Finkelhor (ed.), *Child sexual abuse: A research handbook.* New York: Sage.

Pincus, L. and Dare, C. (1980). *Secrets in the family.* London: Tavistock.

Plummer, K. (1990). Understanding childhood sexualities. *Journal of Homosexuality,* 20, 231–49.

Putnam, F. (1989). *Diagnosis and treatment of multiple personality disorder.* New York: Guilford.

Putnam, F. (1990). Disturbances of "self" in victims of childhood sexual abuse. In R. Kluft (ed.), *Incest-related syndromes of adult psychopathology* (pp. 113–31). Washington: American Psychiatric Press.

Putnam, F. (1993). Dissociative disorders in children: Behavioral profiles and problems. *Child Abuse and Neglect,* 17, 39–45.

Radloff, L. (1977). The CES-D Scale: A self-report depression scale for research in the general population. *Applied Psychological Measurement,* 1, 385–401.

Ramsay, R. and Bagley, C. (1985). The prevalence of suicidal behaviours, attitudes and associated social experiences in an urban population. *Suicide and Life Threatening Behavior,* 61, 63–77, 151–60.

Raychaba, N. (1991). We get a life sentence: Young people in care speak out on child sexual abuse. *Journal of Child and Youth Care,* Fall Special Issue, 129–39.

Reinhart, M. (1987). Sexually abused boys. *Child Abuse and Neglect,* 11, 229–39.

Renovoize, J. (1982). *Incest: A family pattern.* London: Routledge.

Richards, P. and Persinger, M. (1991). Temporal lobe signs, the dissociative experiences scale and the hemispheric quotient. *Perceptual and Motor Skills,* 72, 1139–42.

Ringwalt, C. and Earp, J. (1988). Attributing responsibility in cases of father-daughter sexual abuse. *Child Abuse and Neglect,* 12, 273–81.

Rison, L. and Koss, M. (1987). The sexual abuse of boys: Prevalence and descriptive characteristics of childhood victimization. *Journal of Interpersonal Violence,* 2, 309–23.

Rodberg, G., Bagley, C. and Wellings, D. (1990). Dissociative disorders and abused children. In B. Braun and E. Carlson (eds), *Dissociative disorders: 1990* (p. 65). Chicago: Rush-Presbyterian-St Luke's Medical Center (Proceedings of 7th International Conference on Multiple Personality/Dissociative States, November 9-11).

Rodrigue, M. (1987). Incest: A widespread tragedy. *Canadian Public Health Association Health Digest,* 11(4).

Ross, C. (1984). Diagnosis of multiple personality during hypnosis: A case report. *International Journal of Clinical and Experimental Hypnosis,* 32,

222-35.

Ross, C. (1985). DSM-111: Problems in diagnosing partial forms of multiple personality disorder. *Proceedings of the Royal Society of Medicine*, 78, 933-36.

Ross, C. (1989). *Multiple personality disorder: Diagnosis, clinical features and treatment*. New York: Wiley.

Ross, M., Clayer, J. and Campbell, R. (1983). Dimensions of child-rearing practices. *Acta Psychiatria Scandinavica*, 78, 476-83.

Ross, C., Heber, S., Norton, G. and Anderson, G. (1989a). Differences between multiple personality disorder and other diagnostic groups on structured interview. *Journal of Nervous and Mental Diseases*, 177, 487-91.

Ross, C., Heber, S., Norton, G. and Anderson, G. (1989b). Somatic symptoms in multiple personality disorder. *Psychosomatics*, 30, 155-60.

Ross, C. and Norton, R. (1988). Multiple personality disorder patients with a prior diagnosis of schizophrenia. *Dissociation*, 1, 39-41.

Ross, C., Norton, G. and Anderson, G. (1988). The dissociative experiences scale: A replication study. *Dissociation*, 1, 21-22.

Ross, C., Norton, G. and Wozney, K. (1989). Multiple personality disorder: An analysis of 236 cases. *Canadian Journal of Psychiatry*, 34, 413-18.

Rush, F. (1980). *The best kept secret: Sexual abuse of children*. New York: McGraw Hill.

Russell, D. (1983). The incidence and prevalence of intrafamilial and extrafamilial sexual abuse of female children. *Child Abuse and Neglect*, 7, 133-46.

Russell, D. (1984). *Sexual exploitation: Rape, child sexual abuse, and sexual harassment*. Beverley Hills: Sage.

Russell, D. (1986). *The secret trauma: Incest in the lives of girls and women*. New York: Basic Books.

Rutter, M. (1979). Maternal deprivation, 1972-1978; new findings, new concepts, new approaches. *Child Development*, 50, 283-305.

Ryan, G. and Lane, S. (1991). *Juvenile sexual offending: Causes, consequences and corrections*. Lexington: Lexington Books.

Sandberg, D. and Lynn, S. (1992). Dissociative experiences, psychopathology and adjustment, and child and adolescent maltreatment in female college students. *Journal of Abnormal Psychology*, 101, 717-23.

Sereny, G. (1985). *The invisible children: Child prostitution in America, Germany and Britain*. London: Andre Deutsch.

Sedney, M. and Brooks, B. (1984). Factors associated with a history of childhood sexual experience in a nonclinical population. *Journal of the*

American Academy of Psychiatry, 23, 215–18.

Sheldon, B. (1988). *The psychological sequelae of sexual abuse.* Paper presented to 7th International Congress on Child Abuse and Neglect, Rio de Janeiro, September.

Siegel, S. and Castellan, N. (1988). *Nonparametric statistics for the behavioral sciences.* New York: McGraw-Hill.

Silbert, M. (1982a). Prostitution and sexual assault: Summary of results. *International Journal of Biosocial Research, 3,* 69–71.

Silbert, M. (1982b). *Sexual assault of prostitutes.* San Francisco: Delancey Street Foundation.

Silbert, M. (1984). Treatment of prostitute victims of sexual assault. In I. Stuart and J. Greer (eds), *Victims of sexual aggression: Treatment of children, women and men.* New York: Van Nostrand Reinhold.

Silbert, M. and Pines, A. (1981). Sexual child abuse as an antecedent of prostitution. *Child Abuse & Neglect, 5,* 407–11.

Silbert, M. and Pines, A. (1982a). Entrance into prostitution. *Youth and Society, 13,* 471–500.

Silbert, M. and Pines, A. (1982b). Victimization of street prostitutes. *Victimology, 7,* 122–33.

Silbert, M. and Pines A. (1983). Early sexual exploitation as an influence in prostitution. *Social Work, 28,* 285–90.

Simon, L., Sales, B., Kaszniak, A. and Kahn, M. (1992). Characteristics of child molesters: Implications for the fixated-regressed dichotomy. *Journal of Interpersonal Violence, 7,* 211–25.

Sirles, E. and Franke, P. (1989). Factors influencing mothers' reactions to intrafamily sexual abuse. *Child Abuse and Neglect, 13,* 131–39.

Sorrenti-Little, L., Bagley, C. and Robertson, R. (1984). An operational definition of the long-term harmfulness of sexual relations with peers and adults by young children. *Journal of the Canadian Association for Young Children, 9,* 46–57.

Spitzer, R., Feister, S., Gay, M. and Pfohl, B. (1991). Results of a survey of forensic psychiatrists on the validity of the sadistic personality diagnosis. *American Journal of Psychiatry, 148,* 875–79.

Steen, C. and Monnette, B. (1989). *Treating adolescent sex offenders in the community.* Springfield: Charles C. Thomas.

Stekel, W. (1926). *Peculiarities of behaviour.* London: Williams and Norgate, Volumes I and II.

Stenson, P. and Anderson, C. (1987). Treating juvenile sex offenders and preventing the cycle of abuse. *Journal of Child Care, 3,* 91–101.

Stephens, M., Grinnell, R., Thomlison, B. and Krysik, J. (1991). Child sexual abuse and police disposition: A Canadian study. *Journal of Child and Youth Care,* Fall Special Issue, 53–65.

Straus, M., Gelles, R. and Smith, C. (1990). *Physical violence in American families: Risk factors and adaptations to violence in 8,145 families.* New Brunswick: Transaction Press.

Thomlison, B. and Bagley, C. (1992). *Child sexual abuse: Expanding the research base on program and treatment outcomes.* Calgary: University of Calgary Press (Special issue of Journal of Child and Youth Care).

Trepper, T. and Barrett, M. (1989). *Systemic treatment of incest: A therapeutic handbook.* New York: Brunner/Mazel.

Tse, J., Bagley, C. and Mak, H. (1994). Prevention of suicidal behaviour in Hong Kong: Health intervention training mutual aid network (HIT-MAN). *School Psychology International,* 15, 45–54.

Tzeng, O. and Schwarzin, H. (1990). Gender and race differences in child sexual abuse correlates. *International Journal of Intercultural Relations,* 14, 135–61.

Valliant, P. and Blasutti, B. (1992). Personality differences of sex offenders referred for treatment. *Psychological Reports,* 71, 1067–74.

Vander May, B. (1992). Theories of incest. In W. O'Donohue and J. Geer (eds), *The sexual abuse of children: Theory and research* (pp. 204–60). Hillsdale: Lawrence Erlbaum.

Violato, C. and Genuis, M. (1991). A stepwise discriminant analysis of sexually abused males. *International Journal of Psychology,* 27, 222–23.

Wachtel, A. and Scott, B. (1991). The impact of child sexual abuse in development perspective. In C. Bagley and R. Thomlison (eds), *Child sexual abuse: Critical perspectives on prevention, intervention, and treatment* (pp. 79–120). Toronto: Wall and Emerson.

Walker, L. (1992). Helping heal violated children's trauma. *Contemporary Psychology,* 37, 46–8.

Wasserman, S. and Rosenfeld, A. (1992). An overview of the history of child sexual abuse and Sigmund Freud's contribution. In W. O'Donohue and Geer, J. (eds), *The sexual abuse of children: Theory and research* (pp. 38–48). Hillsdale: Lawrence Erlbaum.

Watkins, J. and Johnson, R. (1982). *We, the divided self.* New York: Irvington Publishers.

Wattenberg, E. (1985). In a different light: A feminist perspective on the role of mothers in father-daughter incest. *Child Welfare,* 64, 203–11.

Weinrott, M. and Saylor, M. (1991). Self-report of crimes committed by sex offenders. *Journal of Interpersonal Violence,* 6, 286–300.

Weisberg, D. (1985). *Children of the night: A study of adolescent prostitution.* Lexington: Lexington Books.

Wells, M. (1990). *Canada's law on sexual abuse.* Ottawa: Department of Justice, Government of Canada.

Will, D. (1983). Approaching the incestuous and sexually abusive family.

Journal of Adolescence, 6, 229–46.

Woody, G., McLellan, A., Luborksy, L. and O'Brien, C. (1985). Sociopathy and psychotherapy outcome. *Archives of General Psychiatry,* 42, 1081–86.

Wyatt, G. (1985). The sexual abuse of Afro-American and White-American women in childhood. *Child Abuse and Neglect,* 9, 507–19.

Wyatt, G., Guthrie, D. and Notgrass, C. (1992). Differential effects of women's child sexual abuse and subsequent sexual revictimization. *Journal of Consulting and Clinical Psychology,* 60, 167–73.

Wyatt, G. and Peters, S. (1986). Methodological considerations in research on the prevalence of child sexual abuse. *Child Abuse and Neglect,* 10, 241–51.

Wyatt, G. and Peters, S. (1988). Issues in the definition of child sexual abuse in prevalence research. *Child Abuse and Neglect,* 10, 231–40.

Wyatt, G. and Powell, G. (1988). *Lasting effects of child sexual abuse.* Newbury Park: Sage.

Yap, P. (1960). The possession syndrome: A comparison of Hong Kong and French findings. *Journal of Mental Science,* 106, 114–37.

Young, L. (1992). Sexual abuse and the problem of embodiment. *Child Abuse and Neglect,* 16, 89–100.

Young, L. and Bagley, C. (1982). Self-esteem, self-concept and the development of identity: Theoretical overview. In G. Verma (ed.), *Self-Concept, achievement and multicultural education* (pp. 41–59). London: MacMillan.

Zingaro, L. (1987). Working with street kids. *Journal of Child and Youth Care,* 3, 63–70.

Subject index

Abusers 9, 29, 47, 78, 112, 125, 135, 142, 173, 193, 197, 198, 205
(see also Offenders, Motivation of offenders)

Adolescent
abusers 9, 10, 29, 37, 44-45, 52, 61, 67, 193-194

Adolescents
therapy with 200

Adolescent victims 3, 9, 11, 34, 47, 112, 122, 126, 130, 134, 136, 137, 141, 142, 158, 160, 161-168, 170, 179, 180, 182, 191-193, 195, 197, 200, 202, 203

Adoption 2, 180

Adult recall studies 4, 30, 31, 33-34, 112, 181-182, 185, 186, 191, 193

Adults
therapy with 111

Adult survivors 2, 4-6, 8, 9, 12, 15, 17, 19, 23, 29, 30, 38, 41, 45, 46, 71, 73, 99, 108, 110, 116, 122, 126, 127, 132, 133, 141, 143, 180, 184, 186, 192, 193, 196, 199, 204
(see also Treatment)

Age of victims 4-6, 9, 11, 15, 17, 22, 30, 31, 32-38, 40-44, 49, 59, 60, 72-74, 77-80, 87, 99, 100, 101, 102, 109-112, 116, 117, 123, 125, 128-130, 132-137, 139, 140, 144, 158, 159, 161, 163, 164, 166, 182-185, 187, 190, 191, 192, 195, 196, 202

Aggression 9, 10, 22, 47, 117, 166

Alcoholism 3, 10, 77, 80, 84, 193

Anorexia 117, 189

Anxiety in victims 10, 19, 21, 22, 68, 86, 100, 108, 109, 113, 115, 116, 118, 122, 124, 131, 132, 136, 137, 139, 141, 142, 178, 180, 187, 189, 191, 196, 200

Attachment issues 123, 127, 129, 140, 141, 188, 196, 197, 205

Motivation of offenders 5, 14, 98, 124, 125, 142, 143, 193-195, 198
(See also Offenders)
Multiple assaults 134-135
Multiple personality disorder 14, 33, 132, 139, 158-162, 165-167, 190
Neglect of children 3, 15, 17-19, 21-23, 25, 77, 79-81, 109, 116, 129, 130, 164, 185, 188, 191, 193, 196, 197, 201, 204
Nightmares in victims 113, 139, 159, 163, 189, 191
Obsessionality in victims 21, 100, 131, 136-137
Offenders 3, 14, 16, 44, 87, 123, 124, 138, 143, 195, 198, 199
adult 124, 138
fixated 3, 123, 199
potential 138, 196
regressed 3, 142, 204
Paedophiles 11, 14, 122-124, 138, 140, 142, 194, 204
Paedophilia 44, 142, 151, 194, 196
Parental absence
(see Separation)
Philippines 1, 11, 12
Physical abuse 3, 4, 8, 15, 20, 21, 22, 23, 77-81, 118, 121, 128, 158, 159, 166, 185, 188, 190, 191, 201, 204, 205
Physical neglect 18, 19, 25, 79, 81, 121
Police action 11, 12, 31, 39, 42, 72, 112, 117, 198
(See also Legal issues)

Policy and abuse prevention 16, 30, 44-47, 111, 181, 185, 198
Pornography 14, 78, 88
Post-traumatic stress 109, 116, 118-121, 132, 136, 137, 139, 159, 189, 191, 196, 199
(See also Trauma)
Poverty (See Social class)
Prevalence of child sexual abuse 5, 12-14, 18, 30, 31, 33, 35, 36, 40, 42, 43, 47, 73-75, 79, 108, 111, 112, 115, 128, 158, 163, 166, 179, 180, 182, 184, 185, 186, 191, 193
Prevention of abuse 3, 12, 13, 30, 44, 47, 117, 122, 132, 141, 143, 181, 196-198, 202, 205
Programs for treatment and prevention of abuse 5, 12, 30, 47, 141, 142, 143, 181, 186, 197, 198, 199, 205
Promiscuity 189
Prosecution of offenders 16, 135, 187, 204
Prostitution 4, 10, 11, 13, 14, 16, 22, 34, 70-82, 87, 90, 93, 186, 191, 192
Psychodynamics 123, 159, 187
Psychoneurosis in victims 19, 21, 23, 26, 100, 101, 105, 108, 113, 118, 120, 131, 136
Psychosis 7, 22, 104, 165, 177
Rape 37, 45, 79, 123, 126, 184, 191, 198, 204
Regressed offender 3, 204
Religion 13, 68, 180